HOW TO MINISTER FREEDOM

DORIS M. WAGNER
GENERAL EDITOR

a division of Baker Publishing Group
Minneapolis, Minnesota

Published by Chosen Books
11400 Hampshire Avenue South
Bloomington, Minnesota 55438
www.chosenbooks.com

Chosen Books is a division of
Baker Publishing Group, Grand Rapids, Michigan

Chosen Books edition published 2014
ISBN 978-0-8007-9750-8

Previously published by Regal Books

Originally published by Wagner Publications as the PROVEN FOUNDATIONS OF DELIVERANCE Series:

Book 1: *Ministering Freedom from Demonic Oppression,* © 2002
Book 2: *Ministering Freedom to the Emotionally Wounded,* © 2003
Book 3: *Ministering Freedom to the Sexually Broken,* © 2003
Book 4: *Ministering Freedom from Occult Bondages,* © 2004

The appendix was originally published as "A Deliverance Session," *How to Cast Out Demons* (Ventura, CA: Renew Books, 2000).

Printed in the United States of America

Library of Congress Control Number: 2014954720

14 15 16 17 18 19 20 7 6 5 4 3 2 1

CONTENTS

How to Minister Freedom to the Emotionally Wounded

How to Minister Freedom to the Sexually Broken

How to Minister Freedom to the Occult Bound

INTRODUCTION

While most Christians believe that demons exist somewhere in the world, a relatively small number of Christians realize that demons can affect their daily lives; and even fewer know how to effectively deal with one. But that is changing! Over the past few decades there has been a great resurgence in both the understanding and practice of deliverance. Because there is a need to understand this type of ministry, I decided to offer a book to help both the local church and the average Christian be equipped to effectively minister freedom from demonic oppression. This book is divided into four sections, each addressing a specific topic and offering practical advice for ministering deliverance in that area.

In the first section, experts in the field of deliverance provide us with a general understanding of how demons work in our lives.

In the second section, experts in deliverance to the emotionally wounded explain how demons can take advantage of our emotions and the traumatic experiences in our lives.

In the third section, experts in deliverance to the sexually broken discuss the complex issues of human sexuality and how the enemy can take advantage of both sin and victimization to bring sexual bondage.

In the fourth section, some of my very special friends, each of whom (with the exception of Frank Hammond) has come out of a background of the occult, share their testimonies. Their experiences can help bring freedom to people who are entangled in the occult and equip those who minister to them.

In the appendix, I share how I prepare for and lead a deliverance session. For a more detailed explanation, please see my book *How to Cast Out Demons.*

Before we begin, I'd like to introduce each of the contributors to you.

Araceli Alvarez

Araceli Alvarez has an extensive background in witchcraft, the occult and New Age. Since her conversion to Christ and subsequent deliverance, she has become one of the leading experts on deliverance from witchcraft, heading up Fountain of Freedom Ministries, a Christian prayer ministry that ministers to believers who desire to be free from spiritual strongholds, demonic influences, recurring sin issues, soul ties, rejection, deep emotional wounds that have resulted in dysfunction and bitterness, and other spiritual bondages that prevent them from enjoying a close walk with our Lord Jesus and experiencing the joy available to all believers. To contact Fountain of Freedom Ministries, please call (818) 729-7980 or visit www.f-o-f.org.

John Eckhardt

John Eckhardt is apostle and pastor of Impact Network in Rossmoor, Illinois. He has traveled throughout the United States and overseas to over 50 nations, imparting biblical truths, which include deliverance and spiritual warfare. He has a passion to see the Church become truly apostolic by developing the saints for ministry through teaching, training and demonstration. Apostle Eckhardt produces a daily radio broadcast in the Chicago area and has written many helpful books to assist the Body of Christ, including *The Demon Hit List, Identifying and Breaking Curses* and *Moving in the Apostolic.* To contact Impact Network, please call (708) 922-0983 or e-mail cmimpac@aol.com.

Tim and Anne Evans

Tim and Anne Evans are employees of Wagner Leadership Institute in Colorado Springs, Colorado. They have worked extensively with teens and frequently hold marriage retreats. Happily married for more than 25 years, they have four grown children. Tim and Anne both served as lay leaders for almost 20 years at Willow Creek Community Church. Tim served on the fire department in Schaumburg, Illinois, and retired as deputy fire chief. Tim and Anne were then called to Lakeland Community Church in Holland, Michigan, where they were ordained and served for 5 years. They relocated to Pasadena, California, and served as deans of students for the inaugural Wagner Leadership Institute: The Call School. Both Tim and Anne graduated from Wagner Leadership Institute with Master of Practical Ministry degrees.

David Kyle Foster

David Kyle Foster is the author of *Sexual Healing* and *Transformed into His Image.* He has served as adjunct professor at Asbury Theological Seminary, the Bible Institute of Hawaii, Trinity Episcopal School for Ministry and Logos Christian College and Graduate School, and is on the faculty of the Wagner Leadership Institute. His articles have appeared in numerous Christian journals and magazines, and he has appeared on countless television and radio programs, Christian and secular, witnessing of God's healing of sin and brokenness. David is the founder and director of Mastering Life Ministries and serves as a canon at Church of the Messiah in Jacksonville, Florida. To contact his ministry, please call (904) 220-7474 or visit www.MasteringLife.org.

Frank D. Hammond

Frank Hammond has been a pastor and teacher in the Body of Christ for more than 55 years. Frank is a graduate of Baylor University and Southwestern Baptist Theological Seminary. He and his wife, Ida Mae (who has gone to be with the Lord), traveled and ministered throughout the United States and internationally with a major emphasis on spiritual warfare and family relationships. The Hammonds are authors of *Pigs in the Parlor, A Practical Guide to Deliverance* and 17 other books on various facets of deliverance. To contact the Children's Bread Ministry, which Frank cofounded, please visit www.thechildrensbread.net or write P.O. Box 789, Plainview, Texas 79073-0789.

Jeff Harshbarger

Jeff Harshbarger was delivered from Satanism by the power of Jesus Christ in 1981. He, along with his wife, Liz, established Refuge Ministries in order to help people who have been involved in Satanism, the occult, Wicca and witchcraft, New Age and false teachings in the Christian Church. Jeff holds a Master of Arts degree in pastoral counseling and travels all over the world, sharing what Jesus Christ has done for him and teaching on the topic of deliverance. For further information, please visit www.refugeministries.cc.

Tom R. Hawkins

Tom R. Hawkins, founder and president of Restoration in Christ Ministries, has helped hundreds of sexual abuse victims since the 1980s. He specializes in those who also experienced ritual abuse and mind-control programming and have developed dissociative identity disorder as a result. With a Ph.D. in biblical studies, he claims no mental health credentials. However, from 1991 to 1993, he worked closely with mental health professionals in one of the few Christian inpatient dissociative disorders units in the United States. He is joined by his wife, Diane, in a prolific seminar ministry. To contact his ministry, please call (540) 249-9119 or visit www.rcm-usa.org.

Chris Hayward

Chris Hayward's call to ministry came in 1983, when he was ordained and served as associate pastor of a Spirit-filled Baptist church in Waco, Texas. Chris then served for 10 years as the first senior pastor with Christian Fellowship Church in Mt. Vernon, Illinois. In 1994 Cleansing Stream Ministries (CSM) was introduced to the church, and beginning with a small group, it eventually ministered to over 90 percent of the congregation. In June 1998 Chris resigned the pastorate to become the executive director of CSM. Chris and his wife, Karen, were married in 1970 and have three children. To learn more about Cleansing Stream Ministries, please call (800) 580-8190 or visit www.cleansingstream.org.

Peter Horrobin

Peter Horrobin is the international director of Ellel Ministries. After graduating from Oxford University, he spent many years lecturing, writing and publishing at the university until Ellel was founded in 1986. Since then, Ellel has steadily expanded both in the United Kingdom and in other countries. There are now three teaching and ministry centers in England, two in Canada, one each in Hungary, Scotland, Australia and South Africa, and one soon to open in the United States. The team now numbers over 150 people with 350 volunteer counselors. In addition to authoring many other publications, Peter has written an excellent two-volume book entitled *Healing Through Deliverance.* Peter and his wife, Fiona, live near Ellel Grange in Lancashire, England. To learn more about Ellel Ministries, please visit www.ellel.org.

Cindy Jacobs

Widely recognized as a prophet to the nations, Cindy Jacobs is the president and cofounder of Generals International, an international missionary organization devoted to training in prayer and spiritual warfare. The global headquarters for Generals International is located in Red Oak, Texas, where Cindy and her husband, Mike, currently reside. In addition to being a widely recognized speaker, Cindy is the author of several books, including the best-selling *Possessing the Gates of the Enemy, The Voice of God* and *Women of Destiny.* She also edited and produced the *Women of Destiny Bible.* To contact Generals International, call (972) 576-8887 or visit www.generals.org.

Charles Kraft

Charles Kraft has been a professor for over 30 years at the School of World Mission of Fuller Seminary, where he teaches anthropology, communication, prayer ministry and spiritual warfare. He is also the president of Deep Healing Ministries and conducts seminars around the world on deep-level inner healing, deliverance and spiritual warfare. Before going to Fuller Seminary, he and his wife, Marguerite, were missionaries in Nigeria from 1957 to 1960. Chuck has written several books, including *Christianity with Power, The Rules of Engagement* and *Deep Wounds, Deep Healing.* To contact Deep Healing Ministries, please call (626) 744-0632 or visit www.deephealing ministries.org.

Ana Méndez Ferrell

Ana Méndez Ferrell was saved in 1985 while she was confined in a mental hospital, after having been a voodoo priestess. The miraculous power of God totally delivered her and transformed her into one of His generals for leading His army to destroy the works of evil. Originally from Mexico, she now resides in Jacksonville, Florida, and is married to Emerson Ferrell. Together they head up Voice of the Light Ministries, equipping the Body of Christ through training and prayer in 40 nations. She is the author of *Shaking the Heavens, High Level Warfare* and *Seated in Heavenly Places.* To contact Voice of the Light Ministries, please visit www.anamendez.org or write P.O. Box 3418, Ponte Vedra, Florida 32004.

Chuck D. Pierce

Chuck D. Pierce is vice president of Global Harvest Ministries, president of Glory of Zion International Ministries and mobilizing apostle for the U.S. Strategic Prayer Network. He has been used by God to intercede and mobilize prayer for local churches, cities and nations. In addition, he coordinates prayer for many of the major spiritual events and gatherings around the world, and is a prophet to territories and cities. Chuck and his wife, Pam, live with their five children in Denton, Texas. He has authored nine books, including *Protecting Your Home from Spiritual Darkness, Prayers That Outwit the Enemy* and *The Future War of the Church.* To contact Glory of Zion, please call (888) 965-1099 or visit www.glory-of-zion.org.

John L. Sandford

John Sandford and his wife, Paula, are cofounders of Elijah House, an international ministry that seeks to spread the word of restoration and reconciliation through prayer counseling ministry, teaching and equipping, and providing audio, video and writing materials for use in home fellowships, Christian adult education and for personal and family ministry. The Sandfords' books are well known and are used around the world. They include *Healing the Wounded Spirit* and *A Comprehensive Guide to Deliverance and Inner Healing,* as well as other numerous titles. To contact Elijah House, please call (208) 773-1645 or visit www.elijahhouse.org.

Dale M. Sides

Dale Sides is founder and president of Liberating Ministries for Christ International. With over 30 years of ministry experience, Dale travels and speaks extensively throughout the United States and abroad. He is the author of numerous books, including *Mending Cracks in the Soul* and *God Damn Satan*. Dale also holds several degrees, including a Doctorate of Theology in religious education from Andersonville Baptist Seminary. He and his wife, Vicki, live with their four daughters in Bedford, Virginia. To learn more about Dale's ministry, please call (540) 586-5813 or visit www.LMCI.org.

Alice Smith

Alice Smith is cofounder and executive director of the U.S. Prayer Center, and a member of America's National Prayer Committee, the International Reconciliation Coalition and the International Strategic Prayer Network. She is an intercessor and an internationally known conference speaker on a variety of subjects, including intimate intercession, spiritual warfare and spiritual mapping. In addition to being a regular contributor to a number of Christian magazines, she has also authored several books, including *Beyond the Veil, Intercessors and Pastors* and *Spiritual Housecleaning,* and is the editor of *PrayerNet,* a biweekly e-mail newsletter. To contact the U.S. Prayer Center, please visit www.usprayercenter.org.

C. Peter Wagner

C. Peter Wagner is the founding president of Global Harvest Ministries, a ministry that brings together prayer networks for the purpose of focusing prayer power on world evangelism. He is also chancellor of Wagner Leadership Institute, located in Colorado Springs, Colorado. Peter and his wife, Doris, were missionaries in Bolivia from 1956 to 1971. Peter then served as professor of church growth at the School of World Mission of Fuller Seminary from 1971 to 1999. He is the author or editor of over 66 books, including *Churchquake!*, *Changing Church* and *Your Spiritual Gifts Can Help Your Church Grow*. To contact Global Harvest Ministries, please visit www.globalharvest.org.

Doris M. Wagner

Doris Wagner, along with her husband, C. Peter Wagner, founded Global Harvest Ministries in 1992, with a vision of bringing together prayer networks for the purpose of focusing their collective prayer power on world evangelism. Doris serves in Global Harvest Ministries as the CEO. A deliverance minister for 20 years, she has helped set countless people free from various addictions and bondages. Because of her desire to see mobilization for deliverance within the local church, she has taught practical seminars in many nations of the world and now specializes in deliverance training and speaking at regional and national conferences. To contact Global Harvest Ministries, please visit www.globalharvest.org.

HOW TO MINISTER FREEDOM TO THE DEMONICALLY OPPRESSED

Chapter 1

WHATEVER HAPPENED TO THE WORDS AND WORKS OF JESUS?

Doris M. Wagner

As we read the New Testament today and pause to observe the followers of Jesus both then and now, we see a huge difference.

Part of that difference is, of course, because the world has changed so much in 2000 years. For example, automobiles and jet planes have replaced donkeys and walking. Computers and printers have replaced the scribe and his pen. Runners are no longer needed to carry messages from place to place; news now comes to us by television, Internet, radio and newspapers. And on it goes. Times have changed!

But what about the words and works of Jesus? How do we respond to them in the twenty-first century?

The Biblical Records

No matter how different the twenty-first century appears in contrast to the days in which Jesus lived, I am a staunch believer that the Bible is the Word of God, and I am totally committed to its teachings as our rules and guidelines for faith and practice today. I am assuming that most of you who read this book hold to those beliefs also.

Simply put, the Bible contains a record of the words and works of Jesus and His followers that are designed to guide us in living a life well pleasing to the Father. This record shows us how much God loves us; it contains the very words and teachings of Jesus; it points us to salvation; and it gives us the rules that will help us live holy lives. If those rules are followed, they not only lead us into holy living but also keep us out of trouble and away from sin. Taking it one step further, the rules are for our good. Obedience to them brings our happiness and well-being. We please the Father.

I personally came to Christ as a teenager, after having read some very powerful words in the Bible. Those words burned within me, and I set out on a quest to discover their meaning. They were words of Jesus—a simple phrase that read, "You must be born again" (John 3:7). Just a five-word sentence that seemed to carry great authority and total truth to my teenaged mind, and I had to know what it meant and how to do it. When someone invited me to a Bible camp and I heard a sermon entitled "You Must Be Born Again," I wept. I was probably the first person who went forward when the invitation to receive Christ was given.

God had answered my prayers and shown me the way. He had given me a voracious hunger to learn all that I could about Jesus and His teachings, and as I began to read the Bible right after asking Jesus to forgive my sins and come into my life, I saw the Word of God through new eyes. Everything made sense. The Holy Spirit was in me, and He indeed was my helper. Ever since that born-again experience, I have treasured the Bible, and I have had an enormous appreciation and reverence for it. I have no trouble whatsoever in believing every word. Its message led me to the truth and to faith in Christ—to salvation, happiness, fulfillment and the great privilege of serving the Lord along my pathway here on Earth.

Along with providing guidance on faith, belief and holy living, the Bible clearly instructs us how to spread the gospel, and it gives numerous examples of the activities of the Early Church as it went about this task. I can see why Satan has done so much throughout history to keep the Scriptures out of the hands of the common people. The Scriptures are powerful, and they contain the words of life. They tell us what to do and how to do it according to the will and plan of God. It takes all of us to accomplish the task.

THE RELIGIOUS LEADERS

As I read the Gospels, I see that Jesus began His public ministry by going to the places where those who were seeking God would be found–in the houses of worship. Mark 11 and 12 tell us about some of the people found in these houses of worship. They were the chief priests, the scribes and the elders who questioned, "By what authority are You doing these things?" (11:27). They were questioning *Jesus' works and authority*. When Jesus refused to tell them, they sent some people of higher influence–the Pharisees and Herodians–"to catch Him in *His words*" (12:13, emphasis added). But when Jesus so wisely answered their questions because He knew of their hypocrisy, they marveled at His words (see 12:15-17).

Another group of religious folk approached Him in the Temple. They were the Sadducees, who claimed that there is no resurrection. They questioned Him concerning the Scriptures. His answer to them was, "Are you not therefore mistaken, because you do not know *the Scriptures* nor *the power of God?*" (12:24, emphasis added). In this verse Jesus affirms two additional important items, added to His works and His words: the Scriptures and the power of God.

After His resurrection, He told the disciples about His authority: "All authority has been given to Me in heaven and on earth. Go therefore and make disciples of all the nations" (Matt. 28:18-19). In Acts 1:8, He added that the power of God would be given to them when the Holy Spirit came upon them.

The religious leaders resented Jesus and were offended by His words, His works, His knowledge of the Scriptures, His authority and His power. They then set out to eliminate Him. But His death proved to be the very pathway to eternal life for those who believe in Him. Praise God!

THE COMMON PEOPLE

There is one more group of people mentioned in Mark 12. They are the common people. Verse 37 states, "The common people heard Him gladly."

I am constantly amazed and humbled by the fact that Jesus turned away from the experts in religious matters of that day and went to the common people. Here was fertile ground. He spent His early days apprenticing with His earthly father in the carpenter shop, and all indications are that He worked there until He was 30 years old. He lived among the common people. He chose as His disciples other common people. They were probably either young men or very young men. Scholars agree that John most likely wrote the book of Revelation in 95 or 96 A.D., so he must have been a very young man as a disciple.

Jesus was also very kind to women, as we see when He includes them in His close circle of friends. To name just a few, "Mary called Magdalene, out of whom had come seven demons, and Joanna, the wife of Chuza, Herod's steward, and Susanna, and many others [women] who provided for Him from their substance" (Luke 8:2-3). There were the famous Mary and Martha, and many other unnamed women who served Jesus. At a time when women were not very high on the social scale of the day, the Gospels carefully point out that these women were special to Him. After His resurrection, He even chose to first appear to Mary Magdalene—a person who had undergone deliverance and whose life was radically changed. In my long Christian experience, I have found fewer people more grateful to the Lord than people such as Mary, who have been set free from demons.

THE WORKS OF JESUS

Now let's briefly look at a few passages of Scripture that talk about the works of Jesus. In Matthew 10:5-8 we read, "These twelve Jesus sent out and commanded them, saying: . . . 'As you go, preach, saying, "The kingdom of heaven is at hand." Heal the sick, cleanse the lepers, raise the dead, cast out demons. Freely you have received, freely give.' " Very specific instructions!

Make no mistake about it. Unbelief actually limits what Jesus can do, and He is the second Person of the Trinity!

Mark 6:5-7 recounts the visit of Jesus and His disciples to Nazareth. "He could do no mighty work there. . . . He marveled because of their unbelief. . . . He called the twelve to Him, and began to send them out two by two, and gave them power over unclean spirits." Something was standing in the way of those people in Nazareth from being able to accept the words and works of Jesus. It was unbelief. Apparently it was time to go on the offensive against unbelief caused by unclean spirits, so Jesus armed His disciples to do battle by giving them power over unclean spirits. In my experience, I have encountered demons of doubt and unbelief, and oddly enough they are frequently tied in with religious spirits, such as the religious spirit of legalism, of idol worship, of false religions and of Freemasonry.

Make no mistake about it. Unbelief actually limits what Jesus can do, and He is the second Person of the Trinity! The inference of Mark 6:5-7 seems to be that if faith had been present in Nazareth, Jesus could have done mighty works there.

These Signs Will Follow

Mark 16:14-20 adds a few more ingredients to Matthew 10:5-8. Jesus appeared to the eleven disciples after His resurrection and rebuked *their* unbelief and hardness of heart. He told them, "'Go into all the world and preach the gospel to every creature. He who believes and is baptized will be saved; but he who does not believe will be condemned. And these signs will follow *those who believe: In My name* they will cast out demons; they will speak with new tongues; . . . they will lay hands on the sick, and they will recover.' So then, after the Lord had spoken to them, He was received up into heaven, and sat down at the right hand of God. And they went out and preached everywhere, the Lord working with them and confirming the word through the accompanying signs" (vv. 15-20, emphasis added).

First, "those who believe" would undoubtedly refer to all of those who have believed down through the ages. So, it would include all true born-again believers today. One of my favorite verses of Scripture is Hebrews 13:8: "Jesus Christ is the same yesterday, today, and forever." So it would follow that He has neither changed His mind nor His commands to His followers. Yes, this includes us!

Second, "in My name" was added to the equation. We have no clearer example of how to actually cast out a demon than found in Acts 16:16-18. In this passage, a girl with a spirit of divination (witchcraft) followed Paul, Silas and Luke and annoyed them so much that Paul finally said to the evil spirit, "I command you in the name of Jesus Christ to come out of her" (v. 18). And it indeed did come out!

Summing It Up

So let's review and sum up what has been said in some simple, brief phrases.

- The Bible is the Word of God and was given to us as a guide for our faith and practice.
- We please the Father when we have great faith and follow the teachings and commands of Jesus.
- The religious leaders of the day resented Jesus and were offended by His words, His works, His knowledge of the Scriptures, His authority and His power.
- Jesus chose His disciples from among the common people and turned to the common people in His ministry.

- Jesus gave them very specific instructions: Preach that the kingdom of God is at hand, heal the sick, cleanse the lepers, raise the dead and cast out demons.
- Unbelief limits what God can do, and we as believers deserve to be rebuked when unbelief is present. We must believe extravagantly and have great faith.
- These same instructions apparently apply to us today. Just as the first disciples had Jesus' authority *in His name* to accomplish the task He had given them, so do we. We are His ambassadors.

Implementing the Task

Now, let's look a little closer at the actual way Jesus and those first workers went about the task.

First John 3:8 reads, "For this purpose the Son of God was manifested, that He might destroy the works of the devil." In other words, as the disciples were given their marching orders and were equipped for the task, spiritual warfare began. Our job is to destroy the works of the devil through the power of God. The Early Church did a great job of it, as the New Testament records. I will list a few examples.

Acts 17:2-3: "Paul, as his custom was, went in to them [the people in the synagogue], and for three Sabbaths reasoned with them from the Scriptures, explaining and demonstrating that the Christ had to suffer and rise again from the dead, and saying, 'This Jesus whom I preach to you is the Christ.' "

Many people in that synagogue in Thessalonica believed in Christ when they heard this message, including a great number of devout Greeks and many leading women. But others did not believe. Some irate, unbelieving Jews started out to persecute the band of believers but could not find them. In the midst of their uprising, these Jews paid quite a compliment to Paul, Silas and the other missionaries of the day when they said, "These who have turned the world upside down have come here too" (v. 6).

Yes, those early evangelists made quite a mark in their course of evangelizing. They heeded the words of Jesus and occupied themselves with doing the works also, as they had been instructed to do. The results were that they turned the world upside down and the Church grew rapidly.

Acts 19:10-12: "And this [Paul's preaching about the kingdom of God (see v. 8)] continued for two years, so that all who dwelt in Asia heard the word of the Lord Jesus, both Jews and Greeks. Now God worked unusual miracles by the hands of Paul, so that even handkerchiefs or aprons were brought from his body to the sick, and the diseases left them and the evil spirits went out of them."

My husband, Peter, is always amused by the phrase "unusual miracles." He reasons that because this phrase is used, there must have been many "usual miracles" that happened so often that they didn't need special mention.

Romans 15:17-19: "Therefore I have reason to glory in Christ Jesus in the things which pertain to God. . . . In mighty signs and wonders, by the power of the Spirit of God, so that from Jerusalem and round about to Illyricum I have fully preached the gospel of Christ."

The apostle Paul wrote this. Note that these also were not usual signs and wonders, but "mighty" ones.

1 Corinthians 2:1-5: "And I, brethren, when I came to you, did not come with excellence of speech or of wisdom declaring to you the testimony of God. For I determined not to know anything among you except Jesus Christ and Him crucified. I was with you in weakness, in fear, and in much trembling. And my speech and my preaching were not with persuasive words of human wisdom, but in demonstration of the Spirit and of power, that your faith should not be in the wisdom of men but in the power of God."

Paul also wrote this. He was a highly educated Pharisee and certainly could have debated most people under the table, but he chose to demonstrate the Spirit and the power of God instead.

When Professionals Take Over

Space in this chapter does not permit me to analyze all of what went awry in the centuries that ensued. I am not qualified to do that anyway! But it appears that when the trend moved from the simple house church model into a more clerical mode of operation, the whole government of the Church shifted. Instead of simply being governed by apostles, prophets, pastors, teachers and evangelists, the Church became governed by a complicated hierarchy, and the common people became less involved. Tragically, the words of Jesus and the works that He commanded us to do shifted to the professionals.

To me the saddest by-product of this was the removal of the Scriptures from the reach of the common people. As God's Word remained in the church buildings and was even written in a language that the people could not understand, the words and works of Jesus faded in meaning. But at last God raised up individuals such as John Wycliffe and Martin Luther and others (for some, at the cost of their very lives) to translate the Bible into the language of the people. Along came the printing press, and the Bible once again became available to the masses of the largest people groups.

In the last few hundred years, the interpretation of the meaning of the words and works of Jesus has taken on many hues and shapes. It is so very amazing that the words have been preserved. But many of the works were lost, because they fell out of use.

Doing What Jesus Says

I once again draw your attention to Hebrews 13:8: "Jesus Christ is the same yesterday, today, and forever." I encourage you to simply do what He says: Go, preach, heal the sick, raise the dead and cast out demons.

The Church is doing a fairly good job of the first two. We know how to go, and we know how to preach. As a matter of fact, the sun never sets on a place where there are no Christians anymore. But think of what could have been done if we had carried out the other instructions down through the ages! The fact that God is now giving us another chance is but His grace and mercy. Let's not lose this opportunity!

We need a massive proliferation of gifted leaders to apprentice people in healing the sick and casting out demons. Let's raise some dead along the way as well, because surely death is an enemy (see 1 Cor. 15:26) and many are dying prematurely at the hand of the devil. Actually, raising the dead is happening much more than most people think. I personally hugged a child that had been dead for at least an hour, and was raised. But lack of faith does not allow many to believe.

Taking Jesus' Words at Face Value

Because my particular area of ministry has been deliverance for 20 years, I am concentrating on doing seminars and teaching as much as I can on the how-to of casting out demons. And in this book I have pulled together many of my friends with special areas of expertise in the field. It is our prayer that many believers will be equipped to cast out demons. We have a great deal of territory to take back from the devil, because this part of the works of Jesus has been on hold for centuries.

Let's have faith, friends. Let's take the words of Jesus at face value and step out boldly in faith to do the works. I'd like to share one more Scripture with you. Jesus said, "I am with you always, even to the end of the age" (Matt. 28:20). This has to include us, because the age hasn't ended yet. He is with us always, cheering us on, honoring our faith and helping us do the works. All we need to do is cooperate, get equipped and go do it.

Chapter 2

CAN A CHRISTIAN HAVE A DEMON?

John Eckhardt

Can a Christian have a demon? This is a question that I personally struggled with in the past. In fact, there was a time in our church when we actually taught that Christians could not have demons. I preached long sermons expounding the fact that Christians could be oppressed, regressed, digressed, obsessed and suppressed, but never possessed. We believed that a demon could be on a Christian, oppressing him or her, but that it could not be inside the Christian. The major issue I could not reconcile (and the major argument used by many people today) was how Jesus and the Holy Spirit could live inside of someone's body along with demons.

Theology Versus Experience

But then we began to face a real problem. We were being confronted with people whom we knew were born-again, Spirit-filled believers who, as we prayed for them, began to manifest demons! Our experience did not line up with our theology. We have found that many times, before God can change a person's theology, He has to bring some experience that will cause this person to reevaluate his or her teaching and doctrine.

We had to deal with the fact that either our experience was wrong or our doctrine was wrong. But we couldn't question our experience, because we knew what we were seeing. Therefore, we had to question our theology. Many who have been taught that no one can have both the Holy Spirit and a demon at the same time have had to reevaluate their position, because their real-life experiences did not bear the doctrine out.

We began to see that in the Bible, Jesus told his disciples to cast devils *out*, not to cast devils *off* (see Matt. 10:8; Mark 3:15; 16:17). In order for something to go *out*, it first has to be *in*. We needed, somehow, to resolve the question of how a person can have Jesus, and even be filled with the Holy Spirit, and yet be in need of deliverance. We finally came to the conclusion that our interpretation of the Bible had been wrong.

In his excellent manual for deliverance, Gene B. Moody quotes Ernest B. Rockstad: "Experience, of course, is not the basis for the interpretation of the Bible. Nevertheless, if consistent experiences run counter to an interpretation, the dedicated seeker after the truth will set out to find the reason. He must be willing to re-study his interpretation under the direction of the Holy Spirit and be prepared to make any necessary corrections in his own belief so as to be in full agreement with the facts as they are."[1] Moody concludes that based on the Scriptures and on experience, Christians, even those who have never participated in the occult, can be oppressed or possessed by evil spirits.[2]

I once had a debate with a minister who said that he never prayed for people in his church to be delivered, because according to Colossians 1:13 we are already delivered. I said, "Fine. Then you'd better not call for another prayer line and lay hands on the sick either, because the Bible also says that by His stripes we are healed. If we're healed, why would you pray for the sick?" He'd never thought about it that way. You see, biblically, we are healed. Yet in reality, we still need to minister to Christians who are sick in their bodies. If the Scripture says we are healed but I keep running into sick Christians, then either those people are not saved or my view of the Scripture has to be interpreted by the fact that though we are healed legally by the stripes of Jesus, that does not automatically mean that every believer will never get sick. Sometimes what the Bible provides for has to be appropriated by the laying on of hands or through faith or anointing with oil or through another means.

Demonically Inspired Doctrine

A common answer you'll hear when someone questions whether a Christian, especially a Spirit-filled Christian, can have a demon is "Definitely not!" As I have already mentioned, the reasoning behind this answer is that the Holy Spirit and a demon cannot reside together. But our experience did not confirm this truth. Nor did the experience of Moody. He writes, "The dismaying fact remains that born-again Christians, including leaders, are having difficulties and problems that cannot be explained as natural infirmities or the endless conflict between the flesh and the Spirit. It is no secret that many believers have become discouraged and filled with awful despair."[3]

We are dealing with real people that have real problems. I have become convinced not only that a Christian can have demons but also that there are demons that operate in the realm of theology that would have us endlessly arguing and debating over doctrine instead of meeting the needs of people who are hurting. Demons actually motivate the teaching that a Christian cannot have a demon, because demons gain strength from staying hidden. They can operate in their destructive ways without being challenged!

God did not save us and commission us to ministry so that we could be people who argue doctrine. He calls us to ministry so that we help people who are hurting, wounded and bruised. When you come into contact with anyone who is controlled by demons, the answer is to cast the devil out, not to argue about whether or not that person is a Christian. The answer is to bring help to that person. Jesus responded to the needs of everyone who went to Him with a demonic problem. Even though we often look at people in the Bible as being less educated than we are, they at least had sense enough to know when a problem was demonic. The fact is that today many people have problems that are driven by demons, but they don't recognize it; and sadly, neither do those who are supposed to be ministering to them.

Clearing the Confusion over Demon Possession

One issue that can trip many people up when thinking of Christians and demons is the idea of being possessed. Hollywood has painted a picture of demon possession that, while it is sensationalized and incorrect, leaves a graphic image in our minds—the image of a person with a spinning head and eyes popping out, having no control at all. In addition, it is unfortunate that one of the meanings of the word "possessed" relates to ownership, because it causes people to assume that if Christians are possessed, then it means that they are fully owned and controlled by the devil. This is obviously wrong.

I do not have as much of a problem with the word "possessed" as some Christians do. In fact, to me the word "demonized" sounds worse.

Derek Prince, in his pamphlet entitled *Expelling Demons*, discusses the biblical Greek words that are used to describe demon possession: "The New Testament Greek word for demon is *daimonion* . . . in the *King James Version* . . . often translated 'devil.' Associated in the New Testament with the noun *daimonion* is the passive verb *daimonizomai*. The literal meaning of this verb is 'to be demoned,' that is, in some way under the influence or power of demons. In the *King James Version* this verb is usually translated by some phrase such as 'to be possessed' or 'to be vexed' by demons or by evil spirits. However, there is no distinction in the original Greek text to support these (translated) distinctions."[4]

Personally, I do not have as much of a problem with the word "possessed" as some Christians do. In fact, to me the word "demonized" sounds worse. And when I looked up the word "possess," one definition simply means to occupy. My contention is that if a demon occupies your big toe, he possesses that part of you. It doesn't mean he possesses your spirit, soul and body. If he occupies just a small portion, such as a physical organ in your body, as a spirit of infirmity does, then there is possession to some degree.

I often ask those who are skeptical of demon possession whether or not cancer is demonic. Most believers will agree that sickness is of the devil. Here's a simple question: Is cancer inside of the body or is there something on the outside that's the problem? If it weren't on the inside, then doctors probably wouldn't be cutting you open in order to remove something. So, evidently you can be a Christian and have something in you that is possessing a certain organ of your body, which definitely is not of God. And if you do believe that sickness is God's will for you, then you would never go to the hospital or take an aspirin. You would just stay at home and enjoy God's will. But even sinners understand that sickness is wrong, and doctors do everything in their power to fight it. There is something in us that fights sickness and death because we know that these things were never intended for Adam and Eve in the Garden.

The Human Makeup

So, if a Christian can be possessed, or demonized, in some part of his or her being, then is anything off-limits to demons? The answer to this question helps reconcile the issue of Jesus' and the Holy Spirit's residing within someone who needs deliverance.

First, it is important to understand that everyone is made up of three parts: spirit, soul and body (see 1 Thess. 5:23). When Jesus comes into a believer's life, He comes into that person's spirit, according to John 3:6: "That which is born of the Spirit is spirit." Second, it is the other components that make up a human being—the soul (the mind, will and emotions) and the physical body—that are the targets of demonic attack. Demons can dwell in those particular areas of a Christian's life, and yet demons cannot dwell inside a Christian's spirit, because that is where Jesus and the Holy Spirit dwell. So when we say that a Christian is possessed, or demonized, we are not saying that a Christian can have demons in his or her spirit, but that this person can have them in parts of the soul or physical body.

To illustrate this, the Lord began to show us the whole idea of Jesus' going into the Temple and cleansing it of thieves and moneychangers. It is mentioned in every one of the four Gospels (see Matt. 21:12-14; Mark 11:15-18; Luke 19:45-48; John 2:14-23). The Greek word for "drove out" is *ekballo,* which means to expel or drive out.[5] This is the same word that is used in Mark 16:17, when Jesus said, "In My name they will cast out demons." Now, according to 1 Corinthians 3:16, we who are God's children are the temple of the Spirit of God. In the Old Testament the Temple had three parts: the holy of holies, the holy place and the outer court. This picture is a type, or representation, of who we are as His temple. The Shekinah glory of God, or God's presence, was in the holy of holies. The holy of holies represents our spirit. When Jesus went into the Temple to drive out the thieves and moneychangers, He did not go into the holy of holies; He went into the outer court, where these evildoers carried on their business. That is a picture of deliverance—of what Jesus wants to do in our temple. There may be demonic thieves in our lives that are operating in our outer courts (body or soul). Even though they cannot enter the holy of holies (our spirit), Jesus wants them expelled, because the temple of God was never intended for thieves to operate in. It is meant to be a place of worship and a place of prayer.

Not for the Unbeliever

Here is another interesting point to ponder when we consider the ministry of deliverance: Deliverance is not for the unbeliever. Let's think about it. What good would it do to cast demons out of an unbeliever, unless that person were going to be saved? Unbelievers cannot maintain their deliverance. In fact, according to Luke 11:24-26, the unbeliever who receives deliverance will later be inhabited by seven times as many demons as before. Add to this the fact that most unbelievers are not seeking deliverance anyway. When I was an unbeliever, I did drugs. I was not at home crying out, "God, deliver me from drugs." I was out looking for more drugs. I was not at the altar of a church praying, "Oh, God, deliver me from anger." But once I became a believer and found out that there were things in my life that were not godly, I began to seek God for deliverance, because then I had a right to it and I had the Holy Spirit to maintain it within me.

The Children's Bread

Since the ministry of deliverance is not for the unbeliever, who then is left? The believer. In fact, the ministry of deliverance is our covenant right. In order to understand this fully, we need to understand what a covenant is. God is a covenant God, and He has a covenant people. In the Old Covenant, His covenant people were the children of Israel. In the New Covenant, His covenant people consist of both Jews and Gentiles who are restored to relationship with God through Christ's blood. Though there are some blessings that God gives all people (see Matt. 5:45), there are many others that He directs toward His covenant people. Every blessing, whether it's healing, prosperity, deliverance or miracles, is promised only to covenant people. God in His mercy will bless people outside of the covenant because He is a merciful God. But primarily, these blessings are based on covenant.

In Mark 7, we read the story of the Syro-Phoenician woman who sought Jesus out to deliver her daughter from an unclean spirit. Verse 27 reads, "But Jesus said to her, 'Let the children be filled first, for it is not good to take the children's bread and throw it to the little dogs.' " Though "children's bread" can refer to any of God's blessings, in this story it refers specifically to deliverance; and Jesus is saying that it belongs to His covenant people. It is a covenant right. Those outside of the Covenant may receive a miracle based on God's mercy, but deliverance is really meant for those who have a covenant with God.

Luke 1:71-73 says that Jesus came "that we should be saved from our enemies and from the hand of all who hate us, to perform the mercy promised to our fathers and to remember His holy covenant, the oath which He swore to our father Abraham." In this passage we see that Jesus' coming brought salvation from our enemies—devils and demons—and then Abraham, with whom God had made a covenant, is brought into the picture. According to Galatians 3:29, we are now the seed of Abraham: "And if you are Christ's, then you are Abraham's seed, and heirs according to the promise." Through Jesus' coming and all the provisions He made for us, God is fulfilling the promises He made with our forefathers in the Covenant. God is a covenant God.

Luke 1:74-75 goes on to say, "To grant us that we, being delivered from the hand of our enemies, might serve Him without fear, in holiness and righteousness before Him all the days of our life." The purpose of deliverance, therefore, is so that we are able to serve God without fear, in holiness and in righteousness all the days of our life. It is very difficult to live a life without fear or in holiness or in righteousness without being delivered. In fact, it is practically impossible.

Working Out Salvation

"Therefore, my beloved, as you have always obeyed, not as in my presence only, but now much more in my absence, work out your own salvation with fear and trembling; for it is God who works in you both to will and to do for His good pleasure. Do all things without murmuring and disputing, that you may become blameless and harmless, children of God without fault in the midst of a crooked and perverse generation, among whom you shine as lights in the world" (Phil. 2:12-15).

Some people would argue that deliverance is entirely dependent on God, so that when you accept Jesus Christ, you're completely delivered and there's nothing you need to do after that but believe. But this passage shows us the human aspect of deliverance, of working out our salvation.

The word for "salvation" in verse 12 is *soteria,* which Thayer's lexicon defines as "deliverance from the molestation of enemies."[6] Building on Thayer's definition, Moody concludes, "*Jesus* has *delivered* our *spirit* from the power of Satan; now He says to us, 'Work out your own *deliverance* from the molestation of enemies until you have freed both *soul and body.*'"[7]

We've had literally thousands upon thousands of believers who have come in need of deliverance. Their purpose in coming is to work out their salvation. Salvation is something that encompasses more than the initial accepting of Jesus Christ. Salvation means healing; salvation means deliverance from sin; salvation means deliverance from poverty or sickness or demonic influence. Jesus came and provided a remedy for these things. Through His shed blood, He also gives us power and authority to deal with anything in our lives that should not be there. The process is ongoing. Deliverance is an important part of working out our salvation.

Not Always a Problem of Sin

Another erroneous belief is that if a Christian does have a demon, it must be the result of a sin in the person's life. Sure, if a Christian is practicing some sin or is living in the flesh, there's no way that he or she can escape a demon. Sin and the flesh go with demons like water and wetness. You can't have water without wetness. Wetness comes with water, and sin comes with demons. If you habitually engage in works of the flesh, you are not only involved in sin but also with the demonic spirits behind it.

However, that is not to imply that if a Christian has a demon, he or she is in sin. For instance, a spirit of rejection or a spirit of trauma can come upon a person, not as a result of that person's own actions, but as a result of someone else's. Some people say that if a person has a demon, then it is impossible for that person to be saved or be a saint, because he or she must be in sin; but these people do not recognize the fact that there are many different kinds of spirits with many different entry points, not all of which are sin. Another demonic entry point may be generational sin—sin that is passed along through family bloodlines.

If You Get Saved, Then Get Delivered!

We have come a long way since the early days when we believed Christians could not have demons. Now, when people get saved in our church, we automatically assume that they need some level of deliverance, and we lead them through the process. We don't question *if* they have a demon, but *how many* they have. That may sound hard, but as I have just pointed out, the presence of demons in the lives of these new believers is not always their fault; they may have inherited them through their bloodlines.

Biblically, if we can be affected to the fourth generation by sin (see Exod. 20:5), and a biblical generation is 40 years, we can then say that we are subject to the demonic influence of what people in our family lines were doing as far back as 160 years. That means that taking the round number of the year 2000, we are affected by what those in our bloodlines were doing as far back as the year 1840. Even if we have great genealogy, we can't know everything that all our ancestors did in secret that long ago. Then, in addition to that, by the time most people come to the Lord, they need deliverance on some level for the influence of sin in their own lives—whether they have been traumatized or victimized, or have gotten involved in sin themselves and have demonic influences of their own. There is just too much defilement and contamination on the earth to escape it.

If we are ministers who have been commissioned to minister to God's covenant people, than we need to be prepared to provide them with their covenant right of deliverance. If we deprive them of deliverance based on some erroneous theological doctrine, then we are denying them what is rightfully theirs, as covenant people; and we cannot call ourselves able ministers of the New Covenant. Let's do as Jesus did and minister the children's bread to those who need it!

Notes

1. Ernest B. Rockstad, *Demon Activity and the Christian,* quoted in Gene B. Moody, "Can a Christian Have a Demon?" *Deliverance Manual.* http://www.demonbuster.com/z1cachad.html (accessed February 11, 2005). For more information about Gene B.

Moody's ministry, Deliverance Ministries, please call (225) 755-8870.

2. Gene B. Moody, "Can a Christian Have a Demon?" *Deliverance Manual.* http://www.demonbuster.com/z1cachad.html (accessed February 11, 2005).
3. Ibid.
4. Derek Prince, *Expelling Demons*, quoted in Gene B. Moody, "Can a Christian Have a Demon?" *Deliverance Manual.* http://www.demonbuster.com/z1cachad.html (accessed February 11, 2005). Italics not in the original.
5. James Strong, *The New Strong's Exhaustive Concordance of the Bible* (Nashville, TN: Thomas Nelson Publishers, 1984), Greek ref. no. 1544.
6. Joseph Henry Thayer, *A Greek-English Lexicon of the New Testament* (Grand Rapids, MI: Baker Book House, 1977), Strong's ref. no. 4991.
7. Moody, "Can a Christian Have a Demon?" *Deliverance Manual.*

Chapter 3

HOW SATAN DIVERTS US FROM THE PATH OF GOD

Chuck D. Pierce

Long before we were born, God set perfect paths for our lives, according to His will. He did this because God longs for us to be successful at every point along our paths. When we submit ourselves to Him and recognize that He has paid the price for our lives, we can enter into the success that He has for us. This is really what redemption means. Success is defined as turning out well or attaining a goal. It means to flourish, to prosper or to thrive. On this topic, Rebecca Sytsema and I have written, "The Lord longs for us to succeed:

- by moving our lives forward so we are not constantly living in the pain and regret of the past;
- by causing us to prevail over the enemy of our souls so that we are able to resist temptation and reclaim our inheritance;
- by causing us to act wisely and strategically;
- by promoting us to new levels at the right season; and
- by helping us to achieve our destined purposes when we cry out to Him along our paths.

In essence, as God's children, He longs for us to succeed even as He succeeds!"[1]

Satan's Plan to Divert Us from God's Path

When we came to the Lord, no matter what age we were, we were all fragmented, with pieces of our lives scattered here and there. Why? Because scattering is a curse that we come under as a result of sin. When we sin, pieces of the people God intends for us to be are left behind. We trade purity, blessing, health and/or a part of God's perfect plan for our lives for a sin we have committed. Therefore, parts of the whole person God intends for us to be lie scattered along the paths of our lives at each point where we have chosen sin. Only God has the power to gather the scattered pieces of our sin-ridden lives and bring them back into wholeness.

Even though God plans for us to be whole and successful, we have an enemy who has a plan contrary to our Maker's. This enemy, Satan, and all of his hordes of demonic spirits, would love to see us fragmented instead of whole. Satan delights in setting us on a wrong path so that we cannot accomplish God's kingdom purposes for our lives and advance His kingdom in the earth. Satan's purpose is to interrupt God's plan for us to have successful lives. At any one of the stages of our lives, the enemy would love to block us from moving any further in God and in His purposes. If he can do this, the destiny that God has for each of us cannot be completed.

In his attempt to keep us from reaching our destiny, Satan uses the following 10 ways to sidetrack us, divert us or fragment us:

1. *Cares of the world*—We divert our eyes and desires to the world around us instead of keeping our eyes on the One who made us.
2. *Anxiety*—Anxiety is friction within our inner person that keeps us from walking in peace, or wholeness.
3. *Weights on our spirit*—These weights are burdens that we bear in the flesh.

4. *Unforgiveness*—Unforgiveness is holding resentment toward an individual who has wronged us.
5. *Poisoned spirit*—We allow the hurts that we encounter in life to cause a root of bitterness to arise within our spirit and eventually defile our whole body.
6. *Grief*—Grief is a function of loss that can be embedded in our emotions. Grief has a time frame. If we go past that time frame, the enemy produces hope deferred within us. We then lose our expectation in God and others.
7. *Unstable emotions*—Instability is the lack of being able to stand. Our emotions eventually rule us, and life becomes a roller coaster.
8. *Accusations*—The accuser of the brethren loves to reproach us and remind us of everything that we have done wrong.
9. *Condemnation*—Condemnation is the opposite of conviction. Whereas conviction leads us to grace, condemnation says that there is no way out for any wrongdoing we've done.
10. *Sin and iniquitous patterns*—Sin's author is Satan. Unconfessed sin can lead us to a pattern of iniquity. Iniquity diverts us from the path of life.

Each of these issues can fragment the way we think and cause our spirit to lose the power that God has made available to us. God has made each of us with a spirit, soul and body; and He ordained us to be whole. If Satan can trap us with any of the above issues, we will become like the person whom James describes: "He who doubts . . . is a double-minded man, unstable in all his ways" (Jas. 1:6-8). Our mind becomes divided (our way of thinking becomes unsure), and we lose the power of the Holy Spirit flowing through our spirit.

When we minister deliverance to others, we need to understand how the enemy attacks us in each of these areas. We need to remember that deliverance is not just setting people free of demonic forces; it is also bringing people into a place of renewal so that the life processes of

God begin to flow through them and they begin to operate in life, not death. In order to do that, we need to minister deliverance to the whole person.

A Divided Mind

Matthew 6:33 tells us that if we learn to seek God first and are able to prioritize properly in our lives, then everything we need will be added to us. In order to do that, our mind is going to have to be renewed, learning to think the way that God wants us to think (see Rom. 12:2). However, hindering demons attempt to stop our mind from thinking that way. Demonic forces know that if our mind is operating with God's anointing, we will be able to prioritize and order our steps in the way that God intends us to on a daily basis. We advance forward and the Kingdom advances. We will be useful tools in God's hands, as well as being prosperous in our lives.

One way the enemy diverts our mind is by forming blocks in our cognitive processes. It's like a natural gas pipeline that flows through a network of connecting lines and systems. Eventually the gas reaches a processing station where it is processed properly and then sent for commercial use. If that pipeline can be blocked at an early point, before the gas flows out through numerous smaller lines, the gas flow to an entire neighborhood can be restricted and cause the neighborhood to remain without gas. Similarly, the enemy attempts to form a block somewhere in our brain by releasing information into it, building information up so that when new information or godly revelation tries to go in, we can't process it at all.

The enemy builds strongholds within our mind to protect his resources. When we are confronted with a truth and our mind seems to go blank, it is often a good indication that a demon is at work, because demons don't want truth to go in like an arrow and shatter strongholds that are there. That's how truth works. When a spirit of truth is inside of us and a godly revelation comes in, it's as if a battering ram hit that stronghold, causing its destruction.

CURSES, LEGALISM AND SUPERSTITION

Curses, legalism and superstition are three tools the enemy uses to gain access to our mind so that truth cannot penetrate it.

Curses are words uttered against us to bring harm. Instead of bringing liberation, these words work in our mind to produce a stronghold. Before long, these words penetrate our heart and attach themselves to our lives, even affecting the way we operate. Curses can alight through witchcraft, legalism and superstition. Surprisingly, they all work the same way.

Legalism is an attempt to please God by following a set of religious rules. We then bind those rules to ourselves and to our thought processes, and make those rules equal to truth, rather than allowing the Holy Spirit to be our guide. Have you ever known someone to take a passage from the Word of God and use it illegitimately as a whipping tool or as binding law? These beliefs, which can seem good, narrow our path and sphere of life in a way that God never intended. Just as a curse binds us to an ungodly belief, so does legalism. Legalism works through religious spirits. Many times religious spirits work within the Church in superstitious, legalistic forms. They take the truth, through which God intends to bring liberty, and misuse it to bring bondage.

In the following passage, Paul warned the church of Galatia that they had been slipped into the bondage of having to keep the Law to be pure before God: "Oh, foolish Galatians! What magician has cast an evil spell on you? ["Who has bewitched you?" in the *NKJV*] For you used to see the meaning of Jesus Christ's death as clearly as though I had shown you a signboard with a picture of Christ dying on the cross. Let me ask you this one question: Did you receive the Holy Spirit by keeping the law? Of course not, for the Holy Spirit came upon you only after you believed the message you heard about Christ. Have you lost your senses? After starting your Christian lives in the Spirit, why are you now trying to become perfect by our own human effort? You have suffered so much for the Good News. Surely it was not in vain, was it? Are you now going to just throw it all away?" (Gal. 3:1-4, *NLT*).

Superstition works very much the same way. It takes a set of rules that must be followed in order to keep evil from our lives. When I was growing up, my family had numerous superstitions. If a triggering event occurred, we had to do 10 other things to neutralize the negative effects that we thought would come as a result of the trigger. The Bible says that superstition is a sign of ignorance. Ignorance has nothing to do with our not being educated, but it has everything to do with our rejecting the truth at some point so that the truth is no longer operating in us. Superstition binds us to certain behaviors, just as legalism does. Therefore, when we embrace superstitious beliefs of any nature, legalistic thought patterns are the result.

Demonization Through Lies

Curses, legalism and superstition all work to bind us into certain behaviors and to keep us from liberation in God. Each of these works against our thinking processes. The minute we receive them as truth, even though they are lies, we are captured by a demonic force. That is why Christians can be demonized. Even though Christians have been saved through Christ, the lies they believe pervert their ability to think and to receive truth into their minds. They end up calling good evil and evil good.

Whenever we buy into a lie, the lie will go into our mind and end up in our heart. Proverbs 4:23 says, "Above all else, guard your heart, for it is the wellspring of life" (*NIV*). The *New King James Version* uses the phrase "the issues of life." A lie will go down into the issues of life that are in our heart and will try to thwart the purpose for which we have been sent to Earth to accomplish.

Therefore, whenever we believe a lie, it actually interrupts the life cycle we discussed in the beginning of this chapter. Instead of life flowing through our blood, it is the wrong word that actually starts flowing through the veins of our body. As the effects of that lie start flowing through the blood pumping through our heart (which has accepted the lie), it begins to darken our conscience. And Satan knows that if he can darken our conscience enough, he can trap us. So as this lie remains in our mind, Satan is able to build a wall that keeps us from recognizing the truth.

Every lie we receive in the mind works like an anesthetic to deaden us. In the Bible it is called a spirit of slumber (see Isa. 29:10). The lie attaches itself to an unbelieving, mocking, blasphemous spirit so that we can't see the truth and be liberated. It will make us go to sleep at the right time to keep us from hearing truth. The enemy will try to use false arguments and philosophies to keep people from knowing the truth about. So we are to cast down these lies (see 2 Cor. 10:4-5).

A Renewed Spirit

Once our mind is infested by evil spirits or once we have allowed a wrong belief system to come into our mind, our salvation may stay intact, but our spirit can become affected so that it's not operating properly. If our spirit is not operating correctly, then the destiny of our lives cannot be completed. Evil surroundings can vex us (to "vex" means to rage or be violent; to suppress or maltreat; to destroy, oppress or do violence; to injure; to exasperate; to entreat evil, harm or hurt).

Psalm 51:10 reads, "Create in me a clean heart, O God, and renew a steadfast spirit within me." Before writing this psalm, David made some big mistakes—adultery and murder, to be precise—so here David prays for God to get him back on the right path. His mistakes had caused his spirit to break alignment and communion with the holy God. He knew that unless his spirit were renewed, he would not have relationship with God, and everything else in his life would fall to ruin. Every one of us makes mistakes and is deceived by lies at some point. The only way we can stay deceived is through pride. Once we humble ourselves, we break the devil's plan against our lives. David humbled himself and asked for a renewed spirit. We must do the same.

A Human Spirit That Is Alive to God

Though the human spirit cannot be seen, it is the driving force of our lives. It is that part of us that becomes alive to God and that must remain alive to God.

Qualities of an Alive Spirit

The following statements list 10 qualities of a human spirit that is alive to God:

1. The spirit is submitted to God (see Matt. 26:41).
2. The spirit can perceive what other people are thinking (see Mark 2:8).
3. The spirit worships and flows in exaltation to God (see Luke 1:47; John 4:23).
4. The spirit can become troubled (see John 13:21).
5. The spirit can travail (see John 11:33,38).
6. The spirit can be fervent (see Acts 18:25).
7. The spirit is determined but not stubborn (see Luke 9:51; Acts 19:21).
8. The spirit sings to God and blesses Him (see 1 Cor. 14:15-16).
9. Faith arises in the spirit and works through love (see 2 Cor. 4:13; Gal. 5:6).
10. The spirit is filled with wisdom and revelation (see Eph. 1:17).

Functions of an Alive Spirit

A human spirit that is alive to God has three functions: intuition, communion and testimony.

Intuition. Activated by the Holy Spirit within us, intuition is a function of the human spirit. It includes the spiritual gifts of wisdom, knowledge and discernment. Ordinary senses become aroused through soulish desire, but the intuition of our spirit comes directly from the Holy Spirit. His anointing arises within us and eventually brings us to spiritual understanding.

Communion. The human spirit is one of two integral parts of communing with God. John 4:23-24 explains that true worshipers worship God in spirit and truth. In worship, we gain a revelation of who God is. Demonic forces try to block our free communion with God so that we cannot receive this revelation. Worship and communion should be daily occurrences, because they keep the flow of God's Spirit moving through us, resulting in cleansing, refreshment and understanding.

Testimony. The human spirit testifies to two things. First, it gives testimony, or bears witness, to biblical truth. Psalm 119:14 reads, "I have rejoiced in the way of Your testimonies, as much as in great riches." It is with the spirit that we rejoice in the truth of God's Word.

Second, the human spirit testifies to the power of God. When we go through a trial and come out victorious, God proves Himself to us. This proof of God is then recorded in the memory of our spirit. When we again come in contact with a situation that we know is contrary to God's ability, we can recall what God did in the past and speak that testimony forth. We can say with confidence, "God has a way!"

What does a testimony do? It overcomes the devil and dismantles demons. Revelation 12:11 reads, "They overcame him [the accuser of the brethren] by the blood of the Lamb and by the word of their testimony." If we want to overcome the enemy, we must allow the testings we go through to become our testimony.

Whining, on the other hand, is the opposite of giving testimony, and it is a part of the soulish nature. It loves self-pity. When we whine, self is trying to draw attention to the circumstances that we are in. Self wants to draw attention to us as individuals and away from God's purpose. Rather than whining, if we testify to God's overcoming power, from that day forward the truth of His power will displace the enemy's foothold within us and overthrow his strategy in the area of our victory.

The Wind of Deliverance Brings Renewal

The Hebrew word *ruwach* and the Greek work *pneuma* can be translated as "wind," "breath" or "spirit." When translated as "spirit," these words refer to spirit beings: God, angels, demons and humans.[2] The Holy Spirit comes like a wind into our human spirit and regenerates and empowers us. This wind has a restoring quality. Where we have grown desolate, the wind of the Holy Spirit breaks the power of desolation and brings life to us. Demons also can come like a wind. But like an adverse wind, they come into a person's soul, set against the movement of the wind of the Holy Spirit in that person.

So this is what deliverance is: It's our Deliverer's coming and bringing a wind of refreshing and cleansing that restores us to the full walk that God has intended for us. To allow His Spirit to move freely in you, confess any sin that you have. As the Holy Spirit begins to move, declare that He will blow the adverse winds of your soul completely out of your body and that you will be set back on the path of life that God ordained for you from the foundations of the earth.

You may want to pray the following prayer to help you and those to whom you minister regain your footing on the path of life that God has set:

Dear Lord, please show me the path of life. Let me feel Your presence. Let me experience the fullness of Your joy. I know that You are at the right hand of the Father and available to me. At Your right hand there are pleasures forevermore. Teach me Your way and lead me in a very plain path. There are enemies all along my path, so please make my way straight so that my enemies will not be able to attach to me or distract me from the fullness You have for me. Even though I walk through narrow ways, You will give me a safe passage. You have already released commandments to instruct me along my path. I delight in these commandments, because they keep my path straight. Your Word is a lamp unto my feet and a light unto my path. You are acquainted with all my ways along this path. You know when my spirit becomes overwhelmed by the anxieties of the world around me. Even though the enemy has secretly laid snares for me, You will make me surefooted as I walk this path of life. Let all my ways be established as I ponder each step that I take before You.[3]

Notes

1. Chuck D. Pierce and Rebecca Wagner Sytsema, *Possessing Your Inheritance* (Ventura, CA: Renew Books, 1999), pp. 25-26.
2. James Strong, *The New Strong's Exhaustive Concordance of the Bible* (Nashville, TN: Thomas Nelson Publishers, 1984), Hebrew ref. no. 7307 and Greek ref. no. 4151.
3. This prayer is composed of excerpts and paraphrases from Psalm 16:11; 27:11; 119:35,105; 139:3; 142:3; Proverbs 1:15; 2:9; 4:14.

Chapter 4

THE BELIEVER'S AUTHORITY OVER DEMONIC SPIRITS

Charles H. Kraft

There is no question that demons have supernatural power to influence our lives. If we are to follow Jesus' command to cast out demons, what can we do to counteract that power? Where do we get the authority to even move into the supernatural realm to do combat with them?

Authority, as it is generally understood, is the right to use power. When we are dealing with deliverance, then, the authority we are discussing is the authority to work in the power of Christ to free people from demons. It is clear from Scripture that Jesus had this authority and used it frequently to set people free from demonic infestation. It is also clear from Luke 9:1 that Jesus granted this authority to His disciples.

Jesus' Authority

Many Christians assume that Jesus worked in the authority of His own divinity. I grew up subscribing to that assumption myself. Holding to this assumption, I then assumed that dealing with demons the way Jesus did required divinity or, at least, the personal commissioning the disciples received from Jesus while He was alive.

Jesus could heal and cast out demons because He was God, I assumed. I could not do these things because I am not God. And that meant that those who claimed to be healers today were mistaken. Nor could anyone expect me to be effective in praying for healing.

With the assumption that Jesus was working out of His divinity firmly in place, however, I found myself at a loss in trying to interpret Philippians 2. For we are told there that Jesus laid aside His divine prerogatives while on Earth (see Phil. 2:6-7). If He had laid aside His divinity, I wondered, how could He do miraculous things and how could He on occasion read people's minds?

It wasn't until the early 1980s, nearly 40 years into my Christian experience, that I began to see that Jesus really did not use His divine powers while on Earth. And the clues to recognizing this fact lie in what we are taught in the Scriptures concerning Jesus' authority.

First of all, while Jesus was growing up, He showed no signs of His deity. We know this because the people of His hometown, Nazareth, were amazed when He began to do miraculous things (see Matt. 13:53-56). These people had known Jesus from birth and had not seen Him do any mighty works. But now, at age 30, a big change had taken place in Jesus. All of a sudden He began healing the sick, casting out demons and teaching—all with incredible authority—and acting as if He owned the world.

We read in Luke that the thing that brought about that change was that He had been given the Holy Spirit by God the Father (see Luke 3:21-22). The next scene in Jesus' life, then, features temptations that begin with, "If you are the Son of God . . ."—temptations to use His deity either to ease His circumstances or to show that God's angels would look after Him if He needed help (see Luke 4:1-12). He, of course, refused, choosing rather to obey the Father by carrying out His mission and ministry entirely as a Man, never resorting to using His divinity.

Although He remained fully God (and still is), Jesus set aside His divine powers while He walked the earth, refusing to use them even to make His life or ministry easier. He even refused to use His divinity at the end of His life on Earth to rescue Himself from the soldiers who had come to capture and kill Him (see Matt. 26:53-54). He did it all as a Man and then predicted that we, His followers, would be able to do everything that He did—and more (see John 14:12).

The Disciples' Authority

Jesus, in sending out the Twelve in Luke 9 and the Seventy in Luke 10 gave them "power and authority over all demons, and to cure diseases" (Luke 9:1). This is an amazing thing, given the fact that Jesus' followers often demonstrated precious little understanding and faith. These were not spiritual giants or people who exhibited spectacular gifting, they would be classed today as "country bumpkins" and be laughed at for their accent.

But to such as these Jesus gave His commission and the same Holy Spirit who had empowered Him. It was these disciples who obeyed Jesus' command to wait in Jerusalem until they received power from on high (see Luke 24:49; Acts 1:4). These disciples, then, according to the book of Acts, went out into the world to demonstrate that the Holy Spirit was indeed empowering them—as He had empowered Jesus—to continue the ministry in power and authority that Jesus had started.

And these disciples were commanded to teach their followers all that Jesus had taught them (see Matt. 28:20). One of these disciples, then, recorded Jesus' amazing prediction that whoever had faith in Him would do what He had been doing and more (see John 14:12).

It is this prediction, and the command that is implicit in it, that we look to as our mandate for continuing the work of Jesus and the disciples in power and authority. Jesus expected His followers, including us, to work in His authority; and He gave us the same Holy Spirit who empowered Him so that we could do the same works that Jesus Himself did.

What Did Jesus Empower Us to Do?

If Jesus has called and empowered us to do what He did while on Earth, we must learn to work in His authority. And we see Holy Spirit power and authority behind all that He spoke and did during His ministry years. We note, however, that what He taught was a matter of deed as well as of word. He indicates this when, in frustration, He tells the unbelieving crowd, "If you won't believe my words, perhaps you will believe my deeds" (see John 10:37-38). Jesus was the demonstration both of who God is and of what humans are supposed to be. Thus, we look to His example as much as to His words to learn about authority.

This being true, what did Jesus teach through word and deed and what has He been teaching us concerning authority?

Recognizing the Reality of Evil

First of all, it is clear that Jesus believed and taught that there is an evil spirit world headed by one He calls "the ruler of this world" (John 14:30). He shows that we are to take this evil spirit world seriously but that we are not to be intimidated by it.

The satanic kingdom is very active in this world, taking advantage of people as often as possible. One important function of this kingdom is to place demonic representatives in people to influence and, if possible, control them. Jesus referred to people as "captives" (Luke 4:18) who need to be freed from the activity of these spirits. Demons apparently have no right to live inside of people who are spiritually clean (see Prov. 26:2; John 14:30). But there are enough people with enough garbage inside them to make it possible for the enemy to be quite successful in his attempts to gain a position inside. We have found that demonization, the right of demons to live inside a person, is a very common problem for Christians and non-Christians alike.

Embracing Our God-Given Authority over Demons

Second, Jesus gave His disciples power and authority to heal and cast out demons (see Luke 9:1) and commanded those disciples to teach their followers what they had learned of this authority and power (see Matt. 28:19-20). He did not simply demonstrate the authority and power as a characteristic of God. He intended that we would imitate Him in confronting the evil spirit world by doing the works that He Himself did (see John 14:12).

Jesus intended that all Christians would follow His example in asserting the power and authority that He gives us over the enemy spirit world.

Jesus, in passing on this authority, seems to make no distinction between people who have special gifting and those who don't. He seems to have made His prediction concerning what those who put their faith in Him would do without restriction. It appears that He intended that all Christians would follow His example in asserting the power and authority that He gives us over the enemy spirit world.

Depending on God the Father

Third, Jesus showed us how to depend on God the Father for leading and empowerment and how to listen to the Father's directions. The authority He took to meet with the Father in secret is intended to be imitated by His followers. There is where He received His instructions concerning ministry, including how He was to use the authority that came from the Father. It was if Jesus carried a credit card with the Father's name at the top and His under it. With that card He had all the authority of the One whose name is on the top of the card. He needed, however, to check with the Father constantly to find out how next to use that authority.

We note that with the Holy Spirit in Him, Jesus had all the power of God at His disposal. The authority, however, plus how to use that authority, came from His intimacy with the Father. Jesus lived, and showed us how to live, in total dependence on the Father. In order to do this, He cultivated His relationship with the Father, doing only what He saw His Father doing (see John 5:19), saying only what the Father had instructed Him to say (see John 8:28). Our authority, like Jesus' authority, then, is a function of our close relationship with the Father.

Following Jesus' Example

We are, therefore, to follow Jesus' example. The fact that He laid aside His deity, working totally out of His humanity empowered by the Holy Spirit, means that we can imitate Him. As He promised, we can do the works that He did. These works don't get done, however, unless we assert ourselves in partnership with Jesus to do them. A credit card is of no use if it just sits on our dresser or in our pocket. It must be taken out and used if it is to be worth anything.

One of the major activities of our enemy, Satan, is to keep us ignorant of the authority we have and how to use it. We may believe that Satan and demons exist but, since we have never seen a demon manifest itself, we live our lives without ever challenging one. Satan and demons, for their part, are intelligent enough to seldom reveal their presence in such a way that people who could successfully oppose them—Christians—will recognize them. They are, of course, helped considerably in American society by the fact that we have developed secular ways of interpreting demonic activity through psychology and medical science. While this is not to say that all troublesome emotional and medical conditions are demonic, our society has a long tradition of interpreting every problem without allowing for the possibility that it might involve a spiritual component.

Whether by ignoring demons, or by believing in them but never challenging them, the result is that captives are not set free. How different this is from what Jesus did.

Choosing Not to Fear Demons

I note that many Christians who have chosen to challenge our Western worldview by believing in demons have allowed themselves to fear them. It seems that once we break through the ignorance barrier, the tendency is to assume that demons have more power than they really do and to become fearful of them. Those who fall into this error have not learned what Jesus taught and what every demon knows—that we humans, working in the power of the Holy Spirit, carry infinitely more power than any demon. So, the fear that demons seek to engender in us is a matter of their ability to bluff and deceive us, not a function of their power.

Indeed, those of us who regularly challenge demons have discovered that they cannot outpower us. And once we are on to their bluffing and deceiving, demons are no match for the power of the Holy Spirit. We see this in Jesus' ministry, in that of His followers in the book of Acts and in our own ministries today. The demons know we have the authority of Jesus Himself. The problem is whether or not we know it and are willing to work in that authority.

So, we who have put our trust in Jesus need not fear Satan and demons. For we have the authority, like Jesus, to challenge demons, the authority to break their power and the authority to free people from demonic influence.

Knowing We Are Not Alone

We also have the authority to gain insight from the Holy Spirit concerning how to deal with demons. For not everything we need to know is recorded in Scripture. Following Jesus' example of depending on the Father, we have the right to ask Him for insight, with the confidence that when we follow Jesus' example by challenging demons, He enables us to know what to do. For we do not work by ourselves to free people from demons. We cannot do it through our own strength and power. We can only banish demons in partnership with Jesus. And in this partnership, Jesus reveals to us what we need to know to do the job. He does this in several ways.

In the Bible, we see God revealing things to people directly. He is still doing that. All of us who work to set captives free from demons have experienced over and over the revealing activity of the Holy Spirit before, during and after deliverance sessions. Whether we work from a questionnaire, as Doris Wagner and others do, through which God reveals what needs to be done, or whether we depend totally on words of knowledge, as many do, Jesus is there to show us what to do. The Holy Spirit even forces demons themselves to bring many things to our attention that we would not have otherwise known—things that we then can use against them. And the experience we gain as we work with Jesus to set captives free is a further important source of His leading.

Using the Accompanying Power to Heal

The authority to heal goes along with our authority to free people from demons. This is especially true of the healing of emotional wounds. Demons do not simply grab people without a reason. They can only live in people if they have legal rights to be there. And these rights are given them in a variety of ways.

Though I will not go into detail here as to how these rights are obtained, the list includes the following: inheritance from parents who have been involved in the occult or being involved in the occult oneself; having been dedicated to spirits; being cursed; making vows; hanging on to damaging emotional reactions such as anger, fear, shame, hatred, rejection, rebellion and the like. When these conditions exist, demons have a legal right to live inside a person.[1]

Getting rid of the demons, then, is most easily done by assuming our authority to break the enemy's power in these areas and to bring healing to emotional and spiritual wounds. Many have assumed that the demonized person's greatest problem is the demon itself. This is seldom true. For demons are like rats. And the ability of rats to stay in a place is dependent on the presence of garbage in that place. With demons, then, it is the presence of emotional and spiritual garbage that gives them the legal rights they need to live in a person. Demons cannot create problems out of nothing. They can only attach themselves to problems that already exist. Their job is to make those problems worse and, thereby, to keep the person in captivity.

If a person is to be healed, then, it is not sufficient to dispatch the rats. The garbage needs to be dealt with. Indeed, those who assume that the demons are the main problem and work hard, often with a fight, to get them out, find that unless they also deal with the emotional and spiritual stuff to which the demons are attached, the person will not get well.

But Jesus gives us the authority to deal with this garbage to set captives free from their emotional and spiritual stuff as well as from the demonic stuff. And we find that if we deal with the garbage first, the rats lose their power and can be cast out without being able to cause violence or embarrassment to the person being freed. Dealing with the garbage is called inner healing.[2]

Though the demons recognize our authority and see their strength diminishing as we administer inner healing, they usually hide until challenged. Typically, they have been working in such a way that the person they inhabit is unaware of their presence and blaming him- or herself for the problems those demons cause. We are, then, to use our authority to flush them out.

Conclusion

Jesus assumed the existence of a satanic kingdom over which both He and we, empowered by the Holy Spirit, have authority over. We have the authority, then, to do all that is necessary to deal effectively with demons. This authority comes from Jesus and is recognized by the whole satanic kingdom. The demons, however, knowing our ignorance, attempt to bluff and deceive us into either ignoring them, or fighting them on their terms, rather than Jesus'.

We note that Jesus did not simply ask God to release people from demons. Assuming the authority the Father had given Him, He commanded it. He worked with the Father and exercised His authority as One commissioned by God to plant His kingdom in the middle of Satan's domain. From this position, then, He won little victories such as healings and deliverances on His way to ultimate victory through the Cross and the Resurrection. Beyond that, He has chosen to partner with us to manifest that victory by continually crushing Satan under our feet (see Rom. 16:20). To that end, He has given us the same power and authority He gave to His disciples (see Luke 9:1). May we learn to work with Him in that authority to do the works He promised we would do (see John 14:12).

Notes

1. For more details, see Charles H. Kraft, *Defeating Dark Angels* (Ventura, CA: Regal Books, 2004).
2. For more information on inner healing, see Charles H. Kraft, *Deep Wounds, Deep Healing* (Ventura, CA: Regal Books, 2004).

Chapter 5

HOW TO MINISTER SPIRITUAL HOUSECLEANING

Alice Smith

It was eerie as the pastor and I stood on the cleared land—stripped by a raging flood. A church building once stood here; however, the flood had swept it away. The pastor began to explain all the problems with the escrow, the building, unexplainable odors on the property and the people's behaving strangely. Now the shattered building was flowing down the San Jacinto River.

"What are we dealing with?" the pastor asked.

"It sounds like defiled land to me," I bluntly answered.

"Well, that could be. The movie *Grave Secrets* was made about this neighborhood. Apparently it was once an Indian burial ground. The developers never told the residents who bought the homes. Many began to have light bulbs burst, smell strange odors and experience increased sickness. Although I don't know the outcome, some of the residents filed lawsuits against the developers. Some of the homes stand abandoned today. Even though we are in the same subdivision, I thought we were far enough away to avoid problems."

Defiled Land

Defiled land is mentioned in the Old Testament 11 times (see Lev. 11:44; 18:25,27-28; Num. 35:34; Deut. 24:4; Jer. 2:7; Ezek. 22:4; 33:26; 36:17-18). The Hebrew word for "defiled" is translated *tame,* which means to be foul, especially in a ceremonial or moral sense.[1] Today our land is defiled. It is spiritually polluted by sin, idols, broken covenants and laws of God, sexual perversion and the shedding of innocent blood.

From the tower of Babel, God dispersed the human race around the world. North American soil, like that of other continents, has suffered the malignancy of the sin of its inhabitants. Because of human sin, "we are conscious that all living things are weeping and sorrowing together in pain until now" (Rom. 8:22, *BBE*). Paul wrote, "Having made peace through the blood of his [Christ's] cross, by him to reconcile all things unto himself . . . whether they be things in earth, or things in heaven" (Col. 1:20, *KJV;* see also Eph. 1:10; Phil. 2:10.)

As carcasses attract the vultures of the air, so defiled land attracts spiritual wickedness. Where the land has been defiled, demons cluster. There they build their strongholds on the very contracts that people have made with sin. Sin's defilement hinders the work of the Spirit of God. It may be in a life, home or city. These are two of the many reasons we need freedom for the homes we live in and for our own lives (see Deut. 19:10,13; Ps. 74:7; 106:37-39; Isa. 24:5; 59:3; Jer. 2:7-8; 3:1-2,9; 7:6-7,30-31; 22:3,17).

Spiritual Housecleaning

God has instructed us, "Abstain from every form of evil" (1 Thess. 5:22), but instead we, the human race, have chosen to defile ourselves and to defile the land we inhabit. In order to cleanse the land and ourselves of this evil, we must do spiritual cleaning both of our homes and of our lives.

Our Homes

The first cleaning involves discovering and removing the spiritual pollution in our homes and sanctifying (dedicating) them unto the Lord. Deuteronomy 7:25-26 says, "The graven images of their gods shall ye burn with fire: thou shalt not desire the silver or gold that is on them, nor take it unto thee, lest thou be snared therein; for it is an abomination to the LORD thy God. Neither shalt thou bring an abomination into thine house, lest thou be a cursed thing like it: but thou shalt utterly detest it, and thou shalt utterly abhor it; for it is a cursed thing" (*KJV*).

Symptoms of spiritual pollution in our homes can include things such as these:

- Sudden ongoing illness
- Continual bad dreams and nightmares
- Insomnia (inability to sleep peacefully)
- Behavioral problems among the adults or children (continual fighting and misunderstandings)
- No peace
- Unexplained illnesses (such as chronic headache or fatigue)
- Heightened bondages (increased mental or physical perversion)
- Ghosts or demonic apparitions
- Poltergeist (the movement of physical objects by demons)
- Foul unexplainable odors
- Atmospheric heaviness (which makes it hard to breathe)

If you have any of these symptoms of spiritual pollution going on in your home, then it is possible that you have spiritual defilement in your home, either by your doing or by the previous owner's doing. You have the right to take action, as the couple in the following story did.

Before I entered the ministry, I was a real estate agent in Houston, Texas. I once listed a very attractive home on the north side of town that had every promise for a good sale. The renters had moved out. The owners, a precious but confused Christian couple, now wanted to sell the house. They confided in me that they felt something was wrong with it.

They were right. Even though I had contracted the house to be painted inside and out and installed new wallpaper and carpet, I still couldn't sell this home.

So one day I took a team of praying people to the vacant house with me. Before we could get out of the car, our son said that he felt the Lord speak to him that a teenage boy had practiced witchcraft in this home. Then he said to us, "There is a black, spray painted pentagram on the ceiling of the house." I told him that this was impossible because I had listed the house and no such thing was there. But realizing the nature of revelation, we determined to look inside the attic. We pulled the rope, opening the door to the attic and climbed in. As we turned on the light, our eyes locked on a huge black pentagram that had been sprayed on the bare wood around the beams.

As the owners repented for the defilement of the home and dedicated it to the Lord, we were confident that He had heard our prayer. Less than 12 hours later the home sold for full price, after having been on the market for over six months.

Acts 19 shows a group of believers who did spiritual housecleaning. Once the gospel had spread throughout Ephesus, "many who believed came and confessed and showed their deeds. Also many of those practicing the curious arts, bringing together the books, burned them before all. And they counted the prices of them and found it to be fifty thousand pieces of silver. So the Word of God grew mightily and prevailed" (vv. 18-20, *MKJV*). C. Peter Wagner says the people of Ephesus destroyed an estimated $4 million worth of occult items.[2] The remainder of Acts 19 tells how this action of repentance on behalf of the Ephesian people set great anger into motion when a city mob ran as one person into the amphitheatre because of the work Paul was doing in the city.

Deuteronomy 18:9-12 instructs us to avoid all sorts of occult practices: "When you come to the land which the Lord your God gives you, you shall not learn to do according to the abominations of those nations. There shall not be found among you anyone who makes his son or his daughter to pass through the fire, or that uses divination, an observer of clouds, or a fortune-teller, or a witch, or a charmer, or a consulter with familiar spirits, or a wizard, or one who calls to the dead. For all that do these things are an abomination to the Lord. And because of these abominations the Lord your God drives them out from before you" (*MKJV*).

Listed below are items or activities with which we can invite spirits to function in our homes. I recommend that you consider each of these potential entry points and ask the Lord whether it has served to invite a demon into your home and life.

- Objects related to heathen worship (such as Hindu gods, yoga, snakes, dragons, pyramids, crystals, broken crosses, Buddha figurines, Mary statues, rosary beads, Buddhist prophecy sticks, witchcraft objects, Buddhist prayer cloths, tribal face masks, eastern worship artifacts, southwestern Indian art dedicated by a shaman, totem poles, gargoyles, tarot cards, tea leaves, worry stones, voodoo dolls)
- Objects related to the occult (such as Ouija boards, materials related to Dungeons and Dragons and Masters of the Universe, many video games, horoscope or astrology books, demonic tattoos, books on reincarnation, kabala books, Satanism materials and New Age materials)
- Movie videos with immoral behavior or foul language and pornographic books, pictures or websites
- Music that demonstrates a demonic or depraved mental imagery, uses filthy words or creates an interest in death or murder
- Pokemon dolls ("pokemon" means pocket monsters), goddess statues, demon statues, comic books that depict evil, rock posters, troll dolls, Smurf dolls, demonic action figures, Mardi Gras beads (variation of rosary beads), dowsing rods or pendulums, and an obsession with turtles (an Egyptian god), owls (witches use for controlling others) or phoenix birds (Egyptian god that controlled the underworld)
- Harry Potter books; certain Disney books and movies that deal with genies and frightening themes; books related to Satanism,

witchcraft, New Age, rebirthing, astrology, Christian Science, Mormonism, Freemasonry, Knights of Malta, Grangers, Taoism, Confucius philosophy, Scientology, Jehovah's Witness, Unity church, Koran, geomancy books, numerology, the Way International, Roy Masters, Transcendental Meditation, Hare Krishna, martial arts, Bahaism and Rosicrucianism
- Art or jewelry with obvious demonic representations, such as snakes, dragons, gargoyles, yin-yang objects, broken crosses, upside-down crosses, swastikas, crystal objects used for the purpose of creating power, shaman worship objects, fetishes (objects with magic powers), phyot armbands, amulets (charms with magic incantations inscribed), good luck charms or beaded bracelets for good luck

In the early 1970s, my husband, Eddie, and I were in a church in South Texas. During the invitation time, a woman came forward crying. She discussed something with the pastor, and then took the microphone. She explained that she was the Sunday School teacher for the fifth grade girls. On Friday night she had a sleepover. One of her girls brought a game with her—the Ouija board (witches board). They began to ask it questions. The triangular piece moved automatically under their fingers to spell out the words. The naïve group asked, "Who are you?" The pointer spelled, "D-E-A-T-H." "Where are you from?" It spelled, "S-A-T-A-N." "How far does your power reach?" It replied, "T-O—T-H-E—B-L-O-O-D."

Our Lives

The second level of spiritual housecleaning involves us. It is possible for things related to our past sin to pollute our lives. If we have been active in an illicit relationship or in an abusive or controlling one, unholy soul ties may have been established. An unholy soul tie is an unseen spiritual alliance or covenant that has supernatural influence over a person. Throughout history, when men made covenants, they sealed them by exchanging gifts. Some of the things that can keep us bound to past sin and susceptible to present evil influences include the following:

- Old photos
- Jewelry
- Love letters
- Clothing
- Furniture
- Stuffed animals

Once, when Eddie and I were guest ministers in a church in Oklahoma, a pastor's wife came to us asking for help. She admitted to a sexual relationship with a teenage boy in the church. This very attractive woman explained how they would meet secretly atop one of the hills that surrounded the city. We helped her repent, pray for forgiveness, break contracts and seek reconciliation with God, her husband, the boy, his family and the church (many of whom already knew something was going on). Incredible joy filled this young woman as she was set free.

Three weeks later, we received a call from her and her husband. Although she was resisting steadfastly, she was feeling drawn back into that sin. Still feeling like something was keeping her bound in the past, they asked us if they had overlooked something.

"Do you have any object, clothing or gift still in your possession that the boy gave to you?"

Surprised that we asked, she answered, "Yes, I sure do. Is this a problem?" She agreed to burn the blouse, necklace, letters and other gifts the immoral relationship had produced. We encouraged them to call us back if this didn't correct the problem. Having never called, we are sure the ties were severed.

The Purification Process

King Hezekiah was only 25 years old when he became king. Second Chronicles 29 tells us that he called in the priests and Levites to consecrate themselves and the Temple of the Lord: "Remove all defilement from the sanctuary. Our fathers were unfaithful; they did evil in the eyes of the LORD. Therefore, the anger of the LORD has fallen on Judah and Jerusalem; he has made them an object of dread and horror and scorn, as you can see with your own eyes. This is why our fathers have fallen by the sword and why our sons and daughters and our wives are in captivity" (vv. 5-6,8-9, *NIV*). The priests consecrated themselves and removed all the defiled things from the Temple, cleansing the utensils, the altar and the table. This is an excellent example for Christians today. Based on this pattern, here are the steps to purification:

1. Repent for the sins, bad attitudes and behaviors of both you and your family members (see 1 John 1:7-10).
2. Repent on behalf of past owners for any defilement in the land or house. God has given us dominion over the earth. "May the LORD who created the heavens and the earth give you his blessing. The LORD has kept the heavens for himself, but he has given the earth to us humans" (Ps. 115:15-16, *CEV*).
3. Remove and destroy (not give away) items related to the occult, heathen worship, past sin and anything else the God convicts you of. However, you do not have the right to destroy other people's property. You are responsible for what God shows you to do, and as you do it, you are sanctified (see Jas. 4:17).
4. Renounce aloud any demonic contract that you have made willingly or unwillingly, and break any unholy covenants with past sin. (Detail your renouncing. For example, you may want to pray, "I sever any and all unholy soul ties bound to me while in the ungodly relationship with [insert the name of the person]. I break them now by the blood of Jesus.")
5. Command the demons, in the name of Jesus, to leave you, your family and your home. Ask the Lord to cleanse you, your possessions and your home.

Understanding the Reasons Why

Joshua 7 records the story of Joshua and Achan. Joshua sent men from Jericho to Ai and told them to spy out the area. So they did. When they returned, they informed Joshua that Ai would be easy to take. They suggested that he send only two or three thousand men. But Ai's army chased the Israelites from the city gates and struck them down. Upon hearing this, Joshua and the elders tore their clothes and fell face down to the ground, asking the Lord what happened. God responded, "Stand up! What are you doing down on your face? Israel has sinned; *they* have violated my covenant, which I commanded them to keep. *They* have taken some of the devoted things; *they* have stolen, *they* have lied, *they* have put them with their own possessions. *That is why the Israelites cannot stand against their enemies*; *they* turn their backs and run because *they* have been made liable to destruction. *I will not be with you anymore unless you destroy whatever among you is devoted to destruction*" (vv. 10-12, *NIV*, emphasis added).

Joshua instructed the Israelites to consecrate themselves. The next morning he searched through each tribe, family and person until he confronted Achan, son of Carmi. Joshua asked him what he had done. Achan admitted, "It is true! I have sinned against the LORD, the God of Israel. This is what I have done: When I saw in the plunder a beautiful robe from Babylonia, two hundred shekels of silver and a wedge of gold weighing fifty shekels, I coveted them and took them. They are hidden in the ground inside my tent, with the silver underneath" (vv. 20-21, *NIV*).

When the messengers went to Achan's tent, they found the defiled things. The Scripture says, "They took the things from the tent, brought them to Joshua and all the Israelites and spread them out before the LORD" (v. 23, *NIV*). The items were acknowledged, destroyed and the result was that God delivered Ai into the hands of the Israelites (see Josh. 8).

Why do we need to cleanse our homes and our personal lives? You will notice that although Achan alone had sinned, God considered the whole nation guilty. He said that *they* (plural) had sinned. Lest you think this applied only in Old Testament times, the apostle Paul in the New Testament tells us that when one member of the Body of Christ suffers, the whole body suffers (see 1 Cor. 12:26). We learn that plural guilt is sometimes due to singular sin. God told the Israelites that as a result of Achan's sin, *they* had sinned. What you do in your home will and does affect the whole Body of Christ. Could it be that we, God's Church, are the greatest hindrance to national revival? Conduct spiritual housecleaning, purify yourself today, and you will hear God say, "Go up and attack your enemies. For I have delivered them into your hands."

Notes

1. James Strong, *The New Strong's Exhaustive Concordance of the Bible* (Nashville, TN: Thomas Nelson Publishers, 1984), Hebrew ref. no. 2930.
2. C. Peter Wagner, *Acts of the Holy Spirit* (Ventura, CA: Regal Books, 2000), p. 479.

Chapter 6

DELIVERANCE IN THE LOCAL CHURCH

Chris Hayward

"I'm not against *deliverance*. I just don't trust *deliverance ministries*." This is a fairly common sentiment among pastors. I know, because I was one of them.

I was saved at the age of 20 in the last few months of my Army tour of duty in Vietnam. I had been thoroughly entrenched in the occult and was delivered out of it, so I definitely knew and understood the need for deliverance. Much later, as an associate pastor, I saw well-meaning "deliverance ministers" come through the church and leave in their wake some real messes that took several months to clean up. As a result, once I became a senior pastor, I found myself reluctant to embrace deliverance as a ministry due to some of the excesses I had witnessed. These excesses came in the form of "goofy" or "weird" hyper-spirituality on the part of deliverance ministers who also suffered from a gross lack of biblical soundness and relational accountability. Other than that, I didn't have a problem.

Well, actually I did. I began to realize that some Christians had major problems that could not always be written off as psychological in nature. It didn't take long before I recognized the reality of Scripture—that our adversary, the devil, is alive and well (see 1 Pet. 5:8). He is still in the business of stealing, killing and destroying (see John 10:10). For me, the issue isn't, Can a Christian have a demon? No, the real issue is, Can a Christian be deceived, tempted, tormented, influenced—even controlled—by a demon? The answer is an emphatic yes. To deny the existence of demonic activity within the Christian community is to hide one's theological head in the sand. In private, most pastors will acknowledge this. However, so many of our Christian institutions still proclaim that demonic activity is reserved for the lost. There is a great vacuum of understanding among sincere men and women of God who want to deal with this subject within the local church in a biblical and balanced way.

Deliverance Is Not a Program—It's a Lifestyle

Deliverance, in reality, should become a part of the fabric of every local church. The activity of worship is not considered to be a program of the church but rather a part of the life of the church. In the same way, deliverance needs to become a natural aspect of church life. To make deliverance effective within the local church, there need to be certain measures in place. These measures include the following:

- Pastoral covering and involvement
- Sound teaching
- Discipleship training
- Accountability
- Safe environment for ministry
- Preparation *of* the individual
- Ministry *to* the individual
- Follow-through *with* the individual

Anchored in the Word of God

A common danger of deliverance ministry is that of leaning strictly upon experiences. I have observed some embarrassing examples of deliverance. Each incident had one or more of the following flaws:

- Lack of biblical precedent or foundation
- Focus upon the one ministering as having some special talent or ability
- Overly dramatic or theatrical manner on the part of the minister
- Violation of the privacy or dignity of the one being ministered to
- Unnecessary conversation and interaction with demons
- Assumption of powers beyond God-given authority
- Creation of an ongoing dependence upon the minister for future help
- Failure to work in cooperation with local church authority
- The spread of the notion that some sort of manifestation is needed before deliverance has happened

But we just can't go wrong if we adhere to God's Word, His character and His ways. While it is true that the Bible doesn't cover every example of how we are to minister, we can certainly observe the character of Christ and imitate His ways.

I am the son of my father, William Hayward. I loved my dad dearly. He was a good and wonderful man of God. Though he has gone on to be with the Lord, I can still imagine how he would handle certain situations. Because he ingrained certain values in me, I respond and act accordingly. This is also true about the Word of God. Concrete examples and rules are given for the way we are to conduct our lives. But for those situations for which we find no biblical precedent, we have the character and nature of God exemplified through Christ. In the Bible we see numerous examples of His love, sincerity, humility, wisdom and patience. And, we can behave accordingly. For deliverance ministry to become a part of the fabric of every local church, ministers who reflect the character of Christ and the truth of God's Word must accompany it. Without this, deliverance ministry is doomed to justifiable ridicule and exclusion.

Preparing for Battle

What many fail to see is the need for believers to be prepared for deliverance. During my years as a pastor, individuals would often come to me for counseling and prayer. Perhaps there would be a demonic stronghold due to unconfessed sin and ongoing failure. They would confess, repent and be prayed for. There would be an immediate relief and great joy. Then, in a short time, they would be back in my office in need of prayer for the very same problem. What was wrong? Without a fundamental change in their thinking—without an awareness of how they were continuing to open the door to demonic attack—they were bound to repeat the failures of the past.

However, not every demonic attack is a result of *personal* sin. Over the past several years I have prayed for a number of men and women who have experienced severe abuse. They rarely discussed the subject due to an overwhelming sense of shame. In many cases they suffered for years with emotional and demonic torment. But whether the bondage or torment is due to personal sin or the sin of another, there needs to be an opportunity for the truth of God's Word to saturate and prepare the soil of the heart prior to ministry. Only then can there be lasting deliverance: "And you shall know the truth, and the truth shall make you free" (John 8:32).

At Cleansing Stream Ministries, we provide four basic teachings as instruction for the participant, who then becomes increasingly prepared for deliverance.

Walk in the Spirit

"This I say then, Walk in the Spirit, and you shall not fulfill the lust of the flesh" (Gal. 5:16). The first teaching focuses on the need for the troubled believers to walk in the Spirit. During this first period of teaching, they come to understand the uniqueness of body, soul and spirit. Biblical and practical understanding is given so that they might know when they are walking soulishly, or *in the flesh*, versus walking spiritually, or *in the Spirit*. This focus brings a heightened awareness of how responses to life are often born of the soul (mind, emotions, and will) rather than through the Spirit.

It is simple to blame everything we do wrong on the devil. In reality, his greatest weapon is deception. His deception is focused in three areas. The first engagement of battle is in the mind. As such we are tempted to intellectually evaluate matters to the exclusion of biblical truth. Second, the battle is aimed at our emotions, tempting us to make judgment calls based on how we feel, rather than reliance upon the Word of God. Third, the temptation is focused upon our will, bringing confusion, loss of focus and consequently wrong and destructive choices.

Simply stated, our enemy wants us to revert back to the days before we came to know Christ, the days when we relied upon ourselves (mind, emotions and will)—without the influence of the Spirit of God. Many Christians have been so ingrained with the habit of self-reliance that they can hardly distinguish the difference. Their walk is a mixture of flesh and Spirit, producing a lukewarm existence and an entryway for demonic influence.

Commit Everything to God

The second teaching focuses on a consecrated life. This is a natural follow-up to the first teaching because the moment believers begin to walk in the Spirit, they become painfully aware of destructive habits onto which they are holding. Resistance accompanies every walk. These places of resistance usually represent areas of their lives which have not been yielded to God. They might be material possessions, relationships or even ministry.

I once knew of a woman (I'll call her Betty) who had a terrible time releasing her daughter to attend kindergarten. For many parents this can be a challenging occasion. But for Betty it went beyond challenging. Every half hour she would call the school to see if her daughter was safe. "Are you sure she is in the room she's supposed to be in?!" she would ask. "Is the teacher with her?" This went on to the point where the school administration was frustrated beyond belief. Finally, Betty received some ministry. Upon interviewing her, we discovered that as a young girl she had been molested at school. As a result, she needed to be delivered from a spirit of fear. But first she needed to consecrate her daughter to the Lord, otherwise Betty would never be truly delivered. Once she fully committed her daughter's life to the Lord, the spirit of fear had nothing to hang on to and was cast out of her life. Betty was then able to release her daughter to attend school.

Speak Words of Life

We discovered that once troubled believers begin to practice walking in the Spirit, and subsequently commit everything to God, they are presented with another challenge. Their mouths keep getting in the way. It is indicative of the reality that there is a great famine among believers today: a famine of rightly spoken words. The Western mind-set is generally slow to pick up on this important truth, "Death and life are in the power of the tongue, and those who love it will eat its fruit" (Prov. 18:21). We also know that "out of the abundance of the heart the mouth speaks" (Matt. 12:34). For example, if I say, "I will never be free from this habit," there is a very good chance that I will remain in bondage. I will tend to behave in a manner that fulfills what I speak from my heart. Or, if I say to my child, "You'll never amount to anything!" the adversary can use those words to press my child toward a life of failure. The tongue, as James tells us, is like the rudder steering a ship, or a fire igniting a forest (see Jas. 3:4-6). So we must begin to learn (or relearn) how to use words wisely.

Human bondage is a terrible thing. It quenches our confidence and causes us to believe that we are far less than who we really are. We embrace a "worm" mentality that convinces us we are unworthy, worthless creatures and should hide our faces in shame. We underestimate our call and God's love. Consequently, we underachieve, believing that all of our potential is lost. We solidify this hellish notion by the words we speak. If "faith comes by hearing, and hearing by the word of God" (Rom. 10:17), then a wasted life comes by speaking, hearing, believing and acting spoken words that contradict God's Word.

Entering the Cleansing Stream

There is a great joy knowing that God provides a way of escape from the bondage and entrapments of the devil. Once we have prepared believers for deliverance, we then create an opportunity for them to experience it. Every year we conduct hundreds of retreats throughout the United States and overseas. During these retreats, believers are gathered together to receive the ministry of deliverance. It is not mass deliverance, but rather, individual deliverance conducted on a mass scale.

For deliverance to become effective in the local church, the local church must become actively involved in a discipleship process. Deliverance must become more than some ministry coming into town to kick demons out of people in the church. As part of the discipling process, we also must involve those who are being prepared in disciplines of prayer; study and memorization of the Word; worship—as individuals or with their spouse and children; and accountability with a prayer partner. If we don't make this discipling process widespread, we will be forever doomed to the notion that deliverance is for the strange, the weird and the unbalanced. As it is normal for the body to breathe, so it must become just as normal for the local church to practice deliverance.

As it is normal for the body to breathe, so it must become just as normal for the local church to practice deliverance.

We have found that following a time of deliverance some of the participants would slip back to old ways of thinking or behaving, and would open the door again to demonic bondage. To answer this need, we developed a follow-up course to the retreat called "Press Toward the Goal." In this follow-up session, we assist people in making changes in their lives that would maintain the newfound freedom in Christ that they experienced through deliverance. If we don't cover up the pit into which we have fallen, we are likely to fall into it again once we've been pulled out.

This is where accountability comes in. We also attempt to have delivered believers participate in either a small accountability group within their local church or be assigned to a mature believer who will pray for and encourage them before, during and after the seminar and retreat.

A Place of Safety

It is extremely important for those who are coming for ministry at a retreat setting that it be a safe place. Creating an atmosphere of love and acceptance is essential for successful deliverance. Those things that have placed individuals under bondage to demonic attack can be very embarrassing to disclose. The fear of being found out or of being spoken about can keep them from ever stepping forward for ministry. Confidentiality must be at the heart of deliverance ministry, and it can be if the atmosphere is one of grace and love.

How to Get There from Here

How do we get there from here? It is very simple. Train others, who can train others to train others (see 2 Tim. 2:2). It is not my calling to spend the rest of my life going into churches to conduct deliverance meetings. That, ultimately, should be the work of the pastoral leadership and those trained by them. Let's imagine how that scenario would play out in your local church.

Let's imagine that First Church of Yourtown has made deliverance a natural part of its church life. This local church body is ministering deliverance to those in need within it. The members are functioning in spiritual warfare. Through discipleship training they are spreading the burden of ministry beyond that of just the pastoral staff. Trained believers are meeting regularly in the church to grow in their understanding and are helping to train others also. These teams, under pastoral supervision, are conducting intense deliverance sessions. As a result, the pastor's counseling load has been cut back by over 50 percent. All of this is taking place under pastoral covering and accountability.

This is our vision: that the ministry of deliverance will become a natural part of the fabric of every local church throughout the world. At Cleansing Stream Ministries we are beginning to see this happen. At the writing of this chapter, we are involved with over 2,500 churches within the United States, and over 700 churches overseas. In one 12-month period, over 20 teams have been sent out to over 22 countries to conduct deliverance retreats for those who have taken the 12-week preparation course.

God's Heart for Deliverance

Cleansing Stream Ministries continues to experience growth. Pastors are seriously seeking for a balanced, biblical approach to deliverance. Not long ago I asked the Lord, "Why is this becoming so strong? Why is there such a hunger now for what we are doing in this ministry?" I had assumed His answer, namely, that He was preparing a spotless Bride for His soon return.

While that is true, it is not the full reason. In answer, He showed me a great harvest that is beginning to happen—and a great gathering-in that is about to take place. And this is the impression that He left with me: "If those outside of Christ are broken, bruised and bound up, and they come to know My Son as Savior and enter into a church that is also broken, bruised and bound up—what good will it do?" I realize now that deliverance must indeed become the "children's bread" (Matt. 15:26; Mark 7:27). We must first partake of this bread of life, of this gift of deliverance, of this grace to be set free, if we are to ever be used by God to set others free in Jesus' name.

May God grant you understanding and His grace that will enable you to bring the ministry of deliverance into the local church.

Chapter 7

HOW DELIVERANCE SUSTAINS REVIVAL

C. Peter Wagner

Few Christian leaders who hear what the Spirit is saying to the churches would doubt that large-scale revival is about to come to America. Revival reports of many kinds have been proliferating over the last few years. Even those of us who are senior citizens fully expect to see a huge outpouring of the Holy Spirit over our nation before we go to our final rewards. I agree with the title of Chuck Pierce's book that *The Best Is Yet Ahead*!

An Issue of Timing

Understandably some people are surprised that the great revival has not come as yet. We have been praying fervently for it for quite some time. It is certainly God's will—no one is questioning that—so there must be some underlying issues of timing involved. God may well be holding back His timing, waiting for at least two things to happen. I admit that there may well be more than two, but I am writing this chapter from my personal perspective, and I can see these two very clearly. They have to do with the government of the Church and the fitness of the Church for spiritual warfare.

The Government of the Church

Since this book deals with deliverance, I will make only a brief mention of how the government of the Church can help determine God's timing for revival. But it is too important to ignore. Although few have paid much attention to it over the past 1,800 years, the Bible is nevertheless clear that the Church can never be all that God designed it to be without apostles and prophets.

For example, Ephesians 4:11 tells us that Jesus, from the time of His ascension, gave the Church apostles and prophets right along with the more customary evangelists, pastors and teachers. How important are the apostles and prophets? They are actually the foundation of the Church, according to Ephesians 2:20, with Jesus serving as the cornerstone which holds them together. Furthermore, there is a divine order: "And God has appointed these in the church: *first* apostles, *second* prophets, third teachers" (1 Cor. 12:28, emphasis added).

I am happy to be able to report that over the past few years enormous progress has been made in a growing recognition and affirmation of the gifts and offices of apostle and prophet in the Church. My own best observation would be that the renewal of this biblical government of the Church initially was set in place in the year 2001, and since then its acceptance has been rapidly increasing. Those who wish more information now have a high quality list of books to choose from, including five of my own.

Now back to God's timing for revival. It is not surprising that God would insist that the church government He designed would be in place before the great spiritual outpouring. How could we handle it without the proper foundation? We have a high degree of assurance that the foundation is now in place. What we do not know, however, is the exact point to which we need to develop and mature the apostolic movement before God becomes ready to move.

Fitness for Spiritual Warfare

The second factor which I believe is helping to determine God's timing for revival relates to the fitness of the Church for spiritual warfare. I don't think that we are quite as far advanced in this one as we are in church government. Ever since Jesus invaded the kingdom of Satan 2,000 years ago, the Church has been at war. Every soul saved, every healing, every miracle, every demon cast out is a defeat and a setback to Satan. He is losing ground and he has been losing it ever since Jesus said, "I will build My church" (Matt. 16:18). Satan's end is in sight, and no one knows this better than he does. This causes him to have "great wrath, because he knows that he has a short time" (Rev. 12:12).

Every soul saved, every healing, every miracle, every demon cast out is a defeat and a setback to Satan.

No matter what view we might hold regarding the time of Jesus' second coming, one thing is for certain. It is closer today than it ever has been before, and therefore Satan's time is also shorter. Satan has enough wrath as it is right now, but what do you suppose will happen when the greatest outpouring of the power of God in all of history occurs? His wrath will be off the charts! That is precisely why God would not allow it to happen until the Church is properly fit, physically, spiritually and emotionally, for serious spiritual warfare.

In the natural, the United States went to war on September 11, 2001. We have become accustomed to seeing video pictures of our troops on the front lines. Fortunately for us, they are fit. Their eyes are bright and their jaws are set. Their bodies are covered with the gear necessary for fighting and winning, and the soldiers have been trained to use that equipment effectively. There have been casualties, but relatively few. There have been defeats, but many more victories. Our military has what it takes to defeat the enemy, namely terrorism.

I'm afraid that, when we move to the spiritual realm, the Church is not quite as fit as it should be for frontline warfare. Fortunately, we're not totally impotent. We have come a long way, especially since the beginning of the 1990s. We're okay for some of the easier battles. But I don't think that we are as fit as God wants us to be for the ferocious counteroffensive of our enemy, Satan, that will certainly be provoked by the great revival.

Demonic Deliverance and Revival

Rather than dealing with the multiple dimensions of fitness for spiritual warfare that need attention, here I am going to focus on only one, namely, demonic deliverance. To use more technical terminology, this is ground-level spiritual warfare (as contrasted to strategic-level and occult-level spiritual warfare). When the revival comes, we'd better know how to cast out demons really well. That is essential to our spiritual fitness.

Most revivals, at least the initial revival fires, are short-lived. Look at history. The Welsh revival lasted a year, as did the Korean revival of 1907. The Great Awakening lasted two years. The Azusa Street revival went for three years. The Indonesian revival of the 1960s lasted almost four years, longer than most. And many others could be mentioned.

However, two modern revivals have had much longer life spans, namely the Argentine revival (17 years) and the transformation of the city of Almolonga in Guatemala (25 years). A prominent part of the spiritual fuel that sustained both of these revivals was demonic deliverance.

Revival in Argentina

Evangelist Carlos Annacondia was one of God's chief human instruments for sparking the Argentine revival back in 1982. Owner of a successful nuts and bolts factory, he had never been to Bible school, nor had he received ministerial ordination. But he began holding evangelistic campaigns in vacant lots, each one running 30 nights or more, and over the years he saw more than 1 million people, probably closer to 2 million, confess Jesus Christ as their Lord and Savior.

Demonic deliverance was part of every one of his meetings from the start. At a certain time, Carlos would begin coming against the principalities and powers of darkness assigned by Satan to neutralize his meetings and to keep lost souls in darkness. Carlos would even taunt the evil spirits as he was binding them. More than once he would shout his so-called war cry, "Listen to me, Satan!" Every time he did this, demons would start manifesting throughout the crowd, which would range from 2,000 to 20,000 people.

Anticipating this, Carlos would have a trained volunteer team of "stretcher bearers" (strong men, ready to move through the crowd two-by-two, identify those who were obviously demonized and escort, or carry, them around to a 150-foot carnival tent behind the platform). The tent was filled with groups of 3 chairs each, one for the deliverance minister, one for an intercessor and one for the "patient." Carlos called the tent his spiritual intensive care unit. These trained deliverance teams would minister as long as it took to cast the demons out of their victims. Some would still be ministering at daybreak!

The leader of Carlos Annacondia's deliverance ministry was Pablo Bottari, a former barber who has now become one of the world's foremost trainers of deliverance ministers. More recently he has joined the pastoral team of the prestigious Central Baptist Church in Buenos Aires as staff deliverance minister, and that church is now looked upon as a model of deliverance ministry in a local church. I highly recommend Bottari's book *Free in Christ*, as well as Annacondia's book *Listen to Me, Satan!*

We can learn many things from the Argentine revival, but one of the most important lessons is that an ongoing ministry of casting out demons helps greatly to sustain a revival once it begins.

Revival in Almolonga, Guatemala

Those who have viewed George Otis, Jr.'s epochal video, *Transformations*, will remember Almolonga, Guatemala. This city of 20,000 was festering in the pits of social degradation 25 years ago. Disease, immorality, poverty, violence, malnutrition, ignorance, crime, family abuse, drought and depression were rampant. Drunkenness was the escape mechanism of choice, and on Mondays the streets would be lined with bodies of men who, instead of taking their Friday pay envelope home to their families, had taken it to the bars and drank themselves into a lifeless stupor.

A handful of evangelical churches had been planted in Almolonga, none of which had more than a few struggling families trying to keep their heads above the water of despair. Not one of them was able to influence the city. They were all under the perverse control of Maximón, the territorial spirit whom Satan had assigned to keep the area in darkness.

Today everything is different. The largest buildings dotting the hills and streets around Almolonga are evangelical churches. Over 90 percent of the population is born again. Family life is joyful and children are finishing school. Disease seems to bypass the city. Streets and businesses have biblical names. Instead of drought, artesian water comes from the ground to nourish the crops. Cabbages are the size of basketballs. Carrots are as big as a man's forearm. Farmers deliver their produce from southern Mexico to Panama in Mercedes trucks paid for in cash. And the last jail was closed four years ago since crime is virtually nonexistent!

What happened?

Twenty-five years ago, one of Almolonga's struggling evangelical pastors, Mariano Riscajché, had been trying to counsel one of the city's notorious alcoholics. Mariano was very discouraged because he was getting nowhere. Then the Holy Spirit quietly spoke to him and suggested he try something new, namely, casting out a demon of drunkenness. Although he had neither training nor experience in deliverance ministry, in desperation Mariano took authority by the blood of Jesus Christ and commanded the demon to leave. It did! The man was saved and totally freed from his addiction to alcohol. The word quickly got out, and it wasn't long before Mariano had led 400 others to Christ and cast out the demons that had bound them.

Today Mariano has a church of 2,000 right in the central plaza, other churches are growing just as vigorously, and deliverance ministries are in place in all of the churches.

Wouldn't you like your city to be another Almolonga?

CHANGES ARE COMING!

Few would disagree that deliverance ministries in local churches across our nation are very low profile. I am not aware of any city in which deliverance ministry is available to the general public as is, for example, dentistry or automobile repairs or legal services or chiropractic or fast food or, for that matter, Christian worship. This is one thing that I believe must be changed if the expected revival is to come. My hope is that this new handbook on deliverance will help bring us to that point.

The trends, as I view them, are heading in the right direction. In the beginning of the last century, the Pentecostal movement began to draw our attention to the reality of demons. Unfortunately, however, traditional church leaders tended to stereotype Pentecostals as the "lunatic fringe." Then, after World War II, leaders such as Thomas Zimmerman of the Assemblies of God succeeded in mainstreaming Pentecostalism, but at the expense of toning down some of their distinctives, including the practice of casting out demons. The charismatic renewal beginning in the 1960s believed in demons, but, on the other hand, never mobilized for serious deliverance on a large scale.

Still, such developments helped lay the groundwork for positive changes. Christian leaders such as Neil Anderson, Fred Dickason, Charles Kraft, Jack Hayford and John Wimber kept raising our awareness of demons to new levels. Independent charismatics and Third Wave adherents began ministering deliverance more and more. Ministries such as Cleansing Stream Ministries found ways to activate deliverance ministries in local churches across the nation. The net result is that many more local church pastors across denominational lines now believe in literal demons and their activity much more than they did 10 years ago.

Deliverance Ministries in Local Churches

Now it is time to move from believing in demons to incorporating deliverance ministries into the normal life of our churches. The climate is ripe for change. One obvious problem is that many pastors would like to do more, but they have little to draw on. They had no courses in demonology in seminary or Bible school. My suggestion to those pastors who might be reading this book is to begin by teaching the congregation, perhaps through a series of sermons, the seven premises of basic demonology.

1. There are such things as demons.
2. Demons are created beings with distinct personalities.
3. They are active throughout the human population.
4. Their intent is evil—to cause as much misery as they can in this life and in the life to come. They delight in tormenting people.
5. They are organized under a hierarchy of leaders with Satan as the head.
6. Demons have considerable superhuman power to execute their wicked desires.
7. They have been defeated by Jesus' blood, and they are vulnerable to confrontation by believers empowered by the Holy Spirit.

Removing the Barriers

The good news is that an increasing number of pastors and other Christian leaders are accepting and teaching these seven premises of demonology. The bad news is that, among those who believe all seven, some unfortunate notions have developed through the years that actually tend to become barriers to implementing demonic deliverance in real life. In their extreme form, they can even end up quenching the Holy Spirit—which is never good!

I believe that if we are going to get to the place with deliverance ministries where God would be more willing to entrust us with the great revival, we have to do what we can to remove at least three of these unfruitful barriers:

1. *The notion that Christians are immune to the type of demonic activity which requires personal deliverance.* Many of my friends who do believe in demons stumble on this issue. I used to think that it was a rather benign point of view, but no longer. I now am convinced that it is actually a serious barrier to revival. No one has said it better than John Eckhardt, who pastors an African-American church in inner-city Chicago:

   "Soon after I taught in our city on the subject of curses, there came forth some ministries attacking the idea that many believers have curses over their lives that need to be broken. I had been teaching this series for a month and was seeing tremendous results. Many believers were being set free from curses and from the demons operating behind the curses. Nevertheless, there are many who teach that Christians don't need deliverance from demons.

   "We have dealt with the opposition before and will continue to do so. However, this time an anger rose up in me to defend the truth: *Christians need deliverance* from curses and demons. The Lord was telling me that *truth must be defended.*"[1]
2. *The notion that my method of doing deliverance is superior to all others.* There are many different ways to cast out demons. True, some of the methodologies are more compatible than others with the giftings, the temperament, the personality and the past experiences of a given deliverance minister. But this is not sufficient reason for one deliverance minister to conclude that "My way is right and other ways are wrong!" Such thinking, instead of pulling the troops together, tends to fragment them into different camps.

   I am glad to report that although this attitude was quite

prevalent in the past, things are now changing. I have the privilege of providing apostolic leadership to the Apostolic Roundtable for Deliverance Ministers (ARDM) which meets once a year for building relationships aimed at mutual accountability. This group of 20 or so high-profile deliverance ministers never previously had the opportunity to get to know and appreciate each other as colleagues. Now that they regularly sit down together, there is a growing respect for different deliverance methodologies. All rejoice at the bottom line: The demons get cast out!

3. *The notion that demons are equally distributed throughout the human race.* This politically correct, but misguided, idea tends to prevent clear thinking about evangelistic strategy. The fact of the matter is that there is a higher demonic concentration in some geographical areas and among certain people groups than others. There are more demons per capita, for example, in Thailand than in the United States. In the Unites States there are more demons per capita in New Orleans than in Cedar Rapids, Iowa. Demons are more active among Muslims and Hindus and Buddhists than among Christians. Demons are more heavily concentrated in cities than in rural areas. In cities, there are more demons per capita in the inner city than in the suburbs.

Take, for example, the inner city as an illustration of how a strategy should be planned. I once studied the promotional materials of several popular inner-city ministries. I found that they advertised medical and dental services, clothing for the homeless, tutoring for school children, 12 Step addiction programs, crisis pregnancy centers, summer camps, day-care centers, soup kitchens, Bible study groups, employment services, legal assistance and midnight basketball. But, guess what? None mentioned casting out demons! It would be hard to imagine Jesus sending His disciples to evangelize an inner city today without first instructing them to heal the sick and cast out demons! The more committed a group is to ministry in the inner city, the more serious they must become about overt and explicit deliverance ministries. If they don't cast out demons, they have one hand tied behind their back.

Conclusion: Let's Believe Jesus!

Revival—the huge outpouring of the Holy Spirit that we have been praying for—is coming. I would rather see it come sooner than later, and I know you would also. Let's begin to take deliverance ministries more seriously. Let's believe Jesus when He says, "And these signs will follow those who believe: In My name they will cast out demons" (Mark 16:17). Let's install powerful deliverance ministries in the local churches of our cities. Let's remove the barriers that have been thrown up by the enemy. If we do, guided by the Holy Spirit every step of the way, our prayers for revival will soon be answered!

Note

1. John Eckhardt, *Moving in the Apostolic* (Ventura CA: Regal Books, 1999), p. 79.

HOW TO MINISTER FREEDOM TO THE EMOTIONALLY WOUNDED

Chapter 8

FORGIVING THE UNFORGIVABLE

Doris M. Wagner

I hadn't been ministering deliverance over people very long when I began to hear heartbreaking stories from those I was trying to help. Most of these men and women were suffering from varying degrees of emotional wounding that had been inflicted by others. Some of the wounding seemed intentional and some was not; but the fact remained that these people had often been severely emotionally crippled and, at the time, were not able to be all that God wanted them to be.

Rejection

Wounding from others usually results in some form of rejection. I hope you take the time to read carefully Chris Hayward's chapter on rejection (see chapter 10). It is a tool that Satan frequently uses to inflict damage to individuals, both Christian and non-Christian alike. Rejection can be severe, for example, for those who were unwanted children. They know it and it hurts. Often adopted children suffer severe rejection and a feeling of abandonment that leads them to become rebellious and difficult young people. They are plagued by the question: "Why didn't my parents want me?" They are wounded, even though love is lavished on them by their adoptive parents. A demon of rejection often enters this wounding and makes their lives miserable.

Other common forms of rejection show up due to negative circumstances at home or at school: a divorce, a bad job situation, financial disaster, a physical handicap, an accident resulting in disfigurement and so on. People feel unwanted, unloved, unlucky or any number of other things. They sometimes blame themselves or others and, as a result, emotional wounding takes place.

Deliberate Sin

Deliberate sin can lead to emotional wounding that takes the form of all sorts of personal problems, as well as providing an open invitation to demons. I pray for many who have lamented, "How could I have done such a thing?" Some have sought out false religions and have been tempted to do very bad things, resulting in depression, anxiety and even sexual disease and mental problems. It is a very good idea to abide by the Ten Commandments and New Testament teaching. Living according to God's Word spares us all sorts of emotional problems (see John 5:6-14).

Sexual Abuse

Many times, sources of severe emotional wounding have to do with sexual issues. I recall having heard over the radio about a certain court case in the State of California when we lived there, probably during the decade of the 1980s. I do not recall if there was a jury in this case, but probably not, because the female judge passed the ruling in this instance. I wish the judge had been Judge Judy, because she certainly would have done a far better job on this one. It involved the case of a 12-year-old girl who had been raped; and this particular judge let the man who raped her go free because, in her words, "The girl had not been harmed."

I have prayed over a number of rape victims and let me assure you that a person who has been raped, be it male or female, has, indeed, been seriously harmed both physically and emotionally. Life is just never the same. The devil often uses such horrible experiences to open many doors to the demonic. Not all cases are alike, but I have frequently had to deal with a long string of demons including several of the following: trauma, lust, fear, anger, hatred, rejection, self-rejection, self-hatred, a man- or woman-hating spirit, a God-hating spirit, pornography, worthlessness, and in extreme cases, prostitution, abortion, death, suicide, homosexuality, lesbianism, bestiality, and on and on. It is just not a pretty picture.

I get particularly upset and especially angry at the devil when sexual abuse is perpetrated on children. I can hardly speak about it without crying. In the past months a number of these stories have hit the media in great detail. If you have read the accounts of these victims, you see that many of them have suffered emotional shipwreck. The wickedness of those who committed the sins and crimes has, in some cases, been transferred to the victims. "Abused people abuse" and "Hurt people hurt people" are phrases that so often hold true in these cases. Some of those who have been sexually abused will abuse others in the same way. And still other victims suffer continued pain through nightmares, failed marriages, fears in many forms, despair, anxiety, severe depression, uncontrollable anger and rage, lust, pornography, and all manner of sexual sin. Some have even committed suicide. And the picture gets uglier.

Sexual abuse is just one form of victimization, and I have spent quite a bit of time on it because it is common. Although I hate to say it, it seems to be on the rise. I firmly believe that the growing acceptance by the public of raunchy television programs and movies, as well as print and Internet porn, contribute to copycat activities and provide frequent openings for a spirit of lust to invade those who are fascinated by or take part in such activity. When the conservative Christians seek to protect our children from these things, the liberals bemoan the fact that we Christians just don't understand the First Amendment! How sad for them, and for us!

The Occult

People, often children, who have been forcefully introduced into witchcraft or Satanism, with the accompanying rituals, have frequently fallen victim to prolonged, paralyzing fear; unspeakable pain; and, in some cases, the mental scarring that has resulted from torture. These wounded emotions are openings for demons to further torment the victims. Trauma, anger, witchcraft, lust, rejection of the most vile form, depression and a host of other emotional ailments sometimes erupt, each bringing its own set of demons. For those who have been victimized by the occult, their lives will never be the same. The trauma and the negative effects linger.

It is so difficult for me to even imagine anyone wanting to hurt a child, subjecting that young person to abuse that will have severe, long-term physical and emotional consequences. Animals do not treat their young like that! Perhaps the only reasonable explanation is a fallen, sinful nature accompanied by help from Satan and his demons.

Perhaps the saddest aspect of abuse of this nature is the fact that those who come from a background of witchcraft or Satanism often cannot let go of the hurt. It has been my experience that even after they joyously accept Christ as their Savior, these severely emotionally wounded individuals sometimes become angry with the person or persons who have victimized them. Unforgiveness sets in and becomes a demonic stronghold in their lives.

Bitterness, Resentment, Hatred and Anger

Unforgiveness is often accompanied by four other demon buddies: bitterness, resentment, hatred and anger. On top of the emotional wounding that has been inflicted, the abused person then suffers from this additional anguish, making matters even more miserable. Peace and happiness are elusive; relationships fail terribly.

A pivotal question to ask might be, Does the person have reason to be angry, bitter, confused or hurt? Of course! The person has been victimized by others—a crime spurred on by Satan, who has come to steal, kill and destroy (see John 10:10). And much has, indeed, been stolen, destroyed and killed. To make matters worse, perhaps the perpetrator is a relative or some other dangerous individual who is not in jail—justice has not been done. As a result, helplessness is added to the anger, bitterness, confusion and hurt.

Christ Can Heal

It would be wonderful if all of these problems were totally wiped away at conversion, but the reality of the matter is that sometimes they linger on and rob the new Christian of joy. Is Christ capable of healing wounds so severe? Has He already paid the price? Must the new Christian take steps to appropriate more freedom? What keeps the wounding from being totally healed in all cases? These questions keep coming from good people who are trying to understand. The answers are always the same.

Of course Christ is able to heal wounds so severe. Yes, He has already paid the full price. As for freedom, I have found that the key usually lies in forgiveness. In those cases in which total freedom does not come at conversion, a session of forgiveness and inner healing almost always brings full release and freedom.

The Bondage of Unforgiveness

I entitled this chapter "Forgiving the Unforgivable." Some atrocities and horrible sins against children, women and the helpless seem unforgivable, humanly speaking. But we are "not of the world" (John 17:14); and we are commanded to forgive, even when it is a difficult thing to do (see Matt. 18:21-22).

You see, unforgiveness is a bondage. A bondage is like an invisible rope that ties things together, usually in a knot. But the good news is that the bondage can be severed, and those who have been abused can experience complete freedom. Even more exciting is that this freedom often extends to those being forgiven, as well as to those who are extending the gift of forgiveness. I have seen circumstances shift dramatically when a victim has forgiven his or her perpetrator of a terrible injustice. It is somewhat akin to being let out of jail.

There are two often-overlooked aspects of forgiveness. First, to extend forgiveness to a person does not imply condoning the sin, injustice, hurt or even the crime committed by that person. It simply releases the parties held by the bondage. Perhaps I can explain this aspect more easily by relating an experience from my own life.

Forgiveness: The Key to Living Well and Dying Well

A few months ago I had to wait for some lab work to be done in a hospital. This was a fine, large hospital, and many people had come to have blood drawn or undergo tests of some sort. Since the waiting room was crowded, I began to look around for something to read and discovered that the hospital had produced a variety of pamphlets for the varying needs of their patients and families. The one that interested me at the time was one entitled *Preparing to Die Well.* So I picked it up and read what it had to say to those with terminal illness.

My husband, Peter, and I had shortly before held a family conference with our three daughters and their husbands to discuss a bit of our thinking concerning the time that is sure to come when we are both gone. We discussed a number of things, but we soon discovered that something our girls dearly wanted us to do ourselves was to prearrange our own funerals. One of our girls just burst into tears and begged, "Please don't make me pick out your casket!" It was then that we realized what a favor it would be to our kids not to saddle them with all of those arrangements at a time of deep grief, when we could do it ourselves and prepay all of the expenses.

Thinking that the pamphlet had to do with those sorts of arrangements, I was very pleasantly surprised to read that it went much further and gave some very sound and practical advice. I would like to quote a paragraph from this pamphlet written by Kay Talbot, Ph.D.

> Planning your funeral, writing a will, resolving spiritual questions, and saying good-byes are important ways of expressing your individuality, communicating your final wishes, and leaving a legacy for loved ones. To complete your unfinished business and find serenity, you may need to forgive and/or be forgiven. Forgiving does not mean condoning insensitive or abusive behavior, or trusting those who are not trustworthy. Forgiving is something you do for yourself to find peace; it dissolves anger like an antacid. It is a way of looking at others as being unable to love and cherish you in the ways you needed. You forgive the person, not the act. Those who ask and receive forgiveness from others, from God, and from themselves, become able to live their remaining days with greater freedom than ever before. Forgiveness sets your spirit free.[1]

This is one of the most eloquent treatments of the subject of forgiveness I have seen. I certainly hope many persons, not only the terminally ill, will take the advice to heart!

Forgiveness: A Command and a Choice

Probably the second most important aspect is that forgiveness is a choice. Actually, it is a command from our Lord and Savior Jesus Christ; but we as individuals have the option of obeying or disobeying that command, because we have been given a free will to make choices. Making choices often entails living with the consequences of those choices.

The most familiar passage of Scripture that teaches forgiveness is Matthew 6:9-13, commonly known as the Lord's Prayer. When the disciples asked Jesus to teach them to pray, He told them to pray the Lord's Prayer, in which we encounter the phrase, "Forgive our debts, as we forgive our debtors" (v. 12, *KJV*). After the prayer is completed, Jesus goes back and elaborates on verse 12, as though to underscore its importance: "For if you forgive men their trespasses, your heavenly Father will also forgive you. But if you do not forgive men their trespasses, neither will your Father forgive your trespasses" (vv. 14-15). It seems clear that unforgiveness can lock us in prison.

Satan wants us to be locked in the prison of unforgiveness and to lock others in an adjoining cell.

I often deal with people who feel that their sin is too great to be forgiven, and they feel very unworthy. Or they feel as though the wretched sins committed against them are so grievous that it is impossible for them to forgive. How can they forgive the individuals who left their lives in ruins? This, of course, is exactly what Satan whispers in their ears and wants them to believe. He wants them to be locked in the prison of unforgiveness and to lock others in an adjoining cell. But, thanks be to God, He came to "proclaim freedom for the prisoners" (Luke 4:18, *NIV*).

Forgiveness Can Be Difficult

When we come to a point in a deliverance session where I can clearly see that the person I am praying with needs to forgive someone who has committed a sin, an injustice, a false accusation, a betrayal, an abuse, even a crime, we simply pause. I then ask the person to pray to the Lord and extend forgiveness to the person at fault. Sometimes it is very difficult. I then emphasize the fact that what we are thereby doing is bringing freedom to both persons involved. I often encourage the person to pray a prayer something like "As Christ forgave me all my sin, I choose to forgive [insert the person's name] for [insert the offense]." Forgiveness is a choice. Forgiveness is obedience to Jesus Christ. Forgiveness is usually a key to freedom. This freedom is a freedom from the bondage that has tied one person to the sin of another, possibly for years.

A Demon of Unforgiveness

When an injustice or serious sin has been committed, such as child sexual abuse, the child remembers the pain, the violation, the trauma, the panic, the very breath being denied him or her, and visits that situation over and over again in his or her mind. Unforgiveness sets in and eventually invites a demon of unforgiveness to set up housekeeping in the soul of that person. What that demon has acquired is the legal right to be there, because it is feeding off of the injustice and the repeated visitation to that event. It can become very entrenched.

However, when a person extends forgiveness, the demon's legal right to stay has been removed, and it must leave when commanded to do so in the name of Jesus Christ. Sometimes these demons put up a fight to stay, or they may even say that they don't have to leave (which is a lie). Their prop has been knocked out by forgiveness. Of course all of the other traumas need to be prayed over and corresponding demons must be expelled as they are encountered. But their power is that much weaker, since they have become a house divided (see Matt. 12:25). Then serious, concentrated prayer for the healing of memories needs to take place. Be sure to digest Dale Sides's chapter on mending cracks in the soul (see chapter 13). It is a valuable resource in the healing of memories due to trauma.

"I Hate His Guts!"

Let me tell you a dramatic story of a woman I was praying for who had some unforgiveness with which she was dealing. She had some strong disagreements with her husband that concerned household finances. In her own words, looking back, this is how she described her situation: "I hated my husband and had contacted an attorney to get a divorce. I became suicidal and was hospitalized. I had family problems." Their finances were extremely stretched and they owed $5,000 in income tax—which was due in about a month. Because the problem seemed to be primarily the husband's fault, I asked her to forgive him. She answered me, with all the venom she could spew, "I hate his guts!" So I told her to go home and ask God to help her come to the place where she could choose to forgive him. About two weeks later I got a call from her with a simple phrase: "I can forgive, now." She came back and we prayed. She was able to forgive her husband. We prayed and cast out demons of unforgiveness and hatred, along with some others.

When she left, we asked God to supply that enormous need of $5,000. I got a phone call from her just a couple of days later. I love these phone calls that start out with the phrase, "You'll never guess what happened!" She went on to say that she had been awakened at 7 A.M. (we were in California at the time) by a phone call from the East Coast Disability Insurance office. Two years previously she had applied for disability due to a serious illness, but she had never heard back from the insurance company. The person on the other end of the phone said that the application papers had literally fallen between two desks and had just been recovered. That day they were placing in the mail a check in the amount of $5,000 for back disability payments. I am sure there was a cause and effect in operation here. Forgiveness is a powerful weapon against the devil, and I believe that in this case God honored that step of obedience; and to show how much He was pleased with it, He honored her by immediately supplying her pressing need.

I received a note from her a few weeks later that said, "The hate for my husband is gone. Every day I pray and look for ways to please him. Our family is healing. Things turned around 180 degrees. We are excited for each new day to see what God does." A letter like this to a weary deliverance worker suddenly erases the weariness and gives new strength to continue on.

Don't Put It Off

We cannot entertain unforgiveness even for a day. Scripture commands us not to let the sun go down on our anger (see Eph. 4:26). Why? Because anger and the accompanying unforgiveness fester and grow over time, providing an opening for demonic activity. It is good to think of unforgiveness as a luxury that we cannot afford.

We have in our power the ability to forgive because it was given to us as Christians by our Lord. Obedience is the key, and the sooner it is used, the better. The devil wants to tell us that we have a right to hang on to unforgiveness, and by the world's standards, we probably do. But we are not of the world—we are citizens of heaven; and as such, we have the power to forgive the unforgivable. The words of Jesus are truth; and by knowing the truth and being obedient to it, we can then be assured that we "shall know the truth, and the truth shall make [us] free. If the Son makes [us] free, [we] shall be free indeed" (John 8:32,36). No longer in bondage, no longer in pain, no longer a victim, but free indeed. I like that!

Note

1. Kay Talbot, *Preparing to Die Well,* CareNote series (St. Meinrad, IN: Abbey Press, 1999).

Chapter 9

RELEASING BITTER ROOT JUDGMENTS

Cindy Jacobs

One day my husband, Mike, came home from his job at American Airlines in Dallas, Texas, with a shocking announcement—we were going to sell our house and he was going back to school! This was very strange behavior from my husband. For one, neither of us ever just made unilateral decisions like that without consulting one another. For another, he had always told me that he had no reason to get his Master's in Business for his job.

That night I tried to reason with him—all to no avail. "Mike," I began, "let's pray about this together and get the mind of the Lord." However, there was no budging him—the house was to go on the market and we were going to use all of our money for his schooling.

The next morning I set aside time to prayerfully ask the Lord what He was trying to say through this. I really wanted to inquire of God to find out who had kidnapped my husband and replaced him with this alien. As I sat still, I tried to quiet my fuming spirit. My thoughts were churning with statements to God that ran the gamut from "How dare he be so arrogant" to "Lord, he's not living with me in a loving and kind way."

At last I settled down enough for the Lord to really speak to my heart. He murmured to me, "Cindy, Mike is being unreasonable, isn't he?" Sensing that I would only get my self into deeper trouble than I was already in for due to my bad attitude, I sat very still and listened. At last He said, "You are reaping what you have sown."

Right then, I had a picture of myself as a little child, sitting in a car full of our household goods with my pastor daddy and our family. We were leaving a city in the early morning without anyone seeing us off. I really didn't understand where we were moving or why. I only knew that my world was changing and no one had talked to me about anything that was happening.

I'm not trying to fault my parents. They would certainly have taken time to explain to me some of the situation if I had known to ask. However, many years down the road, reeling from the prospect of a similar sudden move, I felt the same feelings that I did then.

The next flash of understanding that came to my mind was a book I had recently read entitled *The Transformation of the Inner Man* by John and Paula Sandford. The chapter called "Bitter Root Judgment and Expectancy" had resonated in my heart and changed my life forward.

Suddenly I knew what was happening. I had bitterness and unforgiveness toward my father for being moved from place to place as a child without explanation. I had sown a judgment that all the men in my life would want to move me from place to place without explanation, and I was reaping through my husband. I quickly repented for this sin, forgave my father and broke the power of reaping through the power of Jesus' shed blood on the Cross.

That night Mike came home from work and was whistling and happy. He didn't even mention selling the house. Later on that night I got the courage to ask him if he was still thinking about school. He smiled and said something like, "No, I thought about it again today and decided against going."

Defilement Through Bitter Roots

After that experience, I went back and studied the Scriptures concerning bitter roots and sowing and reaping. Hebrews 12:15 says, "Looking carefully lest anyone fall short of the grace of God; lest any root of bitterness springing up cause trouble, and by this many become defiled."

Amazing as it sounds, my bitterness had defiled Mike and caused big trouble for me!

The Sandfords have this to say about this defilement:

> Our bitter root, by the force of reaping, actually defiles others. We make them act around us in ways they might successfully resist, apart from us. Every married person or other kind of partner ought to ask, "How come he didn't become a better and stronger person by associating with me?" And, "Can it be that my bitter root is defiling him?" "Am I reaping something through this person?"[1]

Another biblical principle that fed into my situation was Galatians 6:7: "Do not be deceived, God is not mocked; for whatever a man sows, that he will also reap." Not only do the seeds we sow come back to us, but they also come back in a much greater measure than we have sown them. Hosea 8:7 says: "They sow the wind and reap the whirlwind."

I had sown a judgment against my father and I reaped it through my husband! My father, the man in my life when I was a child, had unknowingly caused me pain by not explaining the church situation and our subsequent leaving. Now, God was trying to reveal the bitterness that I had had in that situation by allowing me to reap it through my husband. Once the bitterness had been revealed, the judgment repented for and the power of unforgiveness broken, Mike was free to think for himself. My bitter root no longer defiled him.

Bitter roots often cause us to see situations through defiled lenses. When we judge someone's behavior and thus get bitter about it, our eye suddenly is clouded by what the Bible calls a plank. Matthew 7:1-5 reads,

> Judge not, that you be not judged. For with what judgment you judge, you will be judged, and with the measure you use, it will be measured back to you. And why do you look at the speck in

your brother's eye, but do not consider the plank in your own eye? Or how can you say to your brother, "Let me remove the speck from your eye"; and look, a plank is in your own eye? Hypocrite! First remove the plank from your own eye, and then you will see clearly to remove the speck from your brother's eye.

Bitter Root Judgments Are Not the Same as Unforgiveness

We need to understand that making bitter root judgments is not the same as unforgiveness. The judgments that we make in bitterness actually start an endless-loop tape that will cause us to fall into the same set of situations over and over until we deal with the root issues in our lives. Our merciful, heavenly Father does this because sin, when it is full-grown, brings death (see Jas. 1:15).

The Lord Jesus died on the cross so we can experience life, and life more abundantly (see John 10:10). Therefore, if there's anything in our lives that goes against this, He wants to bring it to death on the Cross.

When we judge others, we actually put a binding upon them so that they cannot see their problems. They become imprisoned in our judgment until we free them by releasing our judgment and forgiving them. Then we bring the power of the Cross to bear on the situation and they are freed.

A really dramatic example of this came as a result of praying with a friend for her husband's salvation. During our prayer time she said with a mixture of disgust and sorrow, "George [not his real name] will never get born again! He doesn't even want to accept Christ." At that moment, the Holy Spirit quickened me to say, "Jewel [also not her real name], don't say that! You need to release him from that bitter root judgment so he can be free to receive the Lord into his life."

Jewel looked shocked for a moment, and then she realized what she had done. Right then, she prayed, "Father, I now repent for the judgment I have made of my husband, George, that he refuses to get born again and isn't even interested. In Jesus' name. Amen." The next week her husband was born again.

Bitter root judgments are much more powerful than what counselors call "psychological expectancy." This occurs when someone has been hurt by an authority figure and expects all other such leaders to treat him or her in the same way. Actually, as we said earlier, because of the bitter root, the leaders have been defiled; and so, without their being aware of it, they start to treat the wounded person in the same abusive manner that the authority figure in his or her past did.

A side note on this is if we find ourselves acting in ways that are uncharacteristic of us toward a certain person in our lives, that person may be reaping through us. We may be fighting the defilement that he or she is putting on us through bitterness. It is possible to recognize this and break the defilement off ourselves. I have done this myself on more than one occasion. This really works, as I was able to treat the person quite differently after the prayer of release.

Coals of Fire

The Lord will bring us back to a certain situation in which we first planted bitter roots and failed in our attitudes and judgments in order to ensure that we are healed of those root attitudes. In fact, even after we release those we judge, the Lord will often bring us into a similar situation to make sure that we have dealt with our pattern of thinking in that area. This has happened to me more than once in my life.

Even though I had released my judgments, forgiven the person and broken the curse that comes through judging, my mind still needed to be renewed in that area. You might say that my soul needed to be restored (see Ps. 23:3). For this reason, the Lord again brought me back into a similar situation in which I was falsely judged through an authority figure. But He worked through that situation to bring healing into that area of my life.

This might be called a "coals of fire" experience. Do you remember the story about Jesus' post-Resurrection appearance to His disciples after their disappointing night of fishing (see John 21:4-19)? Jesus stood on the shore and called to the disciples, asking them if they had any food. The key to this story is that He was cooking food for them by a coal fire—the same kind of fire at which Peter had been warming himself when he denied Christ (see John 18:18,25-27). It was in this setting that the Lord said to Peter, "Simon, son of Jonah, do you love Me more than these?" (John 21:15). He went on to tell Peter to feed His sheep and lambs (see vv. 15-17), ending with an invitation to Peter: "Follow Me" (v. 19)

What a powerful picture of true forgiveness! The Lord brought Peter back to the place of his deepest, darkest shame; He fed him; and then He commissioned Peter to follow Him. Essentially Jesus was saying, "Peter, I still love you and want you as My disciple. I forgive you."

I have experienced similar healing through a minister of God, though for years I had been hurt by various male pastors in the Church who had promised to cover me. In the end, the relationships involved both pain and blessings. However, for some, there was more pain than blessing.

When we moved to Colorado Springs and started going to church where our good friend, Dutch Sheets, was the pastor, I found myself struggling. I pinpointed the fact that Dutch had gone from being my friend to being an authority figure in my life. The glorious part of this story is that we are such good friends that I felt the freedom to tell him of my past hurt and old tapes.

I'll never forget the day that he looked into my face and said, "Cindy, I'm going to prove all those other guys to be wrong in how they treated you. This is going to be a wonderful experience for you." You know what? He was right! Mike and I have greatly benefited from being at Springs Harvest Fellowship, and Dutch has been a faithful covering and advocate when we have needed him.

It is critical in our Christian life to come to grips with the fact that old pain and bitterness produce defilement in our own hearts and lives. The Lord will be faithful to let us know the difference when our heart hurts and struggles arise within our souls, if we just ask him to help us. The people in authority over us will bless us as well if we learn to distinguish the truth from the old tapes of the past.

Embracing the Freedom That Comes with Releasing Bitter Root Judgments

The principle of releasing bitter root judgments is one of the most powerful truths I have learned in my own Christian walk. Anytime there is an unreasonable situation surrounding me, I always check to see if I have a root of bitterness.

Years ago I taught on this subject at a women's conference in the Dallas, Texas, area. As I started to pray with people to release judgments against their family, a woman thought about her daughter. The daughter had disappeared a few years before, and the family had not heard a word of her whereabouts since that time. Of course, this was a matter of deep distress for the whole family.

The lady released the judgments that she had made about her daughter. She released her from her judgment that her daughter was no good and that she was a troublemaker. The mother had also judged that her daughter didn't care how the family had been affected by her leaving. After we finished praying, we took a break. The woman was startled during that short break to receive a call from her long-lost daughter. The girl said to her mother, "Mom, I'm sorry that I left home. Can I come home?" Her mom replied through bountiful tears, "Oh, honey, of course you can come home. Come home today!"

My own story of releasing a bitter root judgment took place soon after Mike and I had moved to El Paso, Texas, and bought a big old home with a basement. The washer and dryer were in the basement, and we had inherited them with the house. The dryer was a particular problem because it constantly overheated. I was quite afraid that the clothes might catch on fire; but with a small baby, I had mountains of dirty clothes to wash.

I told Mike the problem and asked him to look at it (he is quite handy and can fix almost anything). Alas, my appeals fell on deaf ears! From there I proceeded to nag, and then cry. I ended my pleas by saying, "Mike Jacobs, you just don't care that our house might catch on fire and that I have piles of stinky clothes in the basement!"

After I calmed down the next day, I had a bolt of revelation that I had judged Mike for not wanting to ever help me around the house. The clothes dryer was just one of a long string of things in this regard. I quickly repented for my judgment and forgave Mike. That night he came home, and *without my asking*, he fixed the dryer. Boy, was I ever excited—I simply danced around the house the next day in my devotional time! (I can't call it my quiet time, because I'm not always quiet in it.)

Taking Steps Toward Releasing Bitter Root Judgments

By now you might be thinking, *Okay, okay, Cindy, I give up! You have made your case. I know that I have lists and lists of judgments against my mother, father, brother, pastor and others. Help me out here!*

I'm so glad you asked that, because I am more than happy, as I am writing these words, to think that you are going to get really, really free in the next few moments.

Here's what you need to do:

1. Make a list of the relationships in your life that may have been tainted by your bitter root judgments. (Don't forget yourself!)
2. If possible, find a friend to pray with you to release them. James 5:16 says, "Confess your trespasses to one another, and pray for one another, that you may be healed. The effective, fervent prayer of a righteous man avails much." If you do not have anyone to pray with you, don't worry. God is there for you, and it is to Him that you are doing the confessing.
4. Ask the Holy Spirit to reveal to you any bitter roots in your life that you are not aware of.
5. Make a list of these judgments.
6. Begin to pray and release the person who has most hurt you or through whom you are reaping the most judgment. It is usual to begin with the family of origin issues. Look for threads running through your life where there is an endless loop of reaping (i.e., you are betrayed over and over).

Here is a sample prayer to release your father:

Father, in the name of Jesus Christ of Nazareth,
I now release the following judgments against my dad:
[insert those particular judgments].

Two examples of judgments that you might need to release are that he would never listen to you or that he was an angry man. This is not to say that your dad listened to you or that he was not angry, but you need to release him so that the defilement you have will not affect any authority figures around you. It is also possible that there was some dishonor in the way you treated your parents, and this will come back on you also. Exodus 20:12 instructs us, "Honor your father and your mother, that your days may be long upon the land which the LORD your God is giving you."

7. Forgive those you have judged and ask the Lord to forgive you for judging.
8. Break the power of the reaping which has the effect of a curse upon your life. Say this, "I now break the curses that have been released against me as a result of my judging."
9. Apply the power of the Cross to any area in your life in which you are reaping from the sowing of bitter root judgments. A sample prayer would be,

Father God, I now bring the power of the Cross to bear
upon these bitter root judgments that I have made. I pray that their
power will be broken today in my life.

I am very excited for you as you start a whole new beginning in your life, from this day forward. The truth will set you and all those you love free as you walk in wholeness in Christ.

Note

1. John and Paula Sandford, *The Transformation of the Inner Man* (Tulsa, OK: Victory House, 1982), p. 263.

Chapter 10

OVERCOMING REJECTION

Chris Hayward

I know of no other act that can bring such pain as rejection. The spirit of rejection can be found in almost every novel or drama. It is ingrained in the very core of our being. Introduced in the Garden of Eden, it has continued to make its indelible mark on each of us. No one is exempt from the effects of rejection and only Jesus can deliver us from its death-producing results.

Some More Than Others

Though each of us can relate to the pain of rejection, some of us have known its pain in greater measure. For example, to have been sexually molested by a family member would inflict a far greater sense of rejection than to have been fired from a job. However, the enemy of our souls will use whatever negative experience he can to cause us to embrace the spirit of rejection. Later in this chapter you will understand just why the devil is so intent on inflicting this upon God's children.

Rejection in any form is painful. There are adults today whose lives are different because of a hurtful statement made by a teacher when they were in elementary school. A child whose parent said to them, "You're stupid—I wish you'd never been born!" can be impacted for a lifetime. Being the last one chosen to play on a team can impact the thinking of a youngster and predispose him or her to failure as an adult. These "little" rejections accumulate over time and become like a mudslide rolling over everything in its path.

Defining the Term

Rejection is an act of throwing away or discarding someone or something. Certainly that implies a lack of value, which is precisely how we feel when we have been rejected. We begin to feel that we have no value as we experience an overwhelming sense of worthlessness. Rejection is also the act of being denied love. Perhaps this is the most significant explanation of all. Consequently, to the degree that we embrace rejection, to that same degree we suffer from a corresponding inability to give or receive love.

When we embrace the spirit of rejection, we have difficulty being able to fully receive the love of God. We might receive His love intellectually but find it awkward to emotionally experience it. This becomes equally true when others try to express their love to us. Depending on the degree of rejection, we resist their affections. Feeling worthless makes any attempt at affection seem unreal. And so we avoid getting too close to others. A polite distance is maintained as we find it very hard both to love and to trust. Correspondingly, we also find it hard to express or receive love from God; and we find that trusting Him is a difficult task. Worship becomes an effort and intimacy with God next to impossible.

The Spider's Web

One summer evening in Texas, I looked out my back door onto the deck. There, under a light above the sliding door, was a spider weaving his web. As the evening wore on, I watched as it wove an intricate design with delicate precision. By the time I went to bed, the web was complete. I mused over the fact that in the morning I would take a broom and with one "swish" wipe away all signs of its having been there. I realized that this is precisely the way the grace of God works: Although the devil might spend years weaving an intricate plan of rejection around our lives, with one sweep of the name of Jesus all traces can be removed.

You might think that the effects of rejection have been with you for so long that you are doomed to despair for the rest of your life. But be encouraged! The power of Jesus' name can deliver you from the ugly entanglements of rejection. "Behold, I give you the authority to trample on serpents and scorpions, and over all the power of the enemy, and nothing shall by any means hurt you" (Luke 10:19).

Satan's Purpose and God's Purpose

Jesus revealed Satan's purpose and His own purpose with these words:

> The thief does not come except to steal, and to kill, and to destroy; I have come that they may have life, and that they may have it more abundantly (John 10:10).

First, Satan came to steal. The word for "steal" in Greek is *klepto*,[1] from which we derive the English word "kleptomaniac." The manner by which the enemy steals is by stealth—imperceptibly, without anyone noticing until it is too late. And what does he want to steal? Our faith, our peace, our joy and our liberation in Christ.

Second, Satan came to kill. The word used in this verse for "kill" is one that refers to sacrifice.[2] It is the intention of Satan that we would give ourselves over to worthless endeavors—that our lives would be void of purpose.

Third, Satan came to destroy. The Greek word for "destroy" means "to ruin."[3] Our enemy would like nothing more than for us to look back at the end of our lives and see a worthless heap of rubble.

But Jesus came to bring us abundant life—life "to the full" (*NIV*). Instead of taking away, He will add. Instead of our sacrificing ourselves to worthless things, we will live out our lives with the purpose and destiny that He has given us. And rather than His witnessing our ruination, He will build something beautiful out of our lives.

Two Kingdoms

The Kingdom of Darkness

Based on John 10:10 and other verses, we know that Satan's kingdom is one where there is no love, no joy, no peace, no acceptance and no forgiveness. There is only rejection, disillusionment, destruction, division and despair. God is love. Satan hates God and therefore is opposed to everything that God is. But why would he want to "steal" the love of God out of our lives? In just a moment we'll see exactly why.

The Kingdom of God

God's kingdom is one of love, acceptance and forgiveness. He offers us mercy and grace. He is the God of all hope. Inherent in the names of God are His attributes. He is the Shepherd who lays down His life for us (see 1 John 3:16). He is the Almighty One for whom nothing is too difficult (see Ps. 46). He is our Healer who binds up our wounds (see Exod. 15:26). He is the Righteous One who makes us fit for heaven (see Jer. 33:16). He is our Peace who calms the troubled waters of our lives (see Eph. 2:14). He will never leave us or forsake us (see Heb. 13:5). And He is our Deliverer who has destroyed the works of darkness (see Rom. 11:26).

The Purpose of Rejection

There is no doubt that the very nature of our enemy is one of hatefulness toward God and humankind. God has placed His glory in humans (see Ps. 8) and has prepared for those who receive His Son an ultimate position even above that of the angels (see 1 Cor. 6:3). Satan knows that he can rarely succeed in having us deny the Lord, or to give up our faith, so he has another way to make us ineffective: encouraging us to reject the love of God.

"For in Christ Jesus neither circumcision nor uncircumcision avails anything, but *faith working through love*" (Gal. 5:6, emphasis added). Here Paul is telling us quite clearly that faith works through love. In other words, if we have great faith, it is because great love is behind it. If we have little faith, it is because there is little love at work in us. I have never seen anyone with great faith, doing great exploits for God, who is at the same time full of rejection. Remember, rejection is the act of being denied love. Those who are subject to the spirit of rejection are too worried about what others think of them. They become so self-centered that they cannot function in faith. This is why Satan's plan works so well. He knows we won't deny the Lord, so he works stealthily as the kleptomaniac, gradually stealing our love for God and filling us with rejection. Through time, and given enough incidents of rejection and pain by others toward us, he gradually steals the love of God and of others from our heart.

We then end up with a church that is full of rejection. We no longer experience the joy of serving Him and the peace of His presence. Hence splits and divisions come within the Body of Christ. The Church becomes anemic and ineffective. The enemy has accomplished what he set out to do: He gets us to become a "faith-less" people.

Over time certain walls are erected around the hearts of people. We have found that behind each wall there is a demonic assignment to perpetuate and maintain that particular wall of rejection.

THE FOUR WALLS OF REJECTION

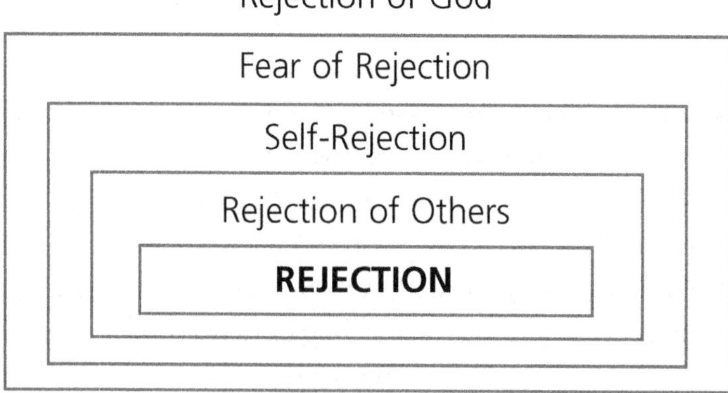

Walls come in many forms. There are physical walls and there are emotional walls. Though not named in the Bible as such, we can clearly see their effects in the lives of many throughout Scripture—in particular in the lives of Adam and Eve. Behind each wall a demonic attack is waged to perpetuate rejection.

The enemy works through deception. For him to be effective we must buy in to his deception, reject God's truth and embrace a lie. Therefore, we must repent of those instances in which we have given in to rejection and failed to trust God. Then we must renounce every place of agreement with the devil's lies. Finally, we break the yoke of bondage to which we have submitted.

Included in this chapter are prayers that I would encourage you to pray from your heart. It is God's desire that you would be set free from the spirit of rejection.

The Rejection of God

> So when the woman saw that the tree was good for food, that it was pleasant to the eyes, and a tree desirable to make one wise, she took of its fruit and ate. She also gave to her husband with her, and he ate (Gen. 3:6).

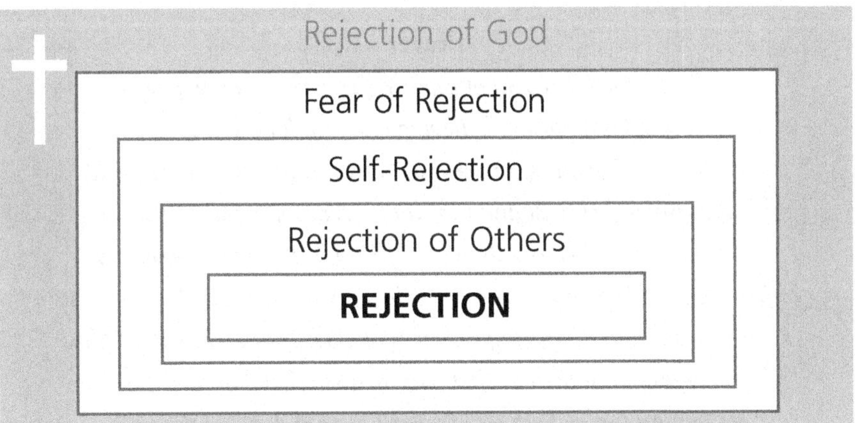

This first wall is what I call a load-bearing wall. Without it, the others cannot be erected. If it goes up, the others are sure to follow. Most of us are more concerned about our own rejection and fail to come to grips with the fact that in many ways we have rejected God. We have rejected His Word, His ways, His character and His love.

Eve was deceived into believing that God no longer cared about her best interests. Perhaps she believed that He had rejected her. The dialogue in the Garden makes it quite clear that the serpent was attempting to place God in an unfavorable light—questioning His motives, etc. Eve was finally convinced that she needed to take matters into her own hands. She rejected God and ate from the forbidden tree. Adam, standing beside her did the same: "She took of the fruit thereof, and did eat, and gave also unto her husband with her; and he did eat" (Gen. 3:6, *KJV*).

We become impatient with God. We start to question His loving providence: Why won't He answer our prayers? Why won't He change this or that situation? When will He come through for us? Why is He restricting us? Then we, like Adam and Eve, take matters into our own hands, rejecting God's love, God's Word and God's ways. The load-bearing wall, built to reject God and keep Him out of our lives, goes up, making possible the construction of all the other walls.

As you examine these walls in your own life, I would invite you to repent of any place you have allowed them to surround you, renouncing the enemy and breaking his stronghold over your life.

Prayer

Father God, I repent of rejecting You and Your Word. Forgive me, Lord, for not believing that You love and accept me. I repent of taking things into my own hands. I repent of my pride, stubbornness, self-will and rebellion. I renounce and cast away all rejection of God and the spirit behind it. I refuse to accept its influence in my life any longer. I break every word, and all agreements I have made with the spirit of rejection of God. I break all connections and generational influences that have to do with the spirit of rejection of God. And now, because of what Jesus has done on the cross, and the authority He has given to me, I come against the wall of rejection of God and break it down in Jesus' name.

The Fear of Rejection

> And they heard the sound of the LORD God walking in the garden in the cool of the day, and Adam and his wife hid themselves from the presence of the LORD God among the trees of the garden (Gen. 3:8).

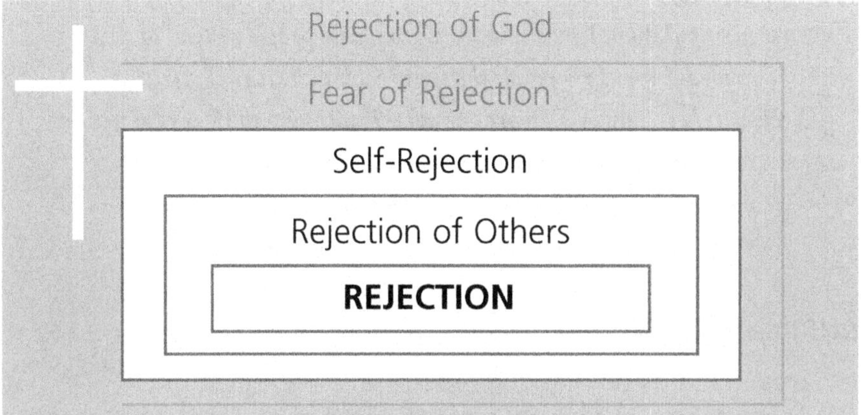

Once we have opened the door to rejection by rejecting God, it is only a matter of time before other walls are erected. One such wall is the fear of rejection. Adam and Eve "hid themselves" from God (Gen. 3:8). They were fearful of God's response to their act of rebellion. They had never before experienced fear. Adam and Eve's fearfulness after the Fall is clear evidence that sin warps our perception of God. We begin to credit Him with sinful motivations because we now see Him through the eyes of rejection. This is why it is so important that our mind be renewed through the washing of God's Word (see Rom. 12:2). The debris must be washed away. We must take on the mind of Christ.

Just as Adam and Eve hid themselves, we also hide ourselves through the fear of rejection. We begin to distrust God and others. We are suspicious of people's intentions. We enter into temporary relationships. Have you ever noticed how some people purposely sabotage relationships? You seem to be getting close to someone, and then suddenly they pull away. When we are being oppressed with self-rejection, we sometimes reject others before they have an opportunity to reject us. We say,

"No one is ever going to hurt me like that again. I will put up a wall and hide from the pain of potentially hurtful relationships." In doing this, we continue to feed rejection. Our greatest fears have come upon us—and this brings still more rejection.

Prayer

Father, I repent of all deception and lying, suspicion, mistrust, control and manipulation. I repent of trying to please people instead of seeking to please You. I renounce the spirit behind the fear of rejection. I reject its lies. I break all words or agreements with the fear of rejection. I break all connections and generational influences with the fear of rejection. Fear of rejection, in the name of Jesus, I come against you and break down your wall.

Self-Rejection

> Then the eyes of both of them were opened, and they knew that they were naked; and they sewed fig leaves together and made themselves coverings (Gen. 3:7).

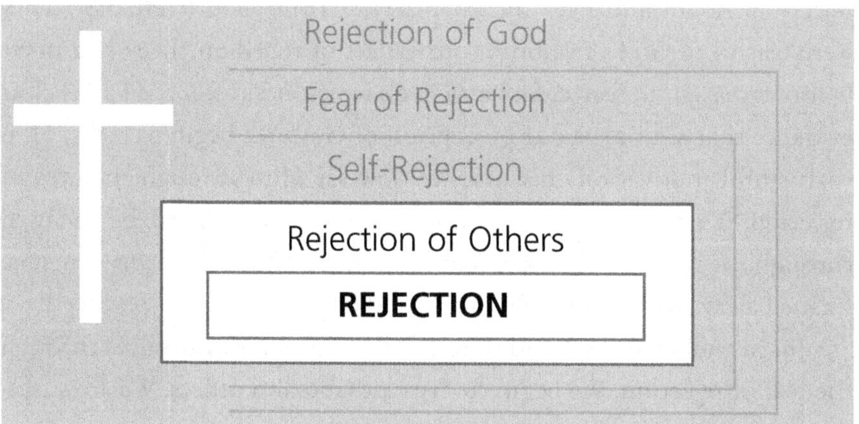

It doesn't take a botanist to realize that fig leaves soon wither and die. They are temporary at best. But how overwhelming and eternal is the love of God! Have you noticed that God sought out Adam and Eve? God didn't demand that they appear before Him in a tribunal;

instead, He sought them out (see Gen. 3:9). It was then that the Lord replaced their coverings of shame for something redemptive. For the first time an animal was slain and its blood shed in atonement for sin; then its skin became a covering for Adam and Eve "Also for Adam and his wife the Lord God made tunics of skin, and clothed them" (Gen. 3:21).

It is natural that we feel shame for the sinful things we have done. It was never God's intention that we "cover" ourselves with shame. Jesus died and rose again to take upon Himself our sin and our "shame." Many hurtful things come from this form of self-rejection. Everything from eating disorders to low self-esteem and suicide are rooted in this malicious spirit.

He does this with us. When we feel our lives are worthless, hopeless—when all thoughts of drawing close to God seem shattered—He shows up. It is for certain that He will not relent until we discard worthlessness in exchange for the eternal. His love demands that.

Dear brother and sister, you can't be replaced! There is no soul like yours, and no one else can be you! And God treasures you and who you are. How beautifully this is portrayed by what happened on the Cross. His blood was shed for us to cover sin and shame for each of us. We have been clothed in Christ—the Eternal One, the Redeemer!

Prayer

Father, I repent of rejecting myself. I repent of hating Your creation. I repent of resisting Your plan for my life. I repent of trying to be someone I was never meant to be. I repent of always needing the approval of others. I choose to accept Your love for me and what I am meant to be. Spirit of self-rejection, I renounce you. I break your power. I break your authority. I break every curse and vow that has given you permission to operate in my life. I choose to accept God's Word, God's love and God's ways for my life. Lord, break the stronghold of self-rejection off my life now. I ask this in Jesus' name.

The Rejection of Others

> Then the man said, "The woman whom You gave to be with me, she gave me of the tree, and I ate." And the LORD God said to the woman, "What is this you have done?" The woman said, "The serpent deceived me, and I ate" (Gen. 3:12-13).

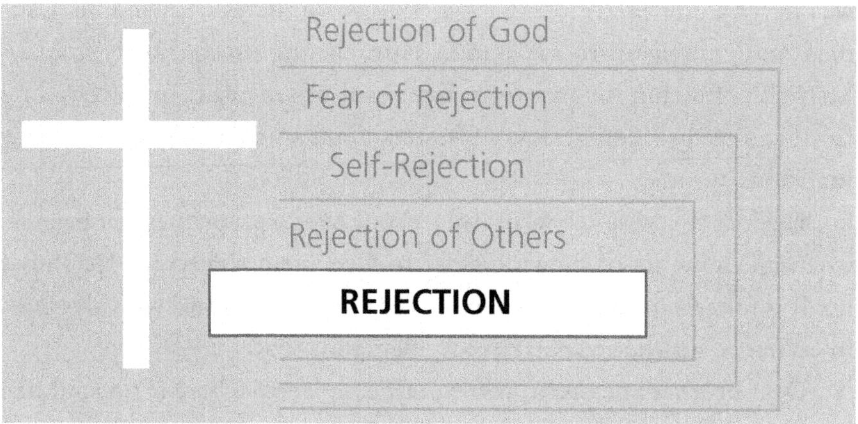

When we don't want to accept personal responsibility for our own actions, we look for opportunities to blame others. We put up walls—first against God, and then very quickly we build walls of rejection against others and ourselves. We begin to look for someone else or something to blame. A husband blames his wife and the wife her husband for unmet expectations and unhappiness. We say, "If she had only been more supportive" or "If he had only been more loving and caring." Racial hatred and bigotry all find themselves under the control of the spirit of rejecting others. We must choose to be a loving and forgiving people. If not, we will be bound and tormented—imprisoned by the spirit of rejection.

> And his master was angry, and delivered him to the torturers until he should pay all that was due to him. So My heavenly Father also will do to you if each of you, from his heart, does not forgive his brother his trespasses (Matt. 18:34-35).

I invite you to come before the Lord right now and choose to forgive the ones that have brought pain into your life. Some feel they cannot forgive because they still nurse the pain and hurt. However, in order to forgive others, you don't have to feel all loving toward those who have hurt you. Forgiveness is a choice, not a feeling. When you choose to forgive, you are obeying God's command.

> For if you forgive men their trespasses, your heavenly Father will also forgive you. But if you do not forgive men their trespasses, neither will your Father forgive your trespasses (Matt. 6:14-15).

The feelings may or may not come later. Your freedom will come immediately. To forgive does not mean to excuse. What others have done to hurt you might have been inexcusable and wicked. Release them and be released. Let God be their judge.

Prayer

Father, I repent of rejecting others. I repent for having been unforgiving, resentful and bitter toward others. I repent for allowing the hurt that I received to move me to reject others before they could reject me. Spirit of rejection of others, I renounce you. I refuse to accept your influence in my life any longer. I choose to be a person of acceptance, not rejection. I break all words, agreements and connections with you. I break all generational influences that would give strength to the rejection of others. Now, spirit of rejection, your stronghold has been dismantled; you have no protection. I come against you and I reject you. Your defeat was accomplished at the cross of Jesus. I tell you that your rule in my life ends here, now! Because of the Spirit of God, who gives me power and authority, I command you to loose me from your hold. I command you to leave me now. I pray in Jesus' name.

The Lord wants His Church to be strong, vibrant and healthy. The Body of Christ is only as healthy as its individual members. For us to be a people that move in great faith, we must be a people who also move in the power of God's love. Rejection must go—it is an enemy of God and a destroyer of God's people. May we all grow in the love and grace of the Lord, Jesus Christ. Amen.

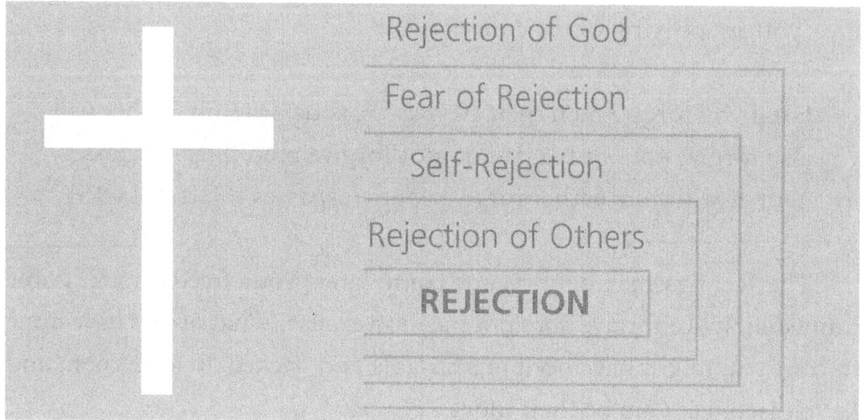

Notes

1. James Strong, *The New Strong's Exhaustive Concordance of the Bible* (Nashville, TN: Thomas Nelson Publishers, 1984), Greek ref. no. 2813.
2. Ibid., Greek ref. no. 2380.
3. Ibid., Greek ref. no. 622.

Chapter 11

DELIVERANCE FROM FEAR AND ANGER

John Sandford

There is an enemy. Normally, we are protected (see Ps. 91:11). We are hidden in Christ (see Col. 3:3). But sins expose us, and the uncrucified aspects of our sin nature offer theaters of operation and control to demonic forces.

But demons can access us through other avenues in addition to our own sins or sin nature. I once ministered to a man whose mother had been a prostitute; she continued her trade until she grew too large to attract customers. Because of her sin, he came out of the womb already inhabited by demons of lust.

Sometimes it is the sins of ancestors that have invited demonic oppression. Many innocent people have been afflicted because a forefather or mother was active in Masonry or Eastern Star, or some other form of magic or witchcraft (see Deut. 5:9; 18:9-13).

If you are struggling with this kind of issue, or are ministering to someone who is, be assured that inherited demonic oppression is often relatively easy to deliver. You simply help the person to repent for his or her own sins and those of his or her forebearers, and you then cast away whatever demons may have found lodging because of it. It will be necessary for the person to renounce the occult and then close all the doors of his or her heart and mind; the open invitations must be removed. But if the doors have been closed, the freedom from demonic possession will most likely be lasting.

Oppression Through Practiced Emotional Habit

It is a different matter to be set free from emotional constructs in our own character—habits of feeling and reacting or "practices" (Col. 3:9, *NIV*). These are more internal than anything we may have inherited. They are practiced ways of responding that we have woven more or less integrally into the very fiber of our character. In the instances cited above, once we have seen the origin of demonization through the sins of others or by inheritance, the battle is largely won. Repentance and authority easily dislodge the demonic. But when a demon has inhabited a practiced emotional habit in our character, much more than simple deliverance will be required if the demon is to be prevented from returning with other demons seven times worse (see Luke 11:26).

Satan is not present everywhere, nor is he omniscient (knowing everything). Consequently, a person may develop a character flaw, a fearful way or a habit of anger over a long period of time before a demon finds that open door. This is not so when a person enters into occult activities. Magic is the home field of the demonic, and instant demonization occurs. But it may be quite some time before demons take up residence in that emotionally sinful "home" in us.

Infestation

When demons do find room in us, then there are several levels of demonization that can occur. The first is *infestation.* Picture a person's head surrounded by buzzing hornets. Demons may be all around, but not yet *in* the person. Whenever he or she falls into acting out a habit of fear or anger (or any other negative emotion), an encircling demon has access to reach in and temporarily increase or even control through that emotion—which then becomes a panic attack or a tantrum (or lust or whatever). But when the person "comes to him- or herself," throws off whatever he or she was feeling and repents of what he or she was doing and is forgiven, demonic influence is snapped off. That door can be kept from reopening when the person sees his or her habitual fleshly way, repents of it and, best yet, discovers how that originated in his or her life and prays for forgiveness, forgives others and carries that practice to death on the Cross.

Inhabitation

The second level is inhabitation. In such cases, there is a degree of demonic entrance and struggle in the individual. A demon has only been allowed to inhabit exterior portions of the mind and character. Nevertheless, warfare is waging, because the Holy Spirit will not allow anything demonic to remain uncontested in the person so near to His own domicile in the heart. The Christian may quickly cast out or encapsulate the demon, like white blood cells, when they surround a tubercular infection, keeping it encased and ineffectual.

That was my case. Researching the occult before I came to Christ, as well as entertaining a long-practiced and hidden emotion of fear, I had allowed a demon to gain access. But the prayers of those around me, and my own strength of character, had forbidden the demon any theater of operation and had imprisoned it. Shortly after I was born anew and had been filled with the Holy Spirit, that demon was forced to the surface. Friends cast it away; I then repented of occultism, renounced it, closed all the doors and was free.

Obsession

The third level is obsession. This is both a spiritual and psychological condition. In cases of obsession, a demon has found access to the mind and character, and it has been allowed to increase its influence and dominion. Almost always, it has invited other demons to help in the warfare to control the person. So, in cases of obsession, seldom are we dealing with only one demon. This was the case for Mary Magdalene, from whom the Lord cast out seven demons (see Mark 16:9). Part of the time an obsessed Christian is freed from demonic control, able to be who God intended. At other times, when something stimulates that person, there is a dramatic switch, and he or she is once again under the control of the demonic. Secular psychologists, seeing that behavior and being unaware of the demonic, have labeled such people "obsessive-compulsive." Insofar as that describes the condition and activity of our flesh, it's probably a fitting diagnosis. But what that term actually describes is the return of the character flaws through which demons can manipulate and increasingly control the person.

In cases of obsession, deliverance cannot be effected merely by naming the condition—whether it be fear, hatred, anger, lust or otherwise—as though the demonic specialists of those emotions are all that is involved. Please understand: Fear and anger are not initially demons. They are usually practiced habits in our flesh. We are not to cast out flesh. Flesh is to be taken to the Cross by confession, repentance, forgiveness and reckoned as dead on the Cross (see Rom. 6:11). Only when Christians continue to practice a forbidden habit, such as fear or anger, does it become obsessive. At some point in the process of the ongoing practice of that habit, a demon finds it to be an available "home" and invites others in to join him. Demons specialize. So if the house is anger, a demon of anger enters, molds itself to the habit of getting angry and has every opportunity to expand the reactions, throwing the perpetrator/victim into ever-accelerating tantrums. A demon of fear may indwell the habit of fear and throw the person into panic attacks (although it is important to note that not all panic attacks are demonic or demonically induced). In any case, such panic attacks are always open invitations for demons to come and increase their impact and frequency.

Sometimes, a demon must first be cast away before you can lead the afflicted person into recognition of the habit. Only then can the person offer repentance for it, forgive those who caused it and bring about the death of the habit through the Cross. Sometimes the Lord guides you differently, and before you can successfully cast away the controlling demon, you must dismantle his house.

It is important to understand that the deliverance ministry is always a matter of following the Holy Spirit's guidance. It is never a set of hard and fast rules and incantations that work every time. Therefore, there are no formulas guaranteed to work, like recipes for baking. *Whenever we are dealing with emotional constructs and the demons that influence or inhabit them, we need to deal with both the demonic and the natural, and we must follow the fresh guidance of the Holy Spirit each time.* We may cast away the demonic and then heal the house, or we may dismantle the house by healing the personality and character and then do away with the demonic. Since the casting and the dismantling are done in the power of the Holy Spirit, whichever must be done first will be dictated by the Holy Spirit's unique guidance in each instance. Paula and I usually find ourselves dismantling the devil's abode first, but not always.

The deliverance ministry is always a matter of following the Holy Spirit's guidance. It is never a set of hard and fast rules that work every time.

Possession

The fourth level is possession. Possession means that demons have gained full control. The original personality is totally suppressed; what remains to speak and be in control is the devil's henchman. Possession is rare. I have never seen a Christian possessed, though I have seen full possession of non-Christians in pagan countries. I do not believe full possession can happen to born-again Christians. He who is in us is stronger than he who is in the world (see 1 John 4:4), and He will not allow it. In this I agree with the many who say that Christians cannot be possessed. But I also know Christians can be demonized on the other three levels, because I have ministered to hundreds of such cases.

The Fruit of the Flesh

We were not created to be hateful or fearful; neither are we created to be filled with lust, envy, malice or any other of the dire fruits of the flesh. God created us in His image to manifest all the fruits of His Holy Spirit. So the first cause of fear or anger lies in original sin. *Though succumbing to fear or anger (or any other fruit of the flesh) is abnormal, far from who we really are, ever since the Fall it has become normal behavior to struggle with all the fruits of the flesh.* It becomes abnormal and then provides a house for the demonic whenever we, as Christians, postpone repentance and aversion, or refuse to take the Christian actions we should: prayer, forgiveness, mercy, loving actions and so on.

Fear

Paul tells us, "For God has not given us a spirit of fear, but of power and of love and of a sound mind" (2 Tim. 1:7); and " 'Be angry, and yet do not sin'; do not let the sun go down on your anger, and do not give the devil an opportunity" (Eph. 4:26, *NASB*). Some Christians think that to be afraid is a sin, continually confessing their fears as though they had broken some eternal laws. But fear is a normal, healthy reaction built into us by our Creator. If we knew no fear, we would not leap out of the way of a speeding car. Or we might step off a building from 20 floors up. Or we might foolishly stand in the line of fire in battle. Fear is good. It is what we do with fear that makes it either good or unhealthy, obsessive if unchecked, and finally demonized.

Anger

The same is true for anger. Anger is healthy. It is a mark of our love for one who is misbehaving, our concern for justice or a reaction to unjust wounding. We do not need to be continually repenting and asking forgiveness for getting angry. Being angry is not sinful. How do we know that? Because our Lord never sinned, yet the Scripture says that Jesus, "when He had looked around at them with anger, being grieved by the hardness of their hearts" healed the man with the withered hand on the Sabbath day (Mark 3:5). Anger is one of the Lord's watchmen for our hearts, informing us when action needs to be taken. For Christians, anger is a call to ministry, understanding, forgiveness and possible reconciliation. Unfortunately, even among Christians, anger has too often been something to use—to dominate, manipulate, control or just bluff people away for self-centered protection. Again, it is what we do with anger that makes us either Christlike or sinful, that invites either the flow of the Holy Spirit or begs demonic help.

The Problem with Suppression

When we don't admit our fear and anger, instead choosing to suppress them, that does untold damage inside our hearts. When suppression becomes a habit—for instance, a false or foolish effort to maintain self-control (rather than releasing the emotion through prayer and understanding)—that begins the construction of a practiced habit, which in turn invites demonic access. Suppression would seem to be the opposite of constantly unleashing fear or anger (and thus building a habit of uncontrolled panic or rage). But, in actual fact, both invite the demonic. The difference is that because fear and anger have been suppressed, the affected person most often doesn't think he or she has either, when in actual fact a volcano is being fed. Someday that volcano will erupt into a panic attack or a tantrum.

Dead to Self and Alive to Him

Whichever is the case, what is really needed is to ferret out, by discussion and listening with the ears of the Holy Spirit, what are the origins of fear and anger in the affected person's life. It will not do simply to perceive demonic operation and command the devil away. As we have said before, both deliverance and healing are needed. Counsel and prayer can heal and deliver and set the person free from recurrences. It is a joyous and fulfilling ministry to be a servant for the Lord, to bring His comfort and freedom to troubled souls. But demons and deliverance are not what is important, however exciting that ministry may become. Nor is inner healing foremost in importance, however satisfying and fulfilling it is to do or to receive. Who and what are important? The Lord—and our obedience to Him.

Whoever would be of service to the Lord and to others in any ministry, but especially in the heart-touching ministries of deliverance and healing, must avoid allowing himself or herself to get carried away in the ministry by running wholly on experience or gifting of the Spirit. We are called every day, in each moment of ministry, to die to what we know and are, in order to be tools of precision in the hand of the Lord. It is the Lord who is important—and His kingdom. It is to Him all glory belongs. In other words, the more successful and power-filled the ministries of deliverance and healing become, the more assiduously we must take care to humble ourselves, remind ourselves of our sinful mortality and return all glory to the Lord.

For example, if on a given day, the Holy Spirit reveals a root cause of fear or anger in the first person who comes to me for ministry, guess what will happen if I do not immediately put that revelation on the altar and die to it? That's what the next several counselees will have, whether they actually have it or not. I'm "into that" today. Ministry to people afflicted naturally and/or demonically by fear and anger demands not so much that we know a lot of stuff, but that we are dead to self and alive to Him each day.

Fear and Anger in the Deliverance Minister

What are the two things that more than anything else keep us enmeshed in self rather than dedicated to ministry to others? Fear and anger! We each have our own fears—that we won't do it right, that this time we'll fail. So we fail to trust the freshness of the Holy Spirit's insights and turn back to rely on what we know or what our experience tells us we can do. We need to continually be aware that anger, based on perceived failures or temporary deliverances, builds even within us.

For example, God may not yet have delivered someone we have prayed for; or a person may seem unable to take hold for himself or herself and may keep coming back refilled with fear and anger, still begging for deliverance. You name it. It's your problem. What I am saying is as old as Jesus' telling us that, if we would take a splinter out of our brother's eye, we had better first take the "log out of our own" (Matt. 7:3-5). Whoever enters upon the battlefield of deliverance and healing ministry will find himself or herself skewered by the Lord's lance more often than he or she will defeat the devil or pierce anyone else's heart with insights and truth (see Gal. 6:1-2). If a minister of deliverance does not find it so, either he or she isn't listening, or something is causing him or her stubbornly to head for his or her own demonic enmeshment and need for deliverance. How many ministers of the Lord have we seen fall by the wayside?

Fear and anger beset ministering Christians every day, perhaps more than the people God sends to be delivered and healed! This means that each of us who would set others free will have to maintain a lively fellowship with God. It is only His perfect love that casts out fear (see 1 John 4:18) and enables us to continue fresh and joyful in Him, while He uses us to scour the debris of fear and anger from others.

THE GOOD NEWS

The good news is manifold: God wants and is able to deliver and heal His children of fear and anger and every other emotional problem and demonic thing. He is still foolishly loving enough to keep on delivering and healing us foolish people, who keep on getting into unnecessary scrapes. He risks the glory of His ministry through us frail vessels—again and again (see 2 Cor. 4:7). The battle is already won, and we have the strength-creating job of a mop-up ministry. He who could do it all with a snap of His fingers still lets us have the joy of delivering and healing alongside our wonderful Lord. We are equipped with power and authority to cast away every kind of demon. And, in the end, we will have worked ourselves out of a job, because someday nobody will ever again need to be delivered and healed of fear and anger—or any other lousy thing! Praise the Lord, and hallelujah!

Chapter 12

HOW TRAUMA AFFECTS THE WHOLE PERSON

Peter Horrobin

Trauma is a side effect of events that happen to us which are beyond our control. A traumatic event can be anything from a road accident or falling down stairs to sexual abuse or the sudden receipt of bad news. None of us can ever plan for such events, and by their very nature we are always unprepared for them.

Traumatic events can have both short-term and long-term consequences. How we are affected by them can depend on a wide range of factors including: the severity of the incident, the local circumstances, who was involved and our attitude toward them, our own temperament, our physical fitness and resilience, our emotional well-being, our upbringing, our age, our former experiences, and our spirituality and personal wholeness in Christ.

An incident that may be very traumatic for one person could prove to be of little consequence to another. Two people of the same age may fall down the same flight of stairs and suffer identical physical injuries. The girl who slipped and fell because she was carrying too much is less likely to carry trauma into later life than the girl who slipped and fell because she was trying to escape the attentions of an abusive father. Two boys may fall off a boat into shallow water. The six-foot-tall teenager may wind up sitting in the water, laughing at his predicament; but the five-year-old may be beneath the surface, face down in mud, inhaling water and fighting for his life. Years later the teenager may not even have a memory of the incident, whereas the five-year-old may as an adult have a chronic fear of water, never learn to swim, suffer regular panic attacks and have breathing problems all his life.

Where We Suffer Trauma

Medically speaking, a trauma is the physical damage that is incurred by an organ of the body as a result of an injury. I took my son 10-pin bowling and was careless enough to drop a bowling ball on my foot. When I limped into the emergency room at 1 A.M., the nurse on duty wrote on her admission form, "Trauma to the left big toe." I tried to correct her by saying, "No, my big toe is broken; the only trauma I experienced was through having done something so stupid in front of my son!"

But technically the nurse was right. It is the part affected by the injury that suffers the trauma. But that statement invites a much broader question. How can we be so sure that when we have a physical injury, the consequences are limited to the physical realm? How can we be certain that other parts of our being are not also affected by the injury and, therefore, traumatized?

Mothers instinctively know the answer to this very basic, but important, question. A three-year-old may suffer one of the hundreds of minor injuries that are part of life's rich learning experience! In the rough and tumble of play, the child falls over and bangs his or her forehead on some concrete. The child instantly bursts into tears and runs to Mommy, who opens her arms wide, takes the child onto her lap and "kisses it better!"

There is absolutely nothing physically therapeutic in that kiss, but its effect is usually instant and dramatic. The kiss does not speed up the rate of physical healing, but the love and the security of mother's embrace almost instantly remove the trauma from the hurting child's inner being! If the mother pushed the child away and refused to show care and love in the child's moment of need, then the crying would go on much longer, and the inner trauma would be at the root of an unhealed memory.

All Parts Are Involved

God created us with spirit, soul, and body. In 1 Thessalonians 5:23, Paul expresses concern that his readers should be whole in all three areas. While we may use the words "spirit," "soul" and "body" to describe three distinct and different aspects of what God created when He made humankind, in reality whatever happens to one part affects the others. During life the spirit, soul and body are indissolubly joined. It is only at death that the body is separated from the rest of our being.

It is impossible for one part of our humanity to experience anything which the other parts are not also involved in or affected by. An athlete may train his or her body to be supremely fit and win a gold medal at the Olympic Games. When the medals are handed out, the neck of the body may be used to hang the medal on, but the athlete whose body has run the race receives the praise. No athlete would say, "Oh, don't praise me, it's my body that did it!" The medal was actually won by a remarkable team effort of spirit, soul and body!

If we, as God's creation, therefore, are so much joined together as spirit, soul and body, cannot the spirit and soul also suffer the consequences of physical trauma? And cannot the body begin to suffer when trauma of a different nature affects the soul? Without a doubt, the answer to these very important questions is a resounding yes!

It was when we first realized, for example, the extent of damage that can result to the inner person (spirit and soul—especially the emotions) through injury or suffering of the outer person (body), that God taught us an incredibly profound healing principle. Through prayerful application of this principle, we have seen a great deal of physical healing take place—often as a result of the consequences of events that took place many years earlier.

Members of the medical profession are rigorously and correctly trained to treat the traumas that affect the body. After an accident, it is their immediate responsibility to take emergency action to save and preserve life, followed by restorative treatment. But what are the further consequences of these traumas if the inner being is not treated with the same care and attention to detail as the medics give to the body? The effects can range from lifelong fears through emotional instability, suicidal tendencies and physical disability.

Lynda's Story

Lynda was a young woman who had suffered from all of these symptoms. Life had become intolerable for her, and she had lost hope. When we first met Lynda, she was 26 years of age, registered disabled with the Australian government and receiving a life-time disability pension. Depressed and even suicidal at times, she was in a great deal of pain and also suffering severe side effects from her medications. When we asked if we could pray for her, she initially refused. She had been prayed for so many times already without effect that she did not want to run the risk of finding out once more that God didn't answer prayer.

She told us her story of how three years previously she had been mountain walking at night with her church youth group. No one had warned her of the dangers of the particular path they were on. She took a step off the pathway and fell off the edge of a cliff into a ravine, falling 35 feet through open space before landing on the rocks below. Her back was broken in 4 places, and it was 10.5 hours before she was airlifted out. What a traumatic experience! The doctors did everything they could possibly have done at the time, and also in the subsequent years. But 3 years after the accident, nothing more could be done for her medically. Her only option was to try to live with the consequences of her accident for the rest of her days.

Gently we began to explain to Lynda how when we suffer physical injury, we are also injured on the inside. Her body had been broken by the fall, but whatever had happened to her body had also happened to her spirit and soul. We told her a few stories of how others had been healed physically when God had brought healing on the inside. We explained how the body (the outer person) is often a reflector of what is happening on the inside (the inner person), and that it is sometimes impossible for the body to be fully healed until the person on the inside has also been healed.

We shared with her from the Scriptures how Isaiah prophesied that one of the ministries of Jesus would be to "heal the brokenhearted" (61:1). When she understood that the word for "broken" used in this verse actually means "shattered into separate pieces" and that not only had her body been broken by the fall, but that her heart (her spirit and soul, her inner being) had also been shattered, she began to understand what must have happened to her in the accident.

The Light of Hope, the Healing of Trauma

Slowly the light of hope began to dawn in her eyes; and she came to a place where she was not only willing to be prayed for once more, but willing also to let others share in what God was doing so that they could learn at the same time. We had met Lynda at a special conference for Christian medics. She was there because she had been a nurse. When the time of prayer came, therefore, she was surrounded by dozens of medical workers, ranging from anesthetists to pain consultants, from surgeons to physiotherapists!

They all watched as God worked a miracle in her body before their very eyes by healing her of the trauma which had been locked on the inside. We asked God to expose the pain that lay in Lynda's broken heart. She instantly fell to the ground, lying in the position she had been in after she had fallen off the cliff. It was as if part of her inner being was still lying at the foot of the cliff—shattered, traumatized, but unnoticed and, therefore, unhealed. We spoke love and gentleness into her spirit and soul; we asked Jesus to begin to heal her on the inside. We led her to forgive those who should have warned her of the danger.

Whenever people go through severe trauma, there is a danger that their extreme vulnerability at the time will be used by the enemy to hold them under demonic control. This had happened in Lynda's case—she was gripped by fear on the inside. We delivered her of the spirits of fear and infirmity that had taken advantage of her traumatized state. We also had to deliver her of things that had taken advantage of subsequent traumas she had experienced through sometimes frightening hospital treatments.

When we had prayed everything the Lord led us to pray, we then blessed some oil and anointed Lynda for physical healing. With all those medics we watched in amazement as God poured His Holy Spirit into her; and we saw her broken body being put back together by the hand of God. The body is normally a natural self-healer, but Lynda's body had been prevented from being healed by all the consequences of trauma that had been locked on the inside at the time of her injuries.

The body cannot be fully healed while it is still reflecting the inner pain of an unhealed trauma.

Five Years Later

Shortly after this conference, Lynda caused consternation in the Sydney Pensions Benefits office. Never before had they had someone who had been affirmed (by three separate doctors) as being disabled for life make a request to discontinue benefits because she had been healed! Five years later Lynda fulfilled what was previously an impossible dream. She found God's man for her life, got married and is now looking forward to having a family!

God truly is a worker of miracles. But as we pray for people, it is important that we also do our part in bringing healing to them. So often when a person is suffering physically, people only pray for the healing of the body. But when the condition has origins which are related to traumatic events, then it is important to pray for the broken heart and not just for the broken body. The body cannot be fully healed while it is still reflecting the inner pain of the unhealed trauma.

The Need for Deliverance

When praying for people who have been traumatized, it is also essential to have a right understanding of the possible need for deliverance. Satan is no respecter of persons; and whether the person is a minister or a non-believer, he will use every possible opportunity to gain access to that person's life through the demonic. The more traumatic the event, the more vulnerable a person is.

Those incidents that carry with them the worst traumas to the inner person are usually those which have been done deliberately by someone who should have been in a position of spiritual covering and protection. When parents, close relations, teachers, ministers and others whom a child would naturally want to trust are the source of the abusive trauma, then the consequent damage and related demonic influence are always greater.

In the area of sexual abuse, the inner trauma is sometimes only exposed when a person gets married. Painful memories, raw emotions and the demonic can all be brought to the surface through the expectation of sexual fulfillment. As a result, physical sexual relations can become a time of intense fear and panic. Instead of being a source of joy and fulfillment, they are destructive of the very relationship that the victim most desires. This also needs to be a part of the healing process.

In a short chapter like this it is not possible to go into greater detail about how to bring healing to those who have been damaged through abuse, but the principles of healing the consequences of trauma, whether the trauma is caused by an innocent accident or by deliberate abuse, are fundamentally the same.

"How Long?"

When Jesus brought healing to the epileptic boy, He asked his father, "How long has he been like this?" (Mark 9:21, *NIV*). That is an important question, since the answer can lead us to understand how to pray for the right things. Perhaps the greatest single reason why people are not healed is often because the wrong thing is being prayed for!

A lady came for prayer wearing a neck brace and asked for prayer for her asthma. It was tempting to anoint her with oil and pray for physical healing, but God prompted me to ask the Jesus question! "Thirty-three years" was her instant answer! "How old are you?" I asked. "Thirty six." "So what happened when you were three years old?" I responded. "I was in a small plane, landing on an Indonesian island. The plane crashed. Everyone else was killed, but because I was a child I had been strapped into a seat and survived."

Immediately I knew what to pray for. I asked God to bring healing to the terrified child on the inside—the child whose chest had been crushed by the seat harness as the plane had hit the ground, and the child whose neck had been thrown forward at the moment of impact. It was as if that brokenhearted, traumatized child was still lying in the remains of the plane on that remote island.

We spoke love and encouragement into her heart, asking Jesus to begin to heal the inner pain—especially the pain resulting from the loss of relatives who had been killed. We asked her to forgive those who had been responsible for the accident. We told the spirits of fear and infirmity, who were still confining the body with the same symptoms some 30 years later, to leave.

This woman then experienced deep deliverance and a profound healing. Normal movement in the woman's neck was restored, and for the first time for as long as she could remember she could breathe deeply once again. She knew that asthma was a thing of the past. God had healed her of the trauma on the inside, leaving her body free to receive the healing that she had been longing for.

We have seen hundreds of people healed in this way. When God heals us on the inside, then we are free to receive His healing on the outside.

When Trauma Goes Unresolved

Finally, just a word about those who begin to suffer physically because of unresolved trauma and inner pain. When, for example, a mother receives news of the sudden death of her child in a road accident, the mother has not suffered physically at all. But the inner pain is immense, and it is through the body that she actually expresses the pain—often through seasons of tears and even, in a case as severe as this, wailing.

But for some of us, the terrible news is so traumatic that we are unable to cope with the shock. The heart is broken, the pain is never expressed, and it all gets locked away on the inside. The inner grief, which is a consequence of the trauma, begins to affect our physical well-being. Some medical professionals now believe that unresolved grief can even be a primary cause of cancer.

One lady with a broken heart shared with me how her young daughter had died in a fire. She described the burning house so vividly that I assumed this had only just happened. But when I asked for more information, I discovered her daughter had died 14 years previously. If God had not come to her on that night and mended her broken heart, she would have lived the rest of her days in a heartbroken, traumatized condition. Who knows what the secondary physical consequences might have been?

Unresolved trauma lies at the root of far more sickness and infirmity than perhaps anyone has previously understood. It is so important that we allow the Lord to heal us on the inside as well as ask Him for healing on the outside!

Chapter 13

MENDING CRACKS IN THE SOUL

Dale M. Sides

The body is lacerated, bruised or broken because of the force of an object on it, but the soul cracks due to trauma and emotional overload. A crack in someone's soul is often much more severe than an injury to the body. If not treated properly, it could result in a warped personality, in much the same way as a broken bone that goes untreated will grow back crooked.

Healing an emotionally wounded individual is complicated, but the problem is compounded by the fact that demons can enter into people at times of trauma. For example, one of the most dysfunctional characters in the whole Bible is the madman of Gadara (see Mark 5:1-5). It is apparent that he had demons and that the demons had to be cast out, but the result of his deliverance was that he was clothed, seated and "in his right mind" (v. 15).

Yes, the demons were a problem, but how they got in was the fundamental problem. The Gadarene man had a crack in his soul that allowed demons to come in; and, consequently, this was the last item that needed to be fixed (see Mark 5:15). It is important to note that this account does not emphasize the demons but the deliverance that came through Jesus to this man. So we should not despair! These spiritual cracks in the soul can be fixed *if* we recognize that there is a problem and refer to the

Word of God as our textbook for treatment. The bottom line is this: If we do not fix the crack whereby the demons came in, we will have to do the deliverance again.

Therefore, my aim in writing this chapter is to give the remedy for fixing the crack through which the demons gain access. I also want to cover some biblical text to document this type of healing. But my main emphasis is to show how the Holy Spirit works with us to repair the crack and, once and for all, close the access portal to demons.

If we do not fix the crack whereby the demons came in, we will have to do the deliverance again.

Before beginning, I would like to emphasize that mending this crack requires a two-part remedy. Like epoxy glue, this remedy has both a filler and a hardener. One without the other looks like it might work—and even may work for a very short duration—but when both of them are used, the crack will be filled in and will be healed to the point of leaving *no scar*. The Holy Spirit provides the initial action of identifying the place of injury and filling in the crack with truth; but the Bible, held and confessed over and over is the hardener that will complete the process.

THE BIBLICAL PROOF

Luke 4:18 verifiably testifies that the Holy Spirit was upon Jesus to heal the brokenhearted. Moreover, it says that He came to set at liberty those who have been bruised. As we more closely examine the word "bruised" (*KJV*), we will see the actual promise in the Word of God to heal those who have been traumatized.

"Bruised" from Luke 4:18 is taken from the Greek word *thrauo*, which means "shatter" or "break in pieces."[1] So, literally this promise says that the Holy Spirit has a ministry to set at liberty those who have been broken or cracked. Furthermore, its root word is akin to the word for "wounds" in the story of the good Samaritan: "So he went to him and bandaged his *wounds*, pouring on oil and wine; and he set him on his own animal, and brought him to an inn, and took care of him" (Luke 10:34, emphasis added).

"Wounds" is derived from the Greek word *trauma*[2]—literally, "trauma." Putting this together, we see the promise of God that the Good Samaritan, Jesus Christ, will heal our trauma through the ministry of the Holy Spirit. In addition, Luke 10:34 says that Jesus will heal the wound (trauma) by pouring on oil and wine. The oil and wine illustrate the two-part remedy: The oil represents the ministry of the Holy Spirit, and the wine refers to the Word of God, specifically regarding forgiveness through the blood of Jesus.

I have literally seen thousands of people revived in hope by seeing these verses, because faith comes from hearing the Word of God (see Rom. 10:17). They realize that this is not just a ploy but a living and vital promise from God Almighty to those who have been struggling under dysfunctions of fear, worry, rejection, abandonment, anger, lust, pride and so on. To paraphrase this truth: God Almighty says, "Jesus came to heal your broken heart of trauma. Through the Holy Spirit and the Word of God, He can put the pieces of your heart together again." Praise God!

From Luke 4:18, we have seen that the Holy Spirit heals the brokenhearted. From doing a simple word search where "heal" and "heart" are used in the same verse, we discover how the Holy Spirit will find and heal this crack in our hearts. Matthew 13:15, John 12:40 and Acts 28:27 all feature the words "heal" and "heart," and they all refer back to Isaiah 6:10. A single verse quoted three separate times shows a magnificent truth. This truth is *how* a broken heart is healed.

> For the hearts of this people have grown dull. Their ears are hard of hearing, and their eyes they have closed, lest they should see with their eyes and hear with their ears, lest they should understand with their hearts and turn, so that I should heal them (Matt. 13:15).

This verse says that if we can see with the true eyes and ears of our heart, or spirit, that we can turn ("be converted," *KJV*) and be healed. The Greek word for "turn" in this verse is *epistrepho*, the base word of which has a literal meaning of "twist."[3] This verse tells us that if we see with the eyes and ears of the spirit, we can turn to the Lord to have our broken hearts healed. As we follow this backward in Scripture, we see the first reference to the eyes being opened, or as we shall see, eyes being closed. This search leads us back to Genesis 3, the fall of humankind.

Seeing with the Real Eyes

What causes a trauma is when we view a situation with our physical eyes instead of our spiritual eyes. The key to having our trauma healed is to view the situation with our spiritual eyes, not the eyes of the flesh.

In Genesis 3:5 the devil told Eve that if she ate of the tree of knowledge of good and evil that her eyes would be opened. In fact, in Genesis 3:7 it says that their eyes were opened. So, did the devil lie? Yes. But you must understand that the devil's preference in lies is deception and telling half-truths. Notice that Genesis 3:7 says that their eyes were opened *and* that they knew they were naked. So, in reality, the eyes of their flesh had been opened because they had lost the true vision of their spiritual eyes.

Viewing traumatic situations with the physical eyes is what causes us to fear because we fear death. We can be overwhelmed with emotional sensations to the end that our souls crack under the strain of emotional pressure. Emotions are wonderful aspects of our soul. They are the spice of life, but too much spice causes heartburn. Likewise, emotions are good in moderation, but when we accidentally dump the whole salt container on our chicken cordon bleu, we have a mess. We either throw away the chicken or scrape the salt off it. When emotions are heaped upon us due to fear of the punishment or death of our physical body, our soul can crack under the strain.

When the crack occurs, demons, being either the perpetrators of the event or capitalizing on it, enter the "opened mind." Once they are in the person, when a similar or associated event occurs and the same emotion erupts, the demons take control of that portion of the brain and make the person think the way the demons want he or she to think. The demons take refuge in the abnormal emotion.

It is quite possible to cast the demons out of the person; but if the memory of the initial event is not healed or the crack repaired, the possibility of the demons returning is very high. So the issue is not just to cast out the demons, but also to heal the crack so that the demons cannot get back in.

How Is the Crack Healed?

The key to mending cracks in the soul is for the Holy Spirit to take the wounded person through past memories and to show that person what was happening in the spirit realm at the time of the trauma. This is called opening the eyes of the heart or spirit. The passage below describes an instance of the Lord's opening the spiritual eyes of an individual.

> And Elisha prayed, . . . "LORD, I pray, open his eyes that he may see." Then *the LORD opened the eyes of the young man*, and he saw. And, behold, the mountain was full of horses and chariots of fire all around Elisha (2 Kings 6:17, emphasis added).

The promise is in the New Testament, too.

> That the God of our Lord Jesus Christ, the Father of glory, may give to you the spirit of wisdom and revelation in the knowledge of Him, *the eyes of your understanding [heart] being enlightened* (Eph. 1:17-18, emphasis added).

The Holy Spirit can open the eyes of our spirit and overwrite the fear and trauma we have experienced. We have been missing a tremendous truth about the Holy Spirit's ability to show us things from the past. We often only think about the possibilities of the Holy Spirit's showing us things in the future (see John 16:13), but He can also show us things in the past. For example, in the book of Genesis, we read about how He took Moses backward and showed him the revelation of things that had happened before him. Likewise, the Holy Spirit took Luke backward and showed him the details of the book of Acts. This is the key to having trauma healed: allowing the Holy Spirit to take you back into the trauma and show you what was happening in the spirit realm at the time of the incident. *He overwrites trauma with truth.* You realize the truth when you see with your real eyes—the eyes of the spirit.

For example, a lady came to me for ministry, because she was having panic attacks while in heavy traffic. She would become so afraid that she would have to pull off the road until the traffic subsided. When I ministered to her, I simply asked the Holy Spirit to take her back in her memory to the incident which had resulted in the trauma, opening the door for this spirit of fear to come in. Almost immediately, she said, "I am five years old and in the car with my mother." She continued, "Another car pulls out in front of us and we hit it. My mother is flying through the windshield. Oh, God," she exclaimed, "we are going to die."

At that point, I asked the Holy Spirit to open the eyes of her spirit and show her what had been happening during the event. It was just like the prayer that Elisha prayed for his servant, that he might see the spirit realm—except the Spirit took her backward. The lady then gasped and said, "Who is that very large man sitting in the seat next to me, with his arm around me?" I replied, "That is the angel of the Lord's presence protecting you!" She said, "Has he always been there?" "Yes," I said. "He was there that day, and that is why you did not fly through the windshield, too."

Once the fear had been dispelled and the hiding place of the demon had been revealed, I simply said to the demon, "Spirit of fear, go in Jesus' name! You have no place to hide." The lady let out a moan and breathed the spirit out of her body. She has never been plagued with panic attacks since.

The root or anchor point of the emotion of fear had been removed when she saw the angel. Now when she is in traffic, or in any other place that is conducive to fear, the emotion of fear has no place to live within her, so she does not register the initial trauma or the effect of it. Since the demon is gone, she is in control of her own mind and will.

I gave her verses of Scriptures to "harden" the filler of the Holy Spirit. Second Timothy 1:7 and Hebrews 13:5 have become memory strongholds for her. Anytime she feels fear coming upon her she *verbalizes* these verses.

> For God has not given us a spirit of fear, but of power and of love and of a sound mind (2 Tim. 1:7).

> For He Himself has said, "I will never leave you nor forsake you" (Heb. 13:5).

I have seen individuals healed of fear, anger, lust, rejection, sexual maladies, eating disorders and shame—and I am continually amazed at the deliverance people have experienced.

Quote the Word

Demons cannot read your mind, so when they return, they will speak to you and try to get you to verbalize an opening. Instead of saying what they want you to say, do what Jesus did. He quoted the Word of God—verbatim, word for word, with the volume and accompanying faith that sent chills up the devil's spine.

There is kinetic power in the Bible. It is released into the senses realm as active energy when it comes out of the mouth of a saint of God. Actually, according to Psalm 103:20, angels heed the commandment of God when they hear the voice of the Lord. Since the Holy Spirit is working in you, when you speak the Bible, angels obey your word just as they obeyed Jesus' word when He walked on the earth.

Holy Scripture has energy that is released when it comes out of your mouth. Quote the Word of God, and add hardener to the patch that the Holy Spirit has fixed in your soul.

Conclusion

The promises of God are always true. He sent the Holy Spirit to help you cure the dysfunctions of your past by removing the lie of emotional imbalance. The lie is removed when the Holy Spirit shows you what happened in the spirit realm when the trauma took place. He overwrites trauma with truth. Once the truth has been sown in your mind, as you quote Bible verses related to the remedy, the patch thoroughly "cures."

God does not want you to live dysfunctionally because of old, ugly memories. Truth overwrites trauma when the Holy Spirit causes you to realize the truth through the real eyes, the eyes of the spirit. Once you have seen the truth, build your mental and emotional strength by quoting the written Word of God.

Truth overwrites trauma, heals broken hearts, balances emotions and cures dysfunction. The truth comes from the Spirit of Truth and the Word of Truth. It is a two-part remedy: Jesus the Good Samaritan pours in the oil of the Holy Spirit *and* the wine of the Word of God. Jesus came to heal the brokenhearted and to set at liberty those who have been traumatized (see Luke 4:18).

Notes

1. Joseph Henry Thayer, *A Greek-English Lexicon of the New Testament* (Grand Rapids, MI: Baker Book House, 1977), Greek ref. no. 2352.
2. James Strong, *The New Strong's Exhaustive Concordance of the Bible* (Nashville, TN: Thomas Nelson Publishers, 1984), Greek ref. no. 5134.
3. Ibid., Greek ref. no. 1994 and 4762.

HOW TO MINISTER FREEDOM TO THE SEXUALLY BROKEN

Chapter 14

MINISTERING TO THOSE IN SEXUAL BONDAGE

Doris M. Wagner

God created human beings with the capacity to reproduce. In the very first chapter of the Bible, Scripture states, "So God created man in His own image; in the image of God He created him; male and female He created them. Then God blessed them, and God said to them, 'Be fruitful and multiply; fill the earth and subdue it'" (Gen. 1:27-28).

In Genesis chapter 2, we find a detailed description of the creation of man and his wife. God "brought her to the man" (v. 22), and then in verse 24 we read, "Therefore a man shall leave his father and mother and be joined to his wife, and they shall become one flesh." Here it seems clear that God Himself established the marriage institution, making Eve to be Adam's wife and giving instructions to future men and their wives. They were to start their own homes and "become one."

Becoming One

"Becoming one" speaks of an inseparable union. Note that Eve was created for two specific reasons: to be a companion and a helper to Adam. "It is not good that man should be alone; I will make him a helper comparable to him" (Gen. 2:18). This speaks to me about God's interest in the emotional side of Adam; and apparently companionship, love, caring, friendship and the like were needed by Adam. It also speaks to me about the practical issues to be handled in life: that having a comparable helper alongside the man was what God intended in order for the job to be complete.

Just as an aside, I have always smiled as I have read the account of creation, particularly God's last act of creation: the making of the woman. Note that as God created things one by one, the phrase appears, "And God saw that it was good" (Gen. 1:18,21,28). Then, as I previously mentioned, God saw that one thing in all of creation was "not good" and that was "that man should be alone" (Gen. 2:18). There was still one thing lacking, and that was the creation of woman to become the other half of man, as it were. Once she had been created, and they became "one," the job was apparently finished. "Then God saw everything that He had made, and indeed it was *very good*" (Gen. 1:31, emphasis added). It took the making of the woman to bring creation to a higher level than it had been previously.

The Enemy and the Curse

But Satan enters the picture in chapter 3. As the angel who wanted glory and worship for himself, he approached Eve and twisted the command and will of God from something good to something bad. Things went downhill fast. Satan was cursed; the husband would rule over the wife and she would bring forth children in pain; the ground was cursed and man would have to work hard to make it produce crops; and they were told that they would eventually die and their bodies would decompose (see Gen. 3:14-19). Lastly, the couple was expelled from the Garden (see v. 23).

Satan has been working to continue to twist the commands and will of God ever since that fateful event. One of the most common ways is to confuse the marriage directives of God and to deceive people into thinking that God's commands concerning sex and marriage can be called into question.

When God told Adam and Eve to "be fruitful and multiply," in order for that to happen, they had to engage in sex. Since God Himself had created their bodies, you can bet that they were beautiful and perfect—the most handsome man and gorgeous woman ever to exist. They would have had the best sexual experiences of all time. And perhaps as a result, human sexuality was one of the things that Satan set out to pervert.

Lust Enters the Picture

When we get to chapter 6 of Genesis, we find that the earth was filled with corruption and violence, except for Noah and his family. So God started all over again after the Flood. Many Bible scholars believe that Genesis 9:24 speaks of homosexuality initiated by Ham against his father, Noah, when he was drunk. So apparently it didn't take long for lust to enter the picture again, even though there were only a handful of people on Earth.

Sex and lust have been problems ever since. The Bible certainly is not silent on these issues, for there is much instruction needed from God to keep His people on course. Sex is a very important part of life; and Satan works overtime to entice, deceive and pervert a God-given gift, bringing confusion at best and horror at worst.

As I have been praying deliverance over people for about 20 years now, there have been very few people to come into my office who have not needed deliverance from sexual demons to some degree. In this chapter, I will deal with a few of the more common ones, and some of my very good friends who work in the field of deliverance will tackle other lust issues.

Pornography

Satan seems to be present when new technology is invented. He invariably goes to work attempting to pervert it to his advantage. He has had great success, particularly in the various forms of communication, as he has used them in the spread of pornography.

My *Random House Webster's College Dictionary* defines "pornography" as "writings, photographs, movies . . . intended to arouse sexual excitement."[1] Among the earliest would probably be art, both drawings and sculpture. People have tried to capture the beauty of God's creation. In days past, frequent subjects of drawings or sculptures would include snow-capped mountains with blue sky, puffy clouds and brilliant autumn-leaf-laden trees; exquisite flowers; birds and butterflies; mouthwatering fruit of many sizes, shapes and colors; a laughing child's countenance; an apple tree in full blossom or laden with perfect fruit; or a magnificent, shiny horse standing knee deep in green grass in the noonday sun.

But somebody, one day very long ago, decided to draw some shameful pictures and make some obscene clay or marble images to sell. The word spread, and many people were drawn to look at them for the excitement such art elicited. It became a lucrative business, and pornography was born. It has thrived ever since.

In my experience praying for people, I find that many struggle with porn. It seems to be highly addictive, producing images in the mind that won't go away and often leaving the person with an insatiable thirst for more. And the afflicted person doesn't have to look very far to find a fix. Porn has pushed its way into books (just imagine—the first printing press was made in order to get the Bible into the hands of the common people!); magazines; photos; and movies. It has greatly proliferated through videos, DVDs and especially the Internet. The porn executives running the industry have figured out how to worm their way into sites used for shopping and research, technical sites and the like, to link Internet users to their well over 1 million porn sites (and constantly multiplying) in hopes of displaying and selling their wares. Their tactic has proven very successful.

Opening the Door for a Demon

Why do people struggle? It is because repeated exposure to porn will open the door for a demon of pornography to enter and set up housekeeping. It will not just leave on its own; rather, it must be confronted with a power that is stronger in order to evict it. Demons (evil spirits) seek human hosts, much the same as parasites, such as lice or pinworms, attach themselves to human bodies and feed off them. The demons must find a place to attach themselves. People who do not mess with porn do not need to worry about demons of porn. In other words: no exposure, no infestation. People must expose themselves to porn in order to become infested by demons of porn. But once they have allowed demons entry through repeated pornography use, they need to find a power that is stronger than the demons in order to be freed of them.

Repeated exposure to pornography will open the door for a demon of pornography to enter and set up housekeeping.

As I said above, demons will not leave on their own. As a matter of fact, they can persuade their hosts to invite more in. Pornography frequently leads to problems such as compulsive masturbation, fornication, victimization and more. These demons must be confronted with the authority and name of Jesus and be ordered out—this action is what gets rid of the demons and decontaminates the person. It should be mentioned that reinfestation is a possibility; and, in that case, the procedure will need to be administered again.

Some folks get the idea that deliverance brings immunity for life, but not so. Jesus' advice to the woman taken in adultery in John 8 holds true: "Go and sin no more" (v. 11). Folks who have been bound by demons of pornography need to take drastic measures to totally shun it forevermore. However, I have found that persons who have been delivered from these demons are so grateful that they do not find it that difficult to overcome the temptation.

Getting Down to the Roots

How do many people get involved in lust to the degree that they become demonized? When I begin to minister to a person who suffers from demons of lust, I ask two basic questions. The first is, Do you really want me to pray for you so you can be free from these bondages? Surprisingly enough, some do not. But if they are desperate for God to clean them up, when it comes to sexual issues that they have invited in, the battle is already half won. Time after time, men and women have come to me asking for help, with tears streaming down their cheeks. In such cases deliverance will usually be an easy job. The demons know that they are on their way out and are trembling already.

The second question I ask is, What is your family like, and when did your problems begin? I find that I always need to probe into the person's history because, as Scripture says over and over again, the sins of the fathers are passed on to the children (see Exod. 20:4-5). Demons of lust have a great tendency to be inherited. What does this mean?

Let me give you an example from my experience. I frequently pray for people who suffer from the problem of compulsive masturbation. I first ask, "When did it begin?" One man told me, "It has been a problem as long as I can remember–I was probably around four." Now, that's unnatural! One needs to conclude that this little kid had some supernatural help.

Inherited Lust

So we probe further to see if we can glean information about his father or mother and both grandparents on both sides of the family. We ask questions such as these: "Were you conceived out of wedlock?" (We find that persons conceived in lust often struggle with lust.) "Was there unfaithfulness that was a well-known fact in your family?" "Did things such as pornography, adultery, child sexual abuse, prostitution or the like find their way into your family?" If there are affirmative answers to these questions, we need to begin by praying against a spirit of inherited lust. That needs to be uprooted before we go on to the problems the individual has in his or her own life.

Just how do we pray against a spirit of inherited lust? I find that there is great relief to the person when I say, "Hey, this was not all your fault—you had some help getting started on this path." Well, then, who is to blame? Obviously, much blame can be placed on the person who allowed this sin into the family line. That person made it easy for a demon of inherited lust to draw its host toward further opportunities for sexual sin. Okay, then, what do we do about it?

It is important that the person seeking deliverance from an inherited spirit of lust forgive the one who allowed it into the family line. It does not matter that the person may have died long ago. Extending forgiveness removes the legal grounds for the spirit of inherited lust to inhabit the host, and that paves the way for commanding the spirit of inherited lust to leave. Even if the evidence is inconclusive that an inherited spirit of lust is present, I try to cover all bases and pray against an inherited spirit of lust anyway, because the person may not have all the facts. Sexual sins are ordinarily not widely broadcast among all family members. If I happen to be wrong, no harm has been done.

After this process, I then proceed to the individual needs of the person for whom I am praying and command each afflicting sexual spirit to leave. When that is complete, I then command the spirit of lust to go, in Jesus' name. By this, I mean the spirit of lust that the person had invited in. This is a spirit different from the inherited spirit of lust. I treat them as two separate demons.

Incubus and Succubus

Inherited spirits of lust are frequently to blame for allowing the sexual spirits of Incubus and Succubus to operate while a person is asleep. What happens is that the individual will have a very vivid dream in which he or she is approached by a "person" who either asks to have sex with him or her, or actually engages in sex. The "person" may act in a heterosexual or homosexual manner, and a sexual climax ensues as the individual awakens. The "person," if acting as a male, is not just a mental fantasy, but actually a demon called Incubus; and if it acts as a female, it is a demon named Succubus. I find these to be very foul, uninvited evil spirits that often, but not always, follow family lines.

Some very bold ones will even attack a person during the day. When evicting them, I call them by name, and they often leave with a pronounced jolt in the body of their host. It seems as though their cover is shattered when they are called by name.

Compulsive Masturbation

In exploring how to minister to those who are in sexual bondage, I think it's important to address the issue of compulsive masturbation. I have prayed with men, in particular, for whom this is an all-consuming, ever-present issue. One man usually masturbated three times a day, and it was ruining his marriage because he was not paying attention to his wife. But how do we go about solving the problem?

After we identify the fact that compulsive masturbation is present in a person's life, we then look for other clues and roots to the problem. Often the person has become addicted to pornography. Sometimes the problem stems from a massive rejection of some sort. Frequently the person was sexually molested as a child or teen. It is very possible for a spirit of lust to take advantage of a sexual trauma, such as a rape, entering at that time—even though the victim was not seeking it. So we continue to gather information.

Clues were apparent in the above-mentioned man's case as to why the demon of compulsive masturbation was present. I don't remember them all; but I was clearly directed by God as to how to pray, and he turned out to be an easy case. He was totally freed from the bondage and went home to announce the victory publicly to his friends. There are few more grateful people on planet Earth than those who have been set free from their long-standing bondage.

Ministering to the Whole Person

I find that praying for people who suffer from sexual bondage seem to fall into two broad categories: those who have invited problems into their lives, and those who have been victimized or seriously abused by caregivers or predators. The former are easy to pray for—those who have tears flowing down their cheeks and want to be free. They are so sorry for their sin, and they want to repent and be healed of its consequences. The latter, those who have been victimized, are extremely complex because a wide range of other very serious problems have often invaded. These might include things such as anger; hatred; self-hatred; suicidal tendencies; homosexuality; dissociative identity disorder (formerly called multiple personality disorder); misplaced affection; and a huge amount of other emotional damage that needs prolonged, tender care and healing, as well as deliverance.

All too often, deliverance ministers have not ministered to the "whole person." Yet the job should not be considered complete until the emotional aspect is healed as well. It is the better part of wisdom not to assume that just because evil spirits have been evicted that the task has been completed. If emotional healing is still needed, pray for what needs to be done, and refer the person to a pastor or counselor who can take them on from there.

Confidentiality

Two very important questions we continually keep in mind are, Why is this person afflicted? and When did it begin? Usually, probing these areas will reveal very important clues as to how to pray. It is vital that the person we are praying for disclose all information relevant to their problems. Partial disclosure is to be discouraged and a promise of confidentiality assured. This must never be violated. As a matter of fact, I do not keep information notes, usually in the form of a questionnaire, but I shred them in the presence of the person. To me, it helps them on their way to "Go and sin no more." I think it is easier for a person to "go and sin no more" (see John 8:11) when he or she knows that what God has forgiven is forgiven, indeed.

Dealing with Guilt and Shame

Over the years, as I have prayed for people with sexual bondage, I find it very important to pray against two other related spirits: guilt and shame.

It is sometimes easy to forget, but I now make it a very important part of my prayers. Since my time is extremely limited due to my obligations as CEO of a Christian ministry, I am able to pray for just a few people, so I have chosen to pray for ministers. Most have no one to turn to when they seek deliverance for fear of losing their jobs, being embarrassed or being exposed to their congregation. But I am safe. I don't know them, and no one needs to know that the person coming to see me for deliverance is a pastor.

One thing that truly bothers pastors suffering from sexual problems of a demonic nature is that they are called to preach the Word of God. But how can they preach against sexual sins if they are victims themselves? They feel like such hypocrites! So I must always remember to pray against the spirits of guilt and shame so that the pastors can then preach as they must. Those condemning spirits have to leave. The Bible has a great deal of instruction concerning the preservation of purity, and every congregation desperately needs this teaching.

Deliverance and Restoration

I recently prayed deliverance over a minister who had been divorced; and since that experience, he has not been allowed to have a pastorate in his denomination. I find myself disagreeing with this policy for several reasons. First of all, I think of Mary Magdalene in Scripture, who, after having been cleansed from seven demons, became one of those very grateful persons who followed and served Jesus (see John 19:25). There is some disagreement as to whether some of those evil spirits may have been sexual in nature, but no matter. Because of the social position of women in that century, I am deeply touched by the fact that Jesus appeared to this formerly demonized woman first after His resurrection, as though she were someone very important in His life, someone that He cared for. Mark 16:9 tells us, "Now when He rose early on the first day of the week, He appeared first to Mary Magdalene, out of whom He had cast seven demons."

The point I am trying to make is that once Mary Magdalene had been cleansed from demons, it would appear that Jesus did not hold her past failure against her; rather, He accepted her appreciation and devotion, giving her the chance to start over. If a person, such as the pastor I refer to above, has been cleansed from his past and shows fruit of repentance, why should he be forever removed from ministry? It does not seem to follow the example of Jesus' treatment of Mary Magdalene. Jesus didn't rebuke Mary for following Him and serving Him as though she were a second-class citizen.

I told that pastor to try to start a church among divorced persons, since so very many marriages end in shipwreck. Many of those wounded people never darken the door of a church, because they feel like social outcasts. But someone needs to present them with the gospel. And who better understands broken marriages than a person who has gone through the pain and has come out of the other side healed?

Pray Cleansing

The last thing I do when praying over a person who has been infested with evil sexual spirits is to pray cleansing over him or her. I ask God to miraculously cleanse that person's mind of pornographic images and ungodly sexual experiences. I also ask God to cleanse the eyes that have looked upon what they should not have; to cleanse the ears from what has been heard; to cleanse the mouth, the skin, the hands and the sexual organs from all sinful thoughts, words and deeds. It is extremely important to break all soul ties with sex partners who are not the person's spouse (see Peter Horrobin's eloquent treatment of this topic in chapter 16). I ask God to bless the person's current marriage relationship, that it be as God intended, complete with joy and sexual fulfillment.

Those of us in the deliverance ministry delight in seeing people made whole again. It is a great embarrassment to Satan, who has come to steal, kill and destroy (see John 10:10). And we really enjoy being part of setting those captives free. We see great potential in any person who wants deliverance, and our prayer is that many will benefit from being set free from sexual bondage and go on to serve the Lord with all of their being.

> Jesus answered, "Most assuredly, I say to you, whoever commits sin is a slave of sin. Therefore, if the Son makes you free, you shall be free indeed" (John 8:34,36).

Note

1. *Random House Webster's College Dictionary*, s.v. "pornography."

Chapter 15

SEXUAL SIN: WHAT IT IS, WHAT IT DOES AND FINDING THE WAY OUT

Peter Horrobin

It is impossible to understand the nature and consequences of sexual sin without first understanding what God's original plan and purpose was for the human race. Then from within an understanding of God's creative purposes, we can begin to understand His plan and purpose for marriage, and then sex within marriage.

Made to Be Creative

We are made in the image and likeness of God (see Gen. 1:27). God is spirit and, therefore, we are also spiritual beings. But God is also creative, being the Creator, and the spirit within us is, therefore, creative by nature.

But we are more than spirit; we are also creatures of flesh. And flesh is more than just the body, for without there being a part of us which gives the body instructions, the body would be incapable of functioning effectively. The soul is that part of us which gives the body its instructions.

A body without a soul would be a bit like a car without a driver. Just as a car only moves when maneuvered by its driver, the body only moves when acted upon by the soul. And just as a bad driver is capable of damaging the vehicle and causing it to be a danger to him- or herself, other cars and other people, so the soul is capable of leading the body into dangerous territory, endangering the individual and possibly others.

Our complete entity, therefore, consists of spirit, soul and body. It is through the spirit that we are able to fellowship with God. The soul stands at the interface between the spirit and the body. The soul and the body together are what the Bible refers to as the flesh, which enables us to function as human beings. The spirit and the soul together form what we call the personality of a human being.

Creativity lies at the center of the human spirit, and God intended that it should find its expression in human beings through the flesh (the body and the soul). Whenever we use the gifts that God has given for godly purposes, it is, indirectly, an act of worship of the God who made us.

So when a child makes a tower out of wooden blocks and when an architect designs a building, they are expressing their God-given creativity. When an artist paints a picture, an author writes a book and a chef prepares a meal, they are also expressing something of the creative gifting they received into their spirit from their Creator. So, too, the use of our gift of sexuality can be used to manifest our creative gifting. Godly sex within the covenant of marriage rejoices the heart of God. When a husband and wife express themselves in a godly sexual relationship, it is both an expression of human creativity and an act of worship to God!

The Challenge of Free Will

When God made us, however, He risked everything by also giving us the gift of free will. God was desirous of a relationship with us that is an expression of love, which means, among other things, that God desires a relationship that is entered into through the exercise of freewill choice, not one that is enforced through domination and control. But this also means that all the creative gifts God has given us can be used for good or evil purposes.

An architect, for example, who is capable of designing a magnificent and inspiring cathedral could also use that creative gifting to design such awful things as the gas chambers of Auschwitz. An artist can use brushes to paint a picture of exquisite beauty, but he or she can also use the same brushes to paint a scene of unimaginable filth, horror and degradation. A film director can inspire, challenge and entertain with a movie of extraordinary power and sensitivity; or he or she can use the same skills to drag viewers into mental participation in violence, pornography and other distasteful situations.

Sadly, there is no limit to the behavior extremes of the fallen human race. Throughout history, humanity has plumbed the depths of behavior that is an abomination to a holy God. And nowhere has humanity done so than in the realm of sexuality, where ungodly desires of the soul can so easily take precedence over the desires of the spirit. The unredeemed have no spiritual brakes to apply to their behavior. They become wise in their own eyes, and "I'll do it my way" becomes the mantra of a world without God.

Only now, with the onset of a worldwide AIDS crisis of epidemic proportions, is the world having the opportunity to reassess some of the physical consequences of having removed restraints on sexual behavior. Tragically, the world's preferred response is not to discourage ungodly sexual activity through a return to godly order, but to encourage further indulgence in Satan's counterfeit regime through an even wider availability of cheap or free protective contraceptives, not solely for contraceptive purposes, but so as to limit the extent of disease transmission during heterosexual intercourse or homosexual activities.

The world is only concerned about the physical dangers of unprotected sex. The god of this world has so blinded the eyes of men and women that the spiritual dangers of ungodly sex have become irrelevant. Ours is a politically correct society in which there are no absolutes. Every faith or belief system, and moral code or lack thereof, has to be given equal political standing; and Christian truth is made to take its place as a supposed equal alongside every false religion, including witchcraft and atheism.

The Spiritual Dangers of Ungodly Sex

The spiritual dangers of ungodly sex are such that no contraceptive in the world can ever provide protection against them. And many of those inside the Church are seemingly ignorant of the spiritual consequences of sexual sin. I say "seemingly ignorant," because if they were fully aware of the dangers, teaching in the Church would at least mirror biblical teaching, and the incidence of sexual sin in the Church would be significantly less than it actually is.

The spiritual dangers of ungodly sex are such that no contraceptive in the world can ever provide protection against them.

In reality there is so much sexual sin inside the Body of Christ that, on occasion, it is difficult to distinguish between the sexual practices of believers and unbelievers! Instead of the Church's being salt and light in the world (see Matt. 5:13-16), the world has been allowed to sow poison inside the Church. And sexual sin is taken so lightly that, for many, the Bible's teaching on sex and sexuality is dismissed as out of date, or even irrelevant, for the permissive age in which we live. I have even had believers suggest to me that the Bible's teaching was true for earlier ages, but now that we have developed reliable contraceptives, biblical requirements for sexual conduct are no longer applicable.

And even in those sectors of the Church in which there is clear and unequivocal teaching regarding the Christian norms for sexual conduct, there is little understanding of the spiritual consequences of sexual sin, leaving believers ignorant of the reasons why purity truly is God's best for His creation. When teaching on the subject, I have found that when people understand what happens when we sin sexually, they come under the conviction of the Holy Spirit, see the need for cleansing, and quickly come to the place of open confession and repentance.

It is for good reason that Paul went out of his way to emphasize this point by telling the Christians in Corinth, "Flee sexual immorality. Every sin that a man does is outside the body, but he who commits sexual immorality sins against his own body" (1 Cor. 6:18). As we will see later (see chapter 16), sexual sin gives the enemy rights within the body through ungodly soul ties.

We live in a rebellious age when respect for authority is no longer enough to restrain the behavior of the willful; and, sadly, within the Church respect for the authority of Scripture has diminished. God's Word is no longer enough to restrain the sexual behavior of believers, let alone unbelievers. The Church may have become more exciting and more charismatic, but in so doing it seems to have lost something of the fear of the Lord. And as is so clearly expressed in Exodus 20:20, "The fear of God will . . . keep you from sinning" (*NIV*). Nothing else will keep a person from sinning when that person is alone and believes that no one else will see what he or she is doing.

The Bible's teaching on sowing and reaping (see Gal. 6:7) has been largely ignored. But Paul warned about not letting the grace of God become an excuse for sinful indulgence. The born-again believer (one whose spirit has been restored again to fellowship with God through faith in Jesus Christ) living in a fallen world will never in this life be free from temptation. The age-old battle between the will of the spirit and the will of the soul (the flesh) is described graphically by Paul in Galatians 5. Paul warns us in verse 21 that "those who practice such things [including adultery, fornication, lewdness] will not inherit the kingdom of God." Understanding the difference between godly and ungodly sex and then choosing to walk in God's ways could indeed be a matter of life and death. The writer of the Proverbs warns that the house of the adulteress "leads down to death and her paths to the spirits of the dead" (2:18, *NIV*).

So what actually is adultery? Jeremiah 3 provides us with a powerful insight into God's understanding of adultery. Here the peoples of Judah and Israel are accused of committing adultery with stone and wood (see vv. 6-10). Not because they were having ungodly sex, but because they had been worshiping idols, worshiping a false god. They were joining themselves through worship to another god. Jehovah was their true God, but they were going after another.

Adultery is, therefore, all wrongful joining together. By this definition, all sexual sin, be it before marriage, after marriage, in homosexual relationships or even with animals, is defined as adulterous. Consequently, the seventh commandment, "You shall not commit adultery" (Exod. 20:14), forbids much more than just heterosexual sin by married people. Its prohibition embraces all forms of ungodly sexual relationships.

As this chapter unfolds, the full spiritual dangers of sexual sin will become clear. My prayer is that as people begin to understand, they will find themselves on the road to restoration and healing.

Healing Grace and Mercy

Although the Scriptures face the reality of the fact that even believers can fall into sexual sin and are clear on what is right and wrong, they are also full of hope, telling us of a God who longs to forgive and to heal. God's promise is that when His people humble themselves, truly confess their sin, repent and turn from their sin, that He will forgive and restore them. While what has been done cannot be undone, David's account of his encounter with God, following the exposure of his adultery with Bathsheba, is eloquent testimony to God's mercy and healing grace (see Ps. 51).

It is absolutely clear, from both Scripture and experience, that when we choose to walk in the ways of the god of this world, we open the door to the enemy, which means that those who have knowingly walked in sexual sin not only need to repent, ask for forgiveness and change their ways; but they will also need deliverance in order to enter into the full healing that God wants them to have.

We cannot sweep these facts under the spiritual carpet. But we do need to be careful to respect the attitude of Jesus toward the woman who was caught in an act of adultery. Her accusers were ready to stone her to death, but Jesus had compassion upon her (see John 8:3-11). It is easy to be judgmental without understanding.

The first time I ministered to a prostitute, I was aware of an inner anger at what this 23-year-old woman had done to men. When I asked how long she had been a prostitute, and she told me 13 years, I began to reassess my thinking. When she told me how her father had left home, that her mother had little money and that she was led into child prostitution by a man who offered her sweets, and then money, for letting him touch her, I began to weep at the terrible damage that had been done by unscrupulous, evil men. I finished up repenting to her on behalf of men for what they had done to her.

We must be very careful not to fall into Satan's trap of heaping condemnation on those who have sinned sexually. There is hope, there is forgiveness, there is deliverance, and there is healing.

Made for Relationship

As explained by Doris Wagner in chapter 14, God designed man and woman for each other. He then provided them with the means through which they could not only express their relationship spiritually and emotionally, but also physically. God's intention for sexual expression between husband and wife was that this should be the high point of human relationship—a deeply spiritual experience of extraordinary oneness—so spiritual that the same Hebrew word, *yada,* is used to describe both sexual relationships between human beings and the intimacy and depth of spiritual relationship that we as humans are able to have with the living God (see Gen. 4:1; Isa. 43:10).[1]

Sex was designed by God to be so enjoyable that the survival of the human race through sexual reproduction would never be jeopardized!

Through the expression of their sexuality, men and women share with God in an act of creation. And sexual relations, as God originally intended, between unfallen man and unfallen woman, was, therefore, a glorious act of worship of the creator God.

While man's body has the physical capacity for casual, animal-like sex with any female, without the requirement of commitment to a relationship, the idea of casual sex is totally foreign to God's plan for humankind. Nowhere in Scripture is any expression of casual sex or sex outside of the marriage covenant approved of or encouraged. Yet, this is the spirit of the age in which we are now living, where hedonism and unrestricted, self-seeking pleasure is rampant throughout much of the world's societies.

Understanding that godly sexual expression is a form of worship is a vital key to understanding why sexual sin leads people into sexual and demonic bondage. For God rejoices to bless His people with His spiritual presence, especially when they are worshiping Him. Since 1662, a traditional marriage service, found in *The Book of Common Prayer*, has included a reference to adoration and worship. In the vows with which the couple would commit themselves to each other, they would say these words: "With my body I thee worship."

Whenever we make freewill choices to please Him, we put ourselves in the place of God's blessing being upon us. And there is no doubt that God rejoices to pour His blessing on godly sexual relationships that are lived out within the covenant of marriage.

The converse of this, however, is that in this fallen world Satan takes advantage of the fact that we were made to worship, and that in worship we make ourselves open to the spiritual. Satan welcomes it when we indulge in sexual practices which are contrary to God's order, because then it is not the living God that is being worshiped, but Satan. God will not give His glory to another and He will not, therefore, remain on the throne of a relationship that is ungodly. He cannot bless or rejoice in those things that are contrary to His created order for humanity.

So, as the god of this world, Satan, steps onto the throne of an ungodly relationship and receives the worship. But far from blessing the participants, who are pleasing Satan with their ungodly use of their creative sexuality, he uses the opportunity to bring them his cursing. And the spirits with which Satan indwells people are not holy, but unholy, or as the Gospel writers describe them, "unclean" (Mark 1:23,26; Luke 4:33,36). Through sexual sin, they are able to access the body which Scripture tells us is, or should be, the "temple of the Holy Spirit" (1 Cor. 6:19).

Guilt and Shame

Before the Fall there was no sin and, therefore, no guilt or shame. Guilt and shame are what we feel when we have offended someone else through our behavior, especially when that someone else is God. In the absence of any other being, we could not experience any feeling of guilt or shame. The very fact that we are aware of guilt and shame is primary evidence of the existence of God.

Guilty is what we are as a consequence of an offense we have committed. Guilt is resolved through restitution and forgiveness. Jesus paid the price for our sin, and through forgiveness we are absolved of the consequences of our sin.

Shame is what we feel on the inside when we have sinned. Shame makes us want to hide from those we have let down, hurt, betrayed or sinned against. A young boy will instinctively want to hide from his parents when he knows he has done something wrong, just as Adam and Eve tried to cover themselves up and hide from God in the Garden (see Gen. 3:6-10).

Shame can only be healed when the sin that caused the shame has been brought to the light and forgiven. There are some people whose entire lives are lived behind a wall of shame. Sometimes the shame is a result of what they have done, but often it is a consequence of what others have done to them. A girl who has been sexually abused can feel the shame of what has been experienced, especially when her abuser lays the blame for what has happened on her, the victim, even though she is not guilty in any way for what has happened. Satan will always try to use shame to prevent people from stretching out their hands and asking for His help.

Jesus is the only One who can touch and heal us if we are living with the consequences of shame in our hearts. He paid the price for our sin; He made it possible for us to be freed from the curse of other people's sin against us (through forgiving them) and to know the reality of His healing presence, which transforms us from the inside out.

Note

1. James Strong, *The New Strong's Exhaustive Concordance of the Bible* (Nashville, TN: Thomas Nelson Publishers, 1984), Hebrew ref. no. 3045.

Chapter 16

SHEDDING LIGHT ON SOUL TIES

Peter Horrobin

God's intentions for our sexual fulfillment lie strictly within the covenant of marriage. Marriage is not just a legal transaction. It is primarily a spiritual transaction—a joining together of two people. Just as each man and woman alive is spirit, soul and body, God also intended the covenant of marriage to lead to a permanent union of spirit, soul and body.

A couple who intend to marry may be spiritually joined in faith, heart and intent; but until after the vows have been made to each other and to God, and intercourse has taken place, the marriage is not complete. Indeed, the Church has always recognized that a marriage which has not been consummated through sexual intercourse is one that can be annulled, because it is not a proper marriage. Intercourse is the union of flesh, a union in which the desire of the soul is completed through bodily sexual union. Through sexual union, therefore, there is both a joining of two people's spirits and souls, as well as their bodies.

After intercourse has taken place, the bodies separate, but the souls are now joined together. At this point, the marriage, as such, is complete. There is then not only a union of spirit, but also a union of soul. Scripture talks about the two having become one flesh (see Eph. 5:31). A soul tie has now been established between husband and wife through the act of sexual union. Something of the man becomes part of the woman and something of the woman becomes part of the man. It is for this reason that as the years go by, married couples can grow to be like each other in so many different ways—even to the extent that it is sometimes possible to see the effect physically in couples that have been married for a long time.

What we have now established is that the physical union of sexual intercourse involves more than the physical joining of bodies, for those who have been joined together in this way also become joined together in their souls with what we call a *soul tie*. This was God's wonderful plan for marriage, to permanently unite couples in a living and dynamic relationship.

Consequences of Sexual Sin

We established in the last chapter that when people enter into sexual sin, they are pleasing the god of this world; and, as a result, they may have welcomed an unclean spirit into their lives for which deliverance is needed. We now also understand that God's intention for marriage was to provide a means through which man and woman would be permanently united in spirit and soul. Paul even tells us that God's intentions for the relationship between husband and wife could even be used to illustrate God's intentions for the relationship between Jesus and the Church (see Eph. 5:22-32). That's the good news!

The bad news for those who are sexually promiscuous is that God does not suspend His plans to establish a soul tie between them in order to accommodate their sin. While God is undoubtedly a God of love, He is also a God of law and order; and God's order for sexual relationships is that *whenever* they occur, a real union takes place and a soul tie is established.

So if a person, for example, has had several sexual partners, he or she now has a soul tie with each one of them. Something of that unique person has been given away to each sexual partner, and something of the partners has become part of that person. Paul explicitly states that this is so even in the case of prostitution; he says that when a man unites himself with a prostitute, the two will become one flesh (see 1 Cor. 6:16).

Instead of this union constituting a godly soul tie—which brings great blessing into the lives of a husband and wife—it becomes a chain of bondage through which people are influenced unknowingly by the life and personality of those to whom they have been sexually joined. Furthermore, an ungodly soul tie provides an opportunity for the demonic to transfer from one person to another, both at the time of sexual intercourse and at any time subsequent.

The whole of Proverbs 5 is a warning against adulterous sexual relationships. Verse 22 sums up the consequences of ungodly sex by saying that "the evil deeds of a wicked man ensnare him; the cords of his sin hold him fast" (*NIV*). An ungodly soul tie is a cord of sin which holds people in permanent bondage—at least until Jesus breaks the chain. Because it is through God's order for humankind that a soul tie was established in the first place, it follows that it is only God who can undo it.

Breaking the Chains of Ungodly Soul Ties

First John 1:9 encourages us to confess our sins to God so that we will be forgiven. But in James 5:16, Scripture tells us to "confess your sins to each other and pray for each other so that you may be healed" (*NIV*). There are clearly two processes going on. One deals with the eternal, spiritual consequence of sin and the restoration of relationship with God through forgiveness; and the other deals with the temporal consequences of sin which have caused a condition requiring healing—healing that can include the need for deliverance.

Of course, God can (and does) heal some people sovereignly when they pray to Him. But for many people there may also be a pride issue that has to be dealt with, and it is only the process of telling someone else about the sin that deals with the pride, which is sometimes a major blockage to receiving healing.

We have seen this to be the case especially in respect to sexual sin in Christians. It is human for us to prefer not to experience the shame of someone else's knowing about our sin. But where there is a pride issue in the heart, it is the humbling of ourselves in this way that enables God to lift us up, restore us fully into His presence and release us into healing and the fulfillment of the calling He has for us.

The humbling of ourselves through the confession of our sexual sin enables God to lift us up, restore us fully into His presence and release us into healing.

There is no sin that God is not able to forgive—and, ultimately, it is only He that can wipe our slate clean. Similarly, it is only God that can undo those soul ties that have been established through ungodly sexual relationships. So in a ministry situation we would encourage a person to confess his or her sin to God, asking Him for forgiveness and restoration. Then we would ask God to break the ungodly soul tie and restore the person to a place where that which was given away to another in a wrong relationship is restored to the person, and he or she is completely released of everything that came to him or her from that sexual partner.

The effect of this can be very profound, bringing transformation to people's lives as they are restored to being the people that God intended them to be in the first place. The final part of the ministry is the deliverance. While we have to ask God to bring the healing (severing) of ungodly soul ties, Jesus gave to us as believers authority to cast out demons. It is our general experience that when an individual has had ungodly sexual soul ties, he or she will also have been menaced by demons that either came in at the time of the sin or which have subsequently used the soul tie to gain access.

Examples

Stories from the Casebook

Some of the real-life stories, gained from our experience within Ellel Ministries, will help you understand the significance of soul ties and the importance of not allowing any of the works of darkness to remain uncleansed in a person's life.

One man I ministered to freely confessed that he had had about 50 sexual partners. The Holy Spirit had brought deep conviction of the sin in his life, and he was truly repentant. After he had fully confessed the sins and asked God to forgive him, I then asked God to break the ungodly soul ties and restore him on the inside. (Prior to this healing, the man had had no teaching on the subject to influence how he would describe what had happened.) This is what he said about the experience: "It feels as though there are parts of me coming back to me. And I can see things that I thought were part of who I am, disappearing as God takes them away." Then he made a very profound statement, "For the first time that I can remember, I know who I am!" He was rediscovering his own true identity.

One of the major consequences of sexual sin is that through the establishment of ungodly soul ties, we begin to lose our own identity. And the more partners with whom we have had sex, the less we know who we really are.

In reality, until God had dealt with the ungodly soul ties, this man couldn't have known who he was, for he had been joined to 50 other people, all of whom were having some sort of an influence on his life. And at the same time, it was as if his own influence was being spread around the world in the lives of all those with whom he had had sex. After God had broken the ungodly ties, the man was free to be himself for the first time since he had begun to be promiscuous as a teenager. The final part of the ministry was deliverance and, not surprisingly, there was a lot of deliverance needed.

Another man, who was a pastor of a local church, came to me because he was concerned that he was unable to make any more headway in his church. It seemed as though every time he tried to move things forward along the pathway of renewal that an impenetrable blockage stood in the way. When I first asked him about any previous sexual partners he may have had, he was surprised by the question, not thinking that this could have any relevance to his situation. He freely admitted that before he became a Christian he had been quite promiscuous—he had had 10 different sexual partners. But he had totally turned his back on this lifestyle after his conversion, and he believed that had all been dealt with at the Cross.

I explained to him that the sin had been totally forgiven and that God had wiped the record of the sin off the slate. But in reality there is also a law of sowing and reaping, which means that not only does sin have to be confessed and repented of in order to deal with the eternal consequences, but there are also instances in which cleansing and healing are also necessary to deal with the consequences in time.

He understood what I was saying and gladly wrote down the names of the 10 girls. One by one I prayed through the list, asking God to break the ungodly soul ties. And one by one the pastor sensed God doing a profound work of cleansing on the inside; and after each name had been prayed over, significant deliverance took place. That is, until we reached the fifth name on the list. I had only just begun to pronounce her name with the syllable "Ang," when I was stunned by a violent and noisy demonic response from the man as he shouted at me, "You are not having her!" He was as stunned as I was; and after he had recovered his composure, I asked him what he could remember about Angela.

He had no difficulty in remembering that Angela was always dressed in black and was actively involved in witchcraft. Here was the major key to the blockage he had been experiencing in his ministry. He was bonded to someone whose witchcraft was still being used against him through the ungodly soul tie which had been established all those years earlier. Satan uses every possible hook to try to limit the effectiveness of our ministries. After I prayed to bind the demons of witchcraft, they were silenced. God broke that soul tie forever, and the pastor was a different man after that. The remaining soul ties and subsequent deliverance presented no problem.

A lady once told me that there was a night in her marriage when she sensed there was someone else present in the bed with her and her husband. She couldn't understand why she was feeling so repulsed by her husband's presence. He had been away on business, and she had been looking forward to the restoration of intimate relations with him on his return. But there was something wrong and she knew it. It was only years later that she found out that when her husband had been away he had committed adultery. What his wife had been sensing was the presence of the other woman, to whom her husband had been joined with an ungodly soul tie. For years since that moment, their relationship had been tarnished by the spiritual presence of the other woman.

Over the years we have ministered freedom from ungodly sexual soul ties to countless thousands of people around the world, people from every racial grouping and from most nations. The fruit has been remarkable. Often Satan uses the ungodly soul ties to hold individuals through demonic symptoms of physical illness, preventing them from ever being fully whole. This type of demonic transference is one of the most common sources of sickness in the Body of Christ.

We have frequently prayed for people who have had previous sexual partners; and, after prayer and deliverance, they have experienced a significant measure of healing. Sometimes the effect has been quite dramatic, as symptoms a person may have been wrestling with for years are suddenly healed as ungodly ties are broken.

On one occasion I taught a large congregation about the nature of sexual sin and its consequences. When teaching in this way, I often use drama to illustrate the key points. I have a young couple on the stage who, in the drama, are about to get married; and I then expose the fact that they both have had previous sexual partners. In the drama these previous partners are hanging on to the young couple as they prepare to get married. But these previous partners have also had other sexual relationships, so there is a second tier of ties, and a third, and so on. When people see just how many different people are tied into such a marriage, they realize how dangerous sexual sin is. They understand why the Scriptures are so clear about the need for sexual purity both before and after marriage.

After the church's congregation had seen the drama and heard the teaching, I then opened up the front of the church for confession, repentance and ministry. A flood of people came forward. There were many tears, as well as major deliverance and extensive physical healing as the hold of the enemy on these dear people's lives was broken forever. The pastors of the church looked on in amazement. They thought they knew their people and were deeply shocked at the extent of their congregation's need in this area.

One lady came for prayer because she was unable to conceive a child with her husband. On asking a few questions, I found out that there had been a previous boyfriend who had wanted to marry her, but she had given him up to marry the man she really loved. Her previous boyfriend, however, with whom she had been having sexual relations, was both heartbroken and very angry. He vowed that she would never have a child by another man.

Such words were, in fact, a curse which Satan used to release demons against her—in this case a spirit of death—to prevent her from ever being able to have her own child. The soul tie between the former boyfriend and the woman had given the enemy easy access to her life. It was only when the soul tie had been broken, and she had been delivered of the spirit of death, that she was then able to conceive.

It has become a common experience for us to minister in this way to women who, for various reasons, are currently unable to conceive. We often find that earlier in life they had had other sexual partners and, in some cases, had had an abortion after becoming pregnant. What a joy it is to bring healing to such people through first dealing with the sin of abortion, and then asking God to break all the ungodly soul ties, followed by deliverance from all the unclean spirits. The icing on the cake is to subsequently receive a photograph of the longed-for baby! We have many such pictures in our files. They are a constant encouragement as we press on to bring healing to God's people.

Special Situations

All that I have said so far about the need for confession, repentance, the breaking of soul ties and deliverance applies to all forms of sexual sin that have been entered into through the freewill choice of the participants.

The primary difference between those who have committed sexual sin before marriage (fornication) and those who have committed sexual sin after marriage (adultery) is that the latter also involves betrayal of the marriage covenant with one's spouse, often resulting in secondary pain and relationship breakdown. Ministry into the marital relationship or into the consequences of relationship breakdown is beyond the scope of this chapter.

It is increasingly common to find that married couples who have a godly sexual relationship within marriage began their sexual relationship with fornication before marriage. In these cases there can be both an ungodly and a godly soul tie between the couple.

It is necessary for the ungodly dimension of the relationship to be fully dealt with, because that soul tie can be a source of spiritual friction—or even be the grounds for an unclean spirit to cause sexual problems and division in the relationship through temptation to subsequent sexual sin. One lady in just such a case was radically healed of epilepsy, which had afflicted her just after her wedding. Having dealt with the fornication, she was then delivered and wonderfully healed.

Abuse and Rape

When sexual relations have been forced upon a person in an abusive or rape situation, an ungodly soul tie is still established between the abuser or the rapist and the victim, even though the sexual union took place against the will of the victim. While much deeper ministry is needed in order to take the victim through forgiveness and healing for the terrible betrayal and ordeal he or she has experienced, it is still necessary at some point in the ministry to deal with the ungodly soul tie that has been formed.

Many people who were abused as children have come to believe that they could never be free of intrusive memories of their ordeal and the perpetrator. But after God breaks the soul ties, they find that they are free to move on in their healing without being chained to the person who had stolen so much from them.

Those who have been abused or raped will also need help with the shame associated with their ordeal. While, in reality, they have done nothing which merits personal guilt or shame, one of Satan's tactics is to overwhelm such victims with false guilt and false shame, often demonically empowered, which entrap them into a false identity from which it is very difficult for them to escape. They need the help of those who can take them by the hand and see them restored under the hand of God. In severe cases, there can also be a breaking of the personality that requires more in-depth personal ministry.

Perversion

Perverted sex is everything that God would define as being ungodly sexual conduct beyond the practice of heterosexual relationships. This would include sex with animals, homosexual and lesbian relationships, oral sex in which a woman is made to experience her partner's ejaculation into her mouth, sexual violence and punishment, and all forms of ritual sex.

The teaching that anything goes within marriage, provided that both partners agree to it, finds no place in Scripture. Perverted sexual practices are wrong, whether they are found inside or outside of marriage. I never cease to be amazed at the extremes of sexual behavior with which some people have experimented. It is little wonder that they are struggling with all manner of spiritual, emotional, physical and sexual problems—not to mention temptations. There is no way out except through uncompromising honesty, a radical determination to turn from all such behavior, deliverance and healing.

Sometimes people have been led into perverted sexual conduct by someone else. For example, a person may have been encouraged by a particular individual to experiment with animal sex. It is our experience that in such cases there is often a soul tie between the participants, even though they may not have had direct, personal sexual contact. The agreement to participate together in ungodliness is enough to unite them in an ungodly soul tie.

Pornography

Pornography of all types provides the means for individuals to participate lustfully, through the eyes, in other people's sexually promiscuous or perverted behavior. Jesus faced this possibility head on in Matthew 5:28 when He said, "Anyone who looks at a woman lustfully has already committed adultery with her in his heart" (*NIV*).

The use of pornography as an aid to masturbation highlights the fact that a sexual union in the mind joins the image that is being looked at with the viewer, resulting in a physical sexual expression. It may be necessary when ministering to those for whom pornography has become an uncontrollable force in their lives to ask God to break the soul ties that have been established through the images they have lustfully used.

None of us can escape the gratuitous onslaught of sexual images that bombard us in the media, especially through television, movies and the Internet. Satan uses this constant bombardment to try to wear us down so that we become increasingly tolerant of blatantly ungodly images. We need to be constantly on our guard and learn to resist the devil's temptations whenever they assault us.

Strength to Stand

When it comes to sexual sin, many people have desperately tried in secret and in their own strength to overcome the temptations of the enemy. Often, largely because they have been ignorant of the nature of the battle, they have not had access to the weapons with which to fight. But once people understand the true nature of sexual sin, soul ties and the need for deliverance, it is as though a huge obstacle to their healing has been removed.

However, deliverance should not be considered the end of the story. We still have to exercise our free will in order to remain free. We do this by making godly choices for, as Peter tells us very graphically, "Your enemy the devil prowls around like a roaring lion looking for someone to devour" (1 Pet. 5:8, *NIV*), which means that Satan doesn't generally give up on trying to tempt us! Peter's simple advice is, "Resist him, standing firm in the faith" (1 Pet. 5:9). For as long as we resist him, the enemy cannot have any ground to stand on in our lives.

May the Lord give you His understanding of any issues you are personally facing and enable you to receive any necessary healing and deliverance. Once you have been healed and delivered, you will have the strength to stand firm as you choose to walk in obedience and fellowship with Him.

Chapter 17

THE EFFECTS OF LUST ON YOUTH

Tim and Anne Evans

It was supposed to be the standard question-and-answer session. After years of speaking to married couples on the topic of intimacy and sexuality, we were excited about the opportunity to present this subject to a younger group. Their ages ranged anywhere from 14 to 18 years old. After working through our outline, we planned to end the night with this session. As our experience grew, it seemed we were almost able to predict the kind of questions that would be asked. Offering biblical principles and godly counsel, we hoped that listeners would be better equipped to make informed choices, reflecting the character of God.

There was a box near the podium filled with questions that the students had written out. Reaching in to pull out the first card, we began, "This is from a 15-year-old female and she asks [long pause], 'If you want to stay a virgin, is anal sex okay?' " An awkward silence filled the room before it was broken by the embarrassed giggle of a few girls in the front row. The older students seemed unaffected, as they quietly waited for our response.

Masking our surprise, we proceeded to respond. It wasn't the question that shocked us; it was the question *behind* the question. What that 15-year-old girl was really asking us was, "Is it okay with God if I engage in *another kind* of sexual activity, one that would allow me to keep my virginity and technically not break God's law?"

Satan loves to take full advantage of a child's immaturity and lack of biblical understanding. If anal sex is reclassified as *another kind* of sexual activity, a child could easily be convinced that this perversion is an acceptable option. Whenever young people begin to focus on the letter of the law by looking for loopholes that could vindicate sinful behavior, it is not long before they are justifying actions that fall outside of God's original design. The question that we often hear from young people regarding sexual behavior is, How far can I go sexually and still fall within God's parameters? The question we want to encourage them to ask is, What is God's best for me?

When we were growing up, anal sex would have been classified as a perverted act, considered only by sexual deviants. The idea of sodomy being a substitute for intercourse for the purpose of maintaining one's virginity would have never even occurred to us. And even if it had, it would not have been a topic for public discussion at a Christian youth group gathering. We have become so desensitized by sin that distortions are becoming more and more acceptable.

Communicating with our youth is the key to keeping a healthy, strong and growing relationship with them. It is so important that children hear an accurate and honest view of God's original design for their lives and for their sexuality. If we can pray and live out opportunities to introduce them to their Father, they will be able to recognize the father of lies. If we can pray and live out opportunities for His design to be taught, it will be easier for them to spot the counterfeit.

> Let us behave properly as in the day, not in carousing and drunkenness, not in sexual promiscuity and sensuality, not in strife and jealousy. But put on the Lord Jesus Christ, and make no provision for the flesh in regard to its lusts (Rom. 13:13-14, *NASB*).

Recent statistics reinforce what we are seeing in this generation: 61 percent of all high school seniors have had sexual intercourse; about 50 percent are currently sexually active; and 21 percent have had four or more partners. The United States has one of the highest teenage pregnancy rates in the world. About a quarter of all sexually active adolescents become infected with a sexually transmitted disease (STD) each year.[1]

While these statistics are compelling, we do not need research companies to tell us values and moral codes are becoming increasingly ambiguous. Students are bombarded with distortions of sex in almost every facet of their lives. Everywhere they turn, the enemy is introducing images that open a door to lust—at school, in the workplace, on television, on the Internet, over the radio and at the movies. The enemy's plan to deceive an entire generation is working. Is it any wonder that he targets our youth? Young children in their formative years are easily deceived, inexperienced and naïve. For the most part, they are unaware of the spiritual battle that is raging for their hearts and souls.

Our evening with the youth group continued as each new question evoked a lively discussion: Can I get an STD if my boyfriend wears a rubber? What are sex toys? Is masturbation a sin? Why doesn't the Church ever talk about this stuff? Is it a sin to lust if you don't do anything about it? Why does sex always feel dirty, even though the Bible says God created it? Is it wrong to look at the Internet sites that pop up on your screen, if you didn't type them in?

Spiritual Fathers and Mothers

During a break time, a young girl asked to talk to us. She expressed her appreciation for the honest and straightforward discussion. She ended by saying, "No wonder we are so confused. Nobody ever talks to us about this stuff." It was a privilege for us to plow through this new ground together. Our interaction with the youth made us more aware than ever of the need for godly spiritual fathers and mothers to be God's voice speaking into the lives of this younger generation, helping them build a strong foundation for living well. Is it difficult? Yes! Discipleship means imparting your very life, but the rewards have eternal impact. It is not wisdom that qualifies us as spiritual parents; it is love.

It was the apostle Paul who said, "For though you might have ten thousand instructors in Christ, yet you do not have many [spiritual] fathers" (1 Cor. 4:15, *NASB*). His words have never been truer, or the need for spiritual fathers and mothers greater, than for this generation. Working with youth reinforces our need to continue crying out to the Lord, asking Him to raise our awareness so that we can come against the enemy in victory. Too many young people are isolated from their family and from the Church. Without godly voices speaking into their young hearts, how will they ever learn to live well? Who will teach them foundational life lessons? Who will teach them the truths that the Bible reveals about what pleases the Lord?

> The body is not for immorality, but for the Lord, and the Lord is for the body. Do you not know that your bodies are members of Christ? (1 Cor. 6:13,15, *NASB*).

> For this is the will of God, your sanctification; that is, that you abstain from sexual immorality; that each of you know to possess his own vessel in sanctification and honor, not in lustful passion (1 Thess. 4:3-5, *NASB*).

> For all that is in the world—the lust of the flesh and the lust of the eyes and the boastful pride of life, is not from the Father, but is from the world (1 John 2:16, *NASB*).

Our Battle Is Not Against Flesh and Blood

As pastors, we have come to realize that an event as mundane as picking up the telephone can often have profound consequences. While walking through our regular morning routine, we received a call from the mother of a teenager. Humbled, she attempted to relay the series of events that had led her to call us. Apparently, a friend of the family agreed to repair her computer and, in the process, discovered that the woman's 13-year-old son was using it to access a large number of pornographic websites. (The enemy places no restrictions on the age of his targets!) Throughout the course of my conversation with her, this mother expressed shock, embarrassment, disappointment and anger. The underlying theme, however, was guilt and shame. Why was this happening to her? What had she done wrong? How long had she been deceived? What will she do?

As we continued to talk together, she confessed that her husband had struggled with pornography for years. While she was aware of his problem, she did not know how to talk to him about it. Helping him to remain in the darkness, she justified his behavior by convincing herself that this particular area of weakness was self-contained. It didn't affect any other area of his life. Or did it? She now wondered out loud if there was a connection between her husband's struggle and her son's.

In an attempt to determine where this behavior could have originated, she learned that her son had discovered his dad's collection of pornographic materials. Unwilling to address the situation with his parents, he never told anyone. Keeping this secret to himself, the sexual images began to consume his mind. Ignoring the guilt inflicted by the illicit photographs that now seemed to control him, he continued to make wrong choices. The trap had been set. In an attempt to satisfy the urges that he was unable to control, he typed the word "sex" into his Internet search engine. The bait had been taken.

> You have heard that it was said, "Do not commit adultery." But I tell you that anyone who looks at a woman lustfully has already committed adultery with her in his heart (Matt. 5:27-28, *NIV*).

Lust is the silent or secret sin. It has been described as a passionate, overmastering desire that eventually seeks to control. Therefore, it is not surprising to hear the number of young people who are addicted to pornography increases every day in our Internet-savvy society. Stories like this one are becoming commonplace. The Internet is just another tool used to lure a generation away from true intimacy. Since lust never satisfies or validates, the victims find themselves needing more—more sex, more pornography, more food, more money, more power, more whatever.

Satan wants you to believe that you can enjoy the benefits of sex apart from a covenantal relationship. Nothing could be further from the truth!

This endless cycle perpetuates an addictive lifestyle that encourages a counterfeit form of intimacy. The shame and the embarrassment that used to be the price you paid in order to purchase illicit sexual materials have been replaced with a false confidence in the anonymity that the Internet provides. The enemy convinces you that no one will ever find out. His strategy is simple: He wants you to actually believe that you can hide without any personal cost. You can enjoy the benefits of sex without the commitment of a covenantal relationship. Nothing could be further from the truth.

The Enemy's Deluge

An entire generation of school-aged youth is coming home to empty houses each day. Healthy family interaction has subtly been replaced by long hours in front of the TV or on the Internet. The average adolescent will view nearly 14,000 sexual references this year. Over half will contain sexual content. Even the prime-time television "family hour" is littered with sexual incidents and innuendos.

By the time an adolescent graduates from high school, he or she will have spent 15,000 hours watching television. As far as the Internet, a leading Web intelligence and traffic measurement service finds "sex" to be the most popular term searched for online. One in every 300 terms searched for online includes the word "sex." People inquire more about sex than they do about games, travel, jokes, cars, jobs, wealth and health *combined.*[2]

God's Redemptive Plan at Work

Sexual promiscuity, rooted in a spirit of lust, continues to inflict the kind of soul wounding that cries out for deliverance and inner healing. Realizing the value of living free in Christ, we encourage spiritual fathers and mothers to recognize the transforming power connected with discipling the next generation. Ministering freedom to our sexually broken young men and women always starts with God. Seeing His redemptive plan realized in young people's lives reminds us that victory over lust is attainable. As spiritual fathers and mothers, we stand in the gap with parents, resolved to confront lust in whatever form it takes. God's unending grace promises to strengthen the weak and purify the lost.

A student in her mid-20s walked into our office. Discouraged, she expressed a desire to return home at the semester break. Beginning the school year searching for intimacy with God, she now felt increasingly distant from Him. Unable to measure any evidence of change, she found herself questioning whether God's promises would ever be realized in her own life. She kept wondering, *What am I doing wrong?* Her quiet times with the Lord felt flat, making them increasingly difficult. Chapel left her uninspired. Obviously something was blocking her from experiencing intimacy with Jesus.

In response, we agreed to meet on a regular basis. The Lord often uses time spent with a young person to give the perspective and understanding needed to identify root issues. In this young lady's case, her childhood was a distorted version of God's family design. At a very young age, she had been exposed to her father's pornography addiction. Those images seemed to be permanently imprinted in her mind's eye. When she was only 10 years old, her mother's drug addiction ended in suicide, leaving a void in her life that had not yet been filled. Forced into adulthood, she made an inner vow to guard her heart from the pain of abandonment. In response to her growing need for love and acceptance, she engaged in multiple sexual relationships.

It was in her late teens that she heard the gospel and realized her need for Jesus. Accepting Him as her Lord and Savior was the beginning. She began believing that God had a plan for her life. Over the next few years, she moved around, attending a number of different churches. Her nomadic existence kept her from building stable relationships. Now in her mid-20s, she found herself sitting in our office at a point of desperation. Tormented by illicit sexual thoughts, she was unable to focus on school or God. The battle left her feeling inadequate and unworthy, thinking, *Why is this happening to me? No matter what I do, I can't seem to break free.*

As we met with her over a period of weeks, we began to see His miraculous power at work in her life. We were not just sitting across the table from a student who needed direction or just listening to another story, looking for the places to insert some godly counsel. Our time together grew into something much deeper as we began to feel an overwhelming sense of love for her. God's heart toward His daughter was being imparted to us. As a result, she was able to take an important step forward and move toward God's best for her.

The Value of Relationship

As we continue to minister to youth, we see God using *relationship* more than anything else as a vehicle for restoration. While deliverance and inner healing are essential to establishing their freedom, they often need something more. The loving guidance of a spiritual parent—in conjunction with prayer, fasting, inner healing and deliverance—often offers the kind of transformation that can be sustained for a lifetime. Young people do not have to have family histories that include broken marriages or severely dysfunctional relationships in order to benefit from the influence of a spiritual parent. We all need people in our lives who are willing to walk with us.

It is naïve of us to assume that families offer the kind of environment to their children that facilitates open communication. The young boy who was involved with Internet pornography came from a loving, Christian home. His father, trapped in his own addiction, had been unable to provide healthy guidance. His mother admitted to having been unable to discuss this sensitive subject with either her husband or her son. Love alone will never be able to equip a child with all that is needed for godly living. This is where the Church must step in and attempt to offer what is lacking.

We see spiritual fathers and mothers not as the answer, but as a vital component of the restoration process. The desire to pray, listen, guide, support, nurture and love another human being comes from the Father. As we grow in intimacy with Jesus, we are better equipped to impart our lives to the next generation. If discipleship doesn't flow out of our own personal intimacy with Jesus, it will lack substance and authority.

We have come to understand that we cannot take our children further than we have gone ourselves. God's plan for the next generation includes our participation. We have been invited to join Him as He weaves His purposes into a remnant of people who long to live for Him. Delivering our youth into the freedom God intends simply begins with being a part of their lives. If we do not give them our time, our energy, our hearts and our passions, it is certain that the enemy will.

Notes

1. American Academy of Pediatrics Committee on Public Education, "Sexuality, Contraception, and the Media," *Pediatrics,* vol. 107, no. 1 (January 2002), pp. 191-194.
2. "Zogby/Focus Survey Reveals Shocking Internet Sex Statistics," *Legal Facts: Family Research Council*, vol. 2, no. 20 (March 30, 2000).

Chapter 18

FREEDOM FROM ABORTION'S AFTERMATH

John Eckhardt

God is raising up women in this hour! He is anointing them prophetically and apostolically to be a strong force for God's kingdom on Earth. God is using deliverance as a tool to release millions of women as ministers of God who can do the works of Jesus Christ; to set them free from curses, generational spirits, from anything that has come upon them. But the truth is that Satan hates women, because it was the seed of a woman that bruised his head (see Gen. 3:15). He is determined to keep women down in such a way that they can never come into the fullness of their true identity. There are certain assignments that demons have against women to keep them oppressed, either as a result of the society in which they live or because of their decisions. Satan is prevailing in the lives of too many women.

One major tool that Satan has used to accomplish this goal is abortion. The devil has often tricked women into believing that if they have an abortion, their problems will be solved. The enemy will give women all kinds of reasons why abortion is the only answer: they can't financially support their child; the child is going to interrupt their career; or perhaps it's an illegitimate child that will bring shame. The enemy will use any number of means to convince women that having an abortion will make everything okay. But the devil is a liar. Instead of solving all of a woman's problems, an abortion works to multiply them.

This chapter is directed to those of us who minister deliverance. It is by no means a message meant to condemn any female who has had an abortion. Most women to whom we have ministered had abortions before they became committed Christians and accepted the Lord Jesus. Abortion is not the unforgivable sin. Nevertheless, we have found that there's a whole system and network of demons that can come in through the door of an abortion, and that can continue to operate in a woman's life long after she has been saved. Even though the sin is forgiven by God, Satan's legal right to torment often needs to be dealt with in order for these women to move into all God has for them.

Many years ago in my church, we did an extensive teaching on abortion in which we used Bill Banks's excellent book *Ministering to Abortion's Aftermath* as a textbook, which I highly recommend. We did this teaching because we found that an amazing number of women coming into our church needed deliverance because of one or more abortions. Many of them were under tremendous oppression as a result.

I also need to make clear that even though we generally minister to women when it comes to abortion, and though this chapter is geared toward women, men can be equally involved in an abortion. Often a man will encourage a woman—whether she's his girlfriend, his wife, his daughter or whatever—to have an abortion. When this has occurred, the man is equally guilty of having shed the blood of an innocent child, and he has also opened the door to demonic oppression.

Abortion is such a prevalent sin in America today that if you are involved in a deliverance ministry, you will likely minister to women who have had abortions and men who have encouraged them. You need to be equipped and understand both the demonic structure behind abortion as well as what the prevailing spirits are that generally oppress those who have been involved in abortion.

The Spirit Behind Abortion

There is no question that God hates the worship of any idol—that's why it is forbidden in the Ten Commandments (see Exod. 20:3-6). But even though there are many, many idols, only a handful of them are mentioned in the Bible. When God specifically mentions a particular idol by name, there must be something about that idol that is especially abominable to God. Behind every idol there is a demon. We know that the idol itself is nothing, but there's a demon force gaining strength from the worship of that idol (see 1 Cor. 10:19-21). Such was the case with one idol named Molech: "And thou shalt not let any of thy seed pass through the fire to Molech, neither shalt thou profane the name of thy God: I am the LORD" (Lev. 18:21, *KJV*).

Later on, God gives a firm warning to those who would involve themselves with Molech:

> And the LORD spake unto Moses, saying, Again, thou shalt say to the children of Israel, Whosoever he be of the children of Israel, or of the strangers that sojourn in Israel, that giveth any of his seed unto Molech; he shall surely be put to death: the people of the land shall stone him with stones. And I will set my face against that man, and will cut him off from among his people; because he hath given of his seed unto Molech, to defile my sanctuary, and to profane my holy name. And if the people of the land do any ways hide their eyes from the man, when he giveth of his seed unto Molech, and kill him not: Then I will set my face against that man, and against his family, and will cut him off, and all that go a-whoring after him, to commit whoredom with Molech, from among their people (Lev. 20:1-5, *KJV*).

These Scriptures are not given just to fill up space. There's something about Molech that we need to know which remains true even today.

Who Was Molech?

Molech is a cruel demon spirit who demands its followers' seed, or children, in sacrifice, and it has an insatiable desire for innocent blood.

Historically, this is an Ammonite spirit. The Ammonites were descendants of Ammon, who was one of the sons of Lot whom he had with his own daughter. Molech was the god of the Ammonites, which means that we are not just dealing with a demon, but also with a principality. So Molech represents a throne of iniquity, as we see in Psalm 94: "Shall the throne of iniquity have fellowship with thee, which frameth mischief by a law? They gather themselves together against the soul of the righteous, and condemn the innocent blood" (vv. 20-21, *KJV*).

Here we see that the very laws of the Ammonites supported the horrible practices that Molech demanded, including the sacrifice of their sons and daughters. But there was more. In the book of Amos, the prophet is prophesying judgment against different nations for their cruelty toward Israel. He pronounces a particular judgment upon the Ammonites because of something they had done. Here is where we see that Molech's desire for innocent blood extends to children still in their mothers' wombs: "Thus saith the LORD; For three transgressions of the children of Ammon, and for four, I will not turn away the punishment thereof; because they have ripped up the women with child of Gilead, that they might enlarge their border" (Amos 1:13, *KJV*).

God pronounces a judgment against the Ammonites because when they came into a land to conquer it, they had a practice of taking pregnant women and ripping them open to pull the baby out. There must be something demonic that would drive them to do that. I believe that it was Molech, the bloodthirsty god of the Ammonites, that caused them to target women with child. God finally pronounces judgment on them for this grave sin: " 'But I will kindle a fire in the wall of Rabbah, and it shall devour the palaces thereof, with shouting in the day of battle, with a tempest in the day of the whirlwind: And their king shall go into captivity, he and his princes together,' saith the LORD" (vv. 14-15, *KJV*).

Israel Violates God's Command

Israel violated the commandment of God set forth in Leviticus and began to get involved with Molech worship. King Solomon was the one who opened the door: "Then did Solomon build an high place for Chemosh, the abomination of Moab, in the hill that is before Jerusalem, and for Molech, the abomination of the children of Ammon" (1 Kings 11:7, *KJV*).

In Psalm 106, we see how the Lord dealt with Israel for this defiling sin:

> And they served their idols: which were a snare unto them. Yea, they sacrificed their sons and their daughters unto devils, and shed innocent blood, even the blood of their sons and of their daughters, whom they sacrificed unto the idols of Canaan: and the land was polluted with blood. Thus were they defiled with their own works, and went a-whoring with their own inventions. Therefore was the wrath of the LORD kindled against his people, insomuch that he abhorred his own inheritance. And he gave them into the hand of the heathen; and they that hated them ruled over them. Their enemies also oppressed them, and they were brought into subjection under their hand (vv. 36-42, *KJV*).

As a result of having sacrificed their children to devils, the Israelites came under the authority of their enemies to the point of oppression. God had to bring judgment against Israel and bring them into Babylonian captivity for 70 years because they had been fellowshiping with demons.

This was not just an Old Testament problem. First Corinthians has this to say about idolatry and fellowshiping with demons:

> Wherefore, my dearly beloved, flee from idolatry. What say I then? That the idol is any thing, or that which is offered in sacrifice to idols is any thing? But I say, that the things which the Gentiles sacrifice, they sacrifice to devils, and not to God: and I would not that ye should have fellowship with devils. Ye cannot drink the cup of the Lord, and the cup of devils: ye cannot be partakers of the Lord's table, and of the table of devils (1 Cor. 10:14,19-21, *KJV*).

The Molech Spirit in Today's World

You may be wondering what all that has to do with abortion today. What we need to realize is that demons and principalities do not die and go to hell. Now, long after the destruction of the Ammonite civilization, the Molech spirit still roams about today to do Satan's bidding. And some things about this evil spirit have not changed. He still craves the blood of innocents. Demons draw strength from blood sacrifices and will work hard for them. Here is where I tie the spirit of Molech to abortion, because I believe this principality is still manifesting, not necessarily through child sacrifice, but through abortion. Why? Because it is the same thing. When you have an abortion, you are destroying your seed. Abortion is murder, and it is the shedding of the most innocent blood of all.

Abortion is murder, and it is the shedding of the most innocent blood of all.

Here in the United States, as in many other nations, Molech gets a lot of blood sacrifices through abortions. Earlier I quoted Psalm 94, which talks about having fellowship with a throne of iniquity because of the mischief framed by the law, specifically as it relates to condemning innocent blood. In other words, a law can be passed that actually promotes something that God hates. One of the things demons try to do is to get involved with governmental structures in order to pass laws that build thrones of iniquity in that society.

I believe that verse 20 of Psalm 94 is a good description of the whole problem of abortion. Abortion has been approved by law in this nation, just as the Ammonites legally approved the sacrificing of their children, condemning innocent blood. And what is behind it, both then and today? It is a throne of iniquity tied to the spirit of Molech.

Millions of babies have been aborted since abortion was legalized. It has opened the door to incredible amounts of oppression and demonization for those involved. Why? Because when an individual commits an act that is tied in with a demonic structure, that person opens the door for that demonic structure to activate in his or her own life. Abortion, therefore, is not just a harmless little sin. It actually connects that person with the particular spirits behind it, which will inevitably affect that person and subsequent generations, as well as leave him or her open to all kinds of curses.

Judgments on Those Who Shed Innocent Blood

Now that we see how abortion is tied in with Molech, it is important to go back and see the judgments that came upon those who shed innocent blood. As we have ministered to countless women who have had abortions, we have seen that many of these same judgments are operating in their lives. The following is not meant to be a fail-safe formula, but it is meant to offer an understanding of why certain spirits can activate in the lives of those involved in abortion.

The first several spirits that we have found operating in cases of abortion can be found in Jeremiah 32:35-36:

> And they built the high places of Baal, which are in the valley of the son of Hinnom, to cause their sons and their daughters to pass through the fire unto Molech; which I commanded them not, neither came it into my mind, that they should do this abomination, to cause Judah to sin. And now therefore thus saith the LORD, the God of Israel, concerning this city, whereof ye say, It shall be delivered into the hand of the king of Babylon by the sword, and by the famine, and by the pestilence (*KJV*).

Spirit of Death

In this passage we see three judgments that the Lord imposed on those who shed innocent blood as a sacrifice to Molech. The first was the sword, which represents death. This is tied in strongly with a spirit of hell, which I will explain in a moment.

Spirit of Poverty

The second judgment was famine, which represents poverty. Women who have had abortions will many times (although not always) have trouble with their finances. Even if that is not the specific problem, they tend to have a famine of some kind in their lives, whether it's related to their careers, finances or certain relationships. *Sometimes the very thing they were trying to save by not having the baby is the very thing that comes under the attack of the devil.* Cain was the first one in the Bible to shed innocent blood. To understand this idea of famine and poverty better, let's look at the judgment that came upon him as a result of his having killed his brother: "And he said, What hast thou done? the voice of thy brother's blood crieth unto me from the ground. And now art thou cursed from the earth, which hath opened her mouth to receive thy brother's blood from thy hand; when thou tillest the ground, it shall not henceforth yield unto thee her strength; a fugitive and a vagabond shalt thou be in the earth" (Gen. 4:10-12, *KJV*).

This curse represents the assignment of a spirit of poverty. No matter how hard those with a spirit of poverty work or how much seed they put into the ground, the ground never gives back its full strength. One of the first curses that can come upon those who shed innocent blood is that the earth does not cooperate with them. All the prosperity that God put on this planet comes from the earth. The gold, silver, agriculture, oil—all of it comes out of the earth. When the earth does not yield its strength, there is no prosperity. We need the earth to cooperate with us. "The earth is the LORD's, and all its fullness" (Ps. 24:1). As we break these curses and minister deliverance, the earth will begin to release its blessings.

Spirits of Sickness and Infirmity

The third curse we find in Jeremiah 32 is pestilence, which represents sickness and disease. We have found that many women opened the door for strong spirits of sickness and infirmity to come in through abortion. Again, this varies from female to female. Some females have abortions and their lives seem to be better, while others have abortions and their lives seem to fall apart. This will obviously depend on the situation and the person you are praying for.

Spirit of Hell

In the Jeremiah 32 passage quoted above, notice that Molech worship was established in the valley of the son of Hinnom, which was a valley outside of Jerusalem. That's very important because the valley of Hinnom in the Hebrew was translated as *Gehenna* in Greek, which represented hell.[1] Jesus used "Gehenna" to typify hell several times as He warned against the consequences of sin (see Matt. 5:22,29-30; 10:28; 18:9; 23:15,33; Mark 9:43,45,47; Luke 12:5). He described it as a place where the worm never dies and the fire is always burning. This was literally true, because after Josiah destroyed this idol in the valley of Hinnom, or Gehenna (see 2 Kings 23), it became a garbage dump where fire was always burning and where the worm never died (see 2 Kings 22:17). This place called hell was tied into the worship of Molech.

But hell is not just a place; hell is also a spirit. There's a demon called hell. Death is not just an event; there's a spirit called death. I believe that also attached to the spirits of Molech and abortion are spirits of death and hell, which are two major end-time principalities found in Revelation 6:8: "So I looked, and behold, a pale horse. And the name of him who sat on it was Death, and Hades followed with him. And power was given to them over a fourth of the earth, to kill with sword, with hunger, with death, and by the beasts of the earth" (*NKJV*).

People who involve themselves with abortions can have a spirit of hell in their lives. They may say, "My life is hell." The spirit of hell's job is to torment people and make their lives so miserable that they become a living hell on Earth. Hell is a place of torment—no rest, no peace. Death works with hell. Those afflicted by these spirits are not even dead yet, but there's something in them that makes them feel that they're not living.

Jesus said, "I come that you might have life and that you might have it more abundantly." The spirits of death and hell in people will keep them from enjoying the abundant life that Jesus provides (see John 10:10). But I believe we don't have to have hell on Earth. I believe we can have heaven on Earth. I believe we can have the glory of God on Earth. I believe we can have the liberty and the joy and the peace of God. As opposed to hell, heaven is a place of peace. Thank God for deliverance!

Vagabond and Fugitive Spirits

Another lesson we learn from the curse on Cain is that those who shed innocent blood are subject to vagabond and fugitive spirits (see Gen. 4:12). A vagabond is one who can never find a resting place. A vagabond spirit manifests by causing those afflicted to be unable to settle down in one relationship, one job, one city, one church and so on. They don't make meaningful commitments. But they will never prosper, always running, hiding, dodging and not getting their roots established. This is a wandering spirit that works much like the poverty spirit.

A fugitive spirit causes people to live in fear as they just try to stay alive. Sometimes women with this spirit end up in abusive relationships. Other times they are tormented. They have no peace or rest and feel as if something is after them. They often can't sleep and live each moment in fear and darkness. Proverbs 28:1 says, "The wicked flee when no one pursues." This is a good description of someone afflicted by a fugitive spirit. But God did not put us on the earth to just stay alive, but to have the abundant life that Jesus provides. That's why deliverance is so important.

The Rachel Spirit

Another spirit we have had to deliver many women from is called Rachel. This comes from Matthew 2:18: "A voice was heard in Ramah, lamentation, weeping, and great mourning, Rachel weeping for her children, refusing to be comforted, because they are no more." This passage refers to the time when Herod had all the children who were two years old and younger murdered in an attempt to kill Jesus (see v. 16). Rachel represents women who weep because of the loss of their children. Many times when we cast this spirit out of a woman, even if the loss of her child was due to an abortion, there is a wail that comes out of her that sounds like a woman who has just lost her child. There is no sound that can be compared to a woman who is grieving the loss of her child. There's a spirit of weeping, sadness, grief, hurt—all of these spirits can operate in women who have had abortions. Because whether we realize it or not, women have not been emotionally wired to deal with the abortion of a child. Of course, there can come a time when the conscience is seared, but that is not natural. More often, a profound grief and sadness come as a result of the abortion.

The natural cycle of childbirth is to go through pregnancy and then go through travail, or labor. But the Bible says that for the joy of having that child, the woman forgets her travail (see John 16:21). That is the natural process. Once she holds that child, there is a joy that comes. But when a woman does not go through that process, she never experiences the joy. The process is short-circuited, and a grief and a travail and a sadness and a heaviness and a depression come. And these negative emotions can now never be overcome by actually having the baby. It's almost as if the woman is in perpetual travail.

This can also happen to women who have had miscarriages or stillbirths. We have had to cast out grief, sadness, travail and the spirit of refusing to be comforted, just as Rachel refused to be comforted. This spirit can actually hinder a woman from receiving the comfort of the Lord. God can't comfort you if you don't let Him.

The Prayer Process

No one can abort a baby and expect their lives to be okay. It's the law of sowing and reaping (see Gal. 6:7). It opens the door for all kinds of tragedy and death, and demonic cycles such as those I've just described. This is a major issue in the heart of God. I've seen women who've had an abortion and the man is gone, but they are still struggling and can't get ahead. Jesus is the answer. He will forgive them. He will deliver them. He will drive those curses and spirits out of their lives.

But in order to get there, she will need ministry. When you're praying for a woman who has told you of an abortion, you need to first get her to repent for having the abortion and ask for God's forgiveness, covered with the Blood. Second, break any curses of murder, death, destruction, poverty or sickness that may have come as a result of the abortion. Third, begin to call out the spirits (as listed above) that came in through the door of abortion and any others that the Holy Spirit may show you.

Many times you will then see a great release and that woman's life will turn around completely. She will be a new woman. God wants to prosper that woman; He wants to bless that woman; He does not want that woman to live a hard, difficult, travailing life. Thank God for deliverance! Thank God that Jesus came that those who have had abortions, and indeed all of us who have ever sinned, might be set free!

Note

1. James Strong, *The New Strong's Exhaustive Concordance of the Bible* (Nashville, TN: Thomas Nelson Publishers, 1984), Greek ref. no. 1067.

Chapter 19

FREEDOM FROM HOMOSEXUAL CONFUSION

David Kyle Foster

Freedom from the Lies

Jesus made it clear that Satan is "a liar and the father of lies" (John 8:44, *NIV*). Because God only blesses faith, the strategy of the evil one has been to gain power by inciting unbelief. Therefore, a significant part of being freed from the power of sin comes in ferreting out the lies that we have believed, renouncing them and aggressively embracing the truth as revealed by God. For God declares in His Word that it is "the knowledge of the truth that leads to godliness" (Titus 1:1, *NIV*).

Lie #1: The Bible Does Not Condemn Homosexual Acts

In reality, you will not find the word "homosexual" in Scripture or any other writing before the nineteenth century. What you do find in the Bible are descriptions of same-sex *behaviors* and condemnation for those who engage in them (e.g., see Lev. 18:22; 20:13; Rom. 1:25-27; 1 Cor. 6:9).

These biblical descriptions are very clear, despite modern attempts to make them appear ambiguous. For example, the Hebrew word for a male "lying with a male" used in Leviticus 18:22 and 20:13, *mishkav zakur,* was translated into Greek in the Septuagint as *arsenos koiten*. The apostle Paul takes those very words and coins a new word, *arsenokoitai,* in 1 Corinthians 6:9, when stating that those who commit homosexual acts will not inherit the kingdom of God. There is no doubt that by his word choice, Paul is declaring that the Torah prohibition of homosexual behavior is part of the unchangeable moral law rather than a part of the ritual/ceremonial law that was fulfilled by Christ.

Romans 1:18-32 is also very clear in its description and condemnation of homosexual acts as being rebellion against God and a part of the disordered human condition. Those who claim otherwise break cardinal rules of interpretation and presume to know better than all of the expert Bible scholar-translators who have ever lived in the 2,000-plus years since the Bible was written.

Lie #2: The Field of Psychology Has Proven that Homosexuals Are Born That Way

In press releases and public debates, modern gay activism likes to give the impression that the field of psychology has proven that homosexuality is healthy and normal, and the claim that it is disordered is a new and dangerous theory held by those who do not know what they are talking about. In truth, if one looks at the thought, research and reported experience of psychologists and other professional counselors throughout history, the novel theory with no basis in reality is the gay activist one.

As the field of psychology emerged more than 100 years ago, its practitioners began to organize human *behaviors* into categories, labeling them as an aid to study and diagnosis. Unfortunately, in our day the artificial construct known as "homosexual" has been misconstrued as a true and inherent identity, something a person is born with; something, therefore, that cannot change. It's as if the word rose up from the page and became the thing itself.

This morphing of terminology did not come about as a result of scientific research and study, but as a consequence of pressure from gay activist groups who threw tantrums and made threats at various professional association meetings in the 1970s, and who have skillfully infiltrated and manipulated media coverage of the issue ever since.[1]

Study after study has failed to show a genetic or other physiological cause for homosexual neurosis. In fact, several have shown just the opposite. At least two studies that were purported to prove a genetic cause for homosexual orientation (the "Hamer" and the "identical twin" studies) actually proved that the orientation could *not* be determined by genetics.[2] The "identical twin" study, for example, found discordant sets of *genetically identical* twins (one was gay and the other straight), an impossible outcome if homosexuality is caused by genetics.

Lie #3: Homosexuality Is Fixed and Unchangeable

A few years ago, Dr. Robert Spitzer, one of the men most responsible for caving in to gay activist pressure at American Psychiatric Association (APA) meetings in the early 1970s (when they removed homosexuality from their official list of disorders), decided to conduct an actual study of homosexuals. He found to his surprise that people with this struggle were *not* hopelessly fixed in their orientation and that many could and have changed.[3] As a result, those who earlier considered Dr. Spitzer to be the darling of the gay movement now vilify him, because he dared to ground his professional opinion in scientific research and to publicly reveal what he had found.

It is critical that we understand the mistake that our culture has made in this matter. Why? Because people generally believe that an *inherent identity* is impossible to change and confer acceptance for its exercise on the one so afflicted. This semantic sleight of hand has provided an excuse for many to yield to unholy desire, and most people who have been misled by it are not even aware of the ruse.

In addition, there is formative power in a name. People tend to become the label that has been given them by authority figures. The more identified a person becomes with the name "homosexual," the more difficult it will be for that person to see him- or herself as anything else. This factor alone can make one person's transformation take much longer than another person's once the process of healing and change has begun.

Lie #4: Homosexuality Is Healthy and Normal

Gay activism and its mouthpiece, the mainstream media, claim that homosexuals are just as happy and healthy as the rest of us (an actual statement in one of their newspaper ads). Once again, nothing could be further from the truth! According to Dr. Jeffrey Satinover, maladies that plague those who participate in homosexual behavior include chronic, potentially fatal liver disease (hepatitis), which often leads to cancer; fatal immune disease (AIDS); frequently fatal rectal cancer; multiple bowel and other infectious diseases; a much higher rate of suicide; and a 25-30 year decrease in life expectancy.[4] You could add to that astronomical rates of alcoholism, drug addiction and (particularly among lesbians) domestic violence.[5]

It is clear that homosexuals are internally driven to self-destructive behavior as a result of the lies that they have believed about themselves, about God and about the purpose of life. Any plan to help them find freedom must deal with the deceptions that the enemy has sown in their hearts and minds. If such lies can be broken and replaced by the truth found only in Jesus Christ, then the destructive power of their bondage can be broken as well.

Freedom from the Brokenness

Other than lies, what else does the person who suffers from homosexual confusion need to be delivered from? Is it a disease that God can instantly heal? Is the condition itself sin that merely requires genuine repentance? Or is it a demon that, when successfully cast out, takes with it the orientation?

None of the above. It is true that upon repentance some people experience such an infusion of God's life and power that it seems as though He has supernaturally removed the brokenness altogether. As time goes on, however, it becomes clear that there is still much that remains to be healed.

It is disappointing to learn at first, but a glorious truth nonetheless, that being transformed into the image of Christ is not achieved by having our susceptibility to temptation supernaturally removed, but by deepening our love for God so that in the midst of such temptation we freely and joyfully choose Him rather than our former idols.

Jesus was tempted in the wilderness and tempted in the Garden—yet without sin. It is into that likeness that we are being formed. Without the temptation, there is nothing to spur growth, nothing to test righteousness, no opportunity to be like Christ.

The transformation process includes great moments of revelation and deliverance interspersed with long roads of hard growth and struggle. There are peaks and valleys, joys and sorrows, times when we feel in perfect union with God and His holiness, and times when we feel as though He has vanished and cast us into the hands of our former gods. Such are the deep waters where faith is born, seemingly empty places where God is ever so close, yet feels ever so far.

The Cause

God creates us to be heterosexual. We are naturally designed to go in male-female pairs. However, at birth our sexuality is in seed form, a kind of time-released seed that is designed to lie dormant for a number of years, and finally germinate and flower during the years of puberty. Though dormant in the early years, the seed needs to be protected and requires proper nurture in order to germinate properly at the appointed time. In those who develop homosexual confusion during their formative years, that seed either has been damaged or has failed to receive the nutrients that it needs to germinate properly. What arises in its place is a false identity derived from ill-conceived attempts to jerry-rig an identity where none exists.

Homosexual confusion, neurosis, orientation—whatever you want to call it—is a form of arrested emotional development that in its early stages is caused by a constellation of environmental factors that usually involve trauma and neglect. These factors negatively affect the sexual identity development of those whose temperament and surroundings make them uniquely susceptible to such influences. This blend of factors interacts and conspires with the temperament, character and personality traits of the individuals as cogs do in a wheel.

This would explain why so many in the gay community are found to have a highly sensitive temperament. These are folks who feel the impact of the traumas and neglects of life more deeply and are broken by them more easily. Their "seed" has been either damaged or improperly fed. Those so afflicted often find themselves saddled with feelings of being different or inadequate, and they suffer an ambiguous sense of incompleteness as males or females. This results in a longing to be made one with their estranged gender.

In an attempt to heal (or complete) themselves, such people often make wrong choices and thus become coconspirators in the worsening of their broken condition. They fix on the creature rather than the Creator as a source of hope and identity, thus, unwittingly at first, making idols of those who seem to epitomize the ideal man or woman. The incredibly powerful force of sexual awakening (whether at puberty, or prematurely via pornography or while being sexually abused) then distorts what is at its root an emotional need, causing it to be perceived as sexual. If they continue to ride this snowball of lust and idolatry, then the demonic realm gains the foothold it needs to create a stronghold, compounding the problem even further.

The most common factor found in males is a failure to emotionally bond or identify with a father figure. (Any number of scenarios could illustrate why this might happen, such as an environment in which the father is absent, abusive, emotionally weak or distant; the feminine influence is stronger; or the mother figure continually communicates disfavor of men or things masculine.) Without the approval, affirmation and modeling of a father figure who can draw them into fixing their identity in masculinity—this could be someone other than the father, such as a scoutmaster, a coach, even an older brother—some preteen boys will remain identified with the feminine (which happened at birth, when they naturally bonded with their mother). Much of the effeminate tendencies can be explained by this failure to switch identity during a boy's early years from mom to dad.

Females sometimes fail to emotionally bond with their mothers, which can be a core factor in the development of lesbian tendencies, although this is not as common as it is in males. In females, by far the most common factor is childhood sexual abuse. Some figures suggest that perhaps 85 percent of all lesbians have been victims of childhood sexual abuse.[6] It's easy to see how such a traumatic event might cause some girls to develop an identity-dominating aversion to the gender of their perpetrator.

What makes the difference between those who develop homosexual tendencies as a result of being sexually abused and those who do not? Once again we need to look at variables such as these: temperament, spiritual and emotional health, a safe and healing environment, the kind of abuse, the age of the child being abused, the frequency and severity of the abuse, and so forth. In any given girl, any number of variables might mitigate the outcome.

Childhood sexual abuse is also prevalent in the backgrounds of male homosexuals, making it the second most common causal factor for them. Some figures suggest that at least half of all males with homosexual orientation have suffered sexual abuse as children or adolescents.[7] The odd difference with males is that many of them do not see their own sexual abuse as abuse, but as being the only source of attention that anyone ever gave them. Thus, many abused males will not admit to being victims. Girls, on the other hand, are much more likely to see their abuse as a violation of their person.

Space does not allow us to discuss many of the other factors that can play into the development of sexual identity confusion. For example, family dynamics can sometimes play a powerful role, such as when a mother gives birth to a baby whose gender is opposite from what mom and/or dad wanted; and the child only receives love, attention and affirmation when he or she behaves and identifies with the opposite gender. This can be profoundly confusing and formative for a sensitive child.

In short, homosexual confusion is usually innocently acquired, but then it is made worse by the sinful reactions of those so afflicted. As homosexuals move into idolatry, whether out of lust or an attempt to heal themselves, God eventually gives them over to the idols that they choose (see Ezek. 16:39; Rom. 1:24). At this point, they can only be brought back to God through repentance and a dogged determination to follow the Holy Spirit as He leads them through multiple layers of repentance, healing and transformation.

Homosexual confusion is usually innocently acquired but then is made worse by the sinful reactions of those so afflicted.

In that process, God exposes and, as the person becomes willing, breaks the demonic stronghold of lies that has given power to sinful desire and the root sin of unbelief. God Himself replaces the former idols and becomes the hope, the life and the love of that person. As that relationship deepens, "the things of earth will grow strangely dim in the light of His glory and grace."[8]

The Cure

Deliverance for those who suffer from same-sex attraction is first and foremost a matter of being set free from the lies that they were born that way, that God cannot change them and that they are excused by some fated condition from the biblical prohibitions of same-sex behavior.

When people renounce and forsake the lies and the false gods that they have used as a means to personal fulfillment or development, the healing begins. As they turn to God to be their source and primary love, He begins to unveil the roots of fallen desire and leads them through a process of transformation. It is critical that whatever other counselors God may use to help them along the way, that the Holy Spirit become their primary Counselor.

Deliverance for a person who struggles with same-sex attraction can be a lengthy process, depending on their willingness to do whatever it takes, their depth of love for God above all others, the passion in their pursuit of Him, their age, the length and depth of their involvement in the sins associated with the condition, and other such variables.

There may be demons that have taken advantage of the person's sin and become a part of the problem, but there is no "demon of homosexuality" that has been the sole cause of this condition. Each person has developed homosexual desire through a unique and complex matrix of elements that must be uncovered and dealt with in an appropriate fashion. As with many other life-dominating bondages, some of the more common elements include idolatry, rebellion, anger, unforgiveness, unbelief, love of sin, a skewed image of God, self-centeredness, performance-orientation, self-hatred, fear. The Holy Spirit knows exactly what the mix is for each individual, the timing and order in which each needs to be addressed and the salutary replacements that need to be imparted. He also has all power in heaven and Earth at His disposal.

In some ways, the process of getting free from same-sex attraction is like the process of salvation. It is three-tiered and multifaceted. Of salvation, the Bible is clear that we are saved (see Acts 15:11; 1 Cor. 15:2; Eph. 2:5,8; Titus 3:5); we are being saved (see 1 Cor. 1:18); and we will be saved (see Matt. 24:13; Mark 13:13). Of this, Dr. John R. W. Stott has written,

> Salvation is a good word; it denotes that comprehensive purpose of God by which he justifies, sanctifies, and glorifies his people: first pardoning their offenses and accepting them as righteous in his sight; then progressively transforming them by his Spirit into the image of Christ, until finally they become like Christ in

> heaven, when they see him as he is, and their bodies are raised incorruptible like Christ's body of glory. I long to rescue salvation from the narrow concepts to which even evangelical Christians sometimes reduce it.[9]

In a similar way, the healing of homosexual orientation is a three-tiered process. Homosexuals receive a degree or dimension of deliverance when they repent and give their lives to Christ. Even so, as the Holy Spirit continues to unveil the secret roots of their condition, they continue to be delivered to a greater and greater degree. Then, on that last day when Christ appears and transforms them into His image completely, they will be delivered fully and for all time.

If God were to instantly zap them free from being homosexually oriented, they would be free from that particular kind of temptation, but they would still be the same immature, broken people as before. Instead, God leads them through a measured, deliberate process of discovering the wrong choices they have made and why they made them; and He offers them an opportunity to willfully forsake those choices, one by one. In essence, He teaches them how to love (defined in 1 John 3:16,18 as "sacrifice" and "commitment"), and He does so in the midst of trial so that their choice to love is hard-won, substantive and, thus, meaningful.

Freedom—A Personal Story

To illustrate, allow me to recount for you parts of my own journey of healing from homosexual confusion. When I got saved at the age of 29, I had been suffering from homosexual confusion most of my life and had been continuously active in the lifestyle for over 10 years. I was hopelessly out of control and was convinced that if God didn't set me free by some supernatural means, it would never happen.

The first thing that God did was to send a great grace upon me that enabled me to recognize the evil that I had embraced so that I could repent from the heart (see 1 John 1:9). I finally knew that I was a sinner and desperately in need of God's grace.

Upon repenting, God swept into my very being, bringing with Him the power to resist what had previously been irresistible temptation (see Matt. 3:11; John 4:10; 7:37-38). It was a great delivering moment that came as I prayed in my room for Him to set me free. I had read in Matthew 5:6 that if I hungered and thirsted for righteousness, He would fill me with it, and He did. Make no mistake, I was still fully capable of committing the same sinful acts as before—and at times I was mightily tempted to do so—but after praying Matthew 5:6 with all my heart, God removed the coercive power that the demonic realm had held over me as a result of my wicked ways. I was then able to freely choose between good and evil for the first time in a long time.

Next, He gave me an awareness that there were demonic spirits that needed casting out. Being alone and too afraid of trusting the church down the street with the knowledge of my sins, I somehow knew that I could cast them out myself. By then, I was fully aware of God's great power over Satan and my new authority as a child of God to call on that power for such a task (see Luke 10:19; John 14:12-14). And I was thoroughly persuaded never to return to that sinful lifestyle. So the Lord led me to call the evil spirits by name (according to what they were tempting me to do), and, in the name of Jesus, I commanded them to leave me and the place where I was staying. Within a week, they were completely gone.

The Lord also gave me revelation as to how my healing was going to come to pass. I was to concentrate on falling in love with Him at deeper and deeper levels, and He was going to reveal and empower everything else that was needed. Through some timely advice from a pastor, God enabled me to see that the battle was the Lord's (see 1 Sam. 17:47; Ezek. 36:25-27). It was going to be His power released on my behalf that would keep me free from bondage (see Jude 24), and that my job was to get into His presence so that I could be led by the Spirit (see Gal. 5:16). In His presence would come the infilling of the Holy Spirit by which the desire to be holy would be replenished. In His presence would be where my yearning to cooperate with Him through the difficult times would be renewed.

God said in His Word that "his divine power has given us everything we need for life and godliness *through our knowledge of him*" (2 Pet. 1:3, *NIV*, emphasis added). It has been through that knowledge and that intimacy that God has delivered me and kept me from falling, because His beauty and the pleasure of His company far surpasses that of all gods.

In coming to know Him more deeply through the revelation of His love demonstrated on the Cross, I have been persuaded that He is worthy to be obeyed and can be trusted. In meditating on the cross that He bore and in experiencing the crosses that He has asked me to bear, I have come to know Him in the fellowship of His sufferings (see Rom. 8:17; Phil. 3:10; 1 Pet. 4:13).

In the revelation of His grace, as He forgives me again and again and again, my heart has been transformed and knit to His (see Titus 2:11-14). I no longer see Him as an adversary. I see Him as love. And that revelation has struck a mighty blow against the rebellion that used to reign in my heart.

He has taught me how to starve the old man and feed the new. And He has transformed my inner motivation for doing so from duty to love.

In intimate moments with the Lord, I often sing love songs to Him; and He sometimes responds with life-changing revelation, healing words of love, visions of glory, or infusions of divine life and power (see 2 Pet. 1:4). As I focus on loving Him, He imparts His very nature (see 2 Cor. 3:18).

Sometimes He reminds me of a particular incident and a person that I need to forgive. At other times, He exposes love for a sin that lingers in the dark inner reaches of my heart so that I can renounce it. And sometimes, He seems to vanish and leave me without any consolation or assurance that He loves me or that He even exists. Yet even those moments are acts of love, designed for my growth in Christlikeness; for it is when we love and obey Him, even when His hand of provision and blessing has been removed, that we grow to be most like Him. For that is also a part of the nature of Christ, as He demonstrated in the Garden of Gethsemane when all seemed lost and forsaken.

Over the years, God has led me to unite with various fellowships and small groups of Christians where I could learn to know and be known as I truly am. He has sent me to life-changing conferences and arranged other divine appointments with those who had just the right word, hug or blessing.

He has put me in places where I could get prayer to break the soul ties that were formed with former sexual partners as well as prayer to break family-line curses (see Num. 14:18; Ezek. 18:14-17).

He has enabled me to forgive people whom I didn't think I could ever forgive. He has shown me how to love, how to serve and how to sacrifice for others.

God has also imparted to me a mature sense of masculinity, which had always been missing. He has spoken words of love and sonship into my spirit that have healed deep inner wounds and insecurities. He has given me a healthy view of men and removed my fear of women, enabling me to see them as the glorious creatures that they are.

He has taught me how to rejoice in my weaknesses and to use them as reminders of my absolute dependence on Him (see 2 Cor. 12:9-10). I now enjoy staying under the shelter of His almighty hand.

God has imparted to me, through many trials and testings, a capacity to trust and obey Him that is far beyond all that I could have ever imagined.

He has healed my desperate sadness and broken spirit and filled me with divine life (see Isa. 61).

He has renewed my mind (see Rom. 12:2; Eph. 4:23) and shown me how to guard it (see Phil. 4:7).

He has replaced what I lost and healed what I damaged (see Joel 2:25).

He has taught me the schemes of the enemy and the greater strategies that heaven has devised to overcome them (see Eph. 6:10-18).

He has taught me how to put to death that which feeds the old broken self (see Rom. 8:13-14), and how to feed and nurture the new creation that I have been made by Christ (see 2 Cor. 5:17; Eph. 4:24). In doing so, the heterosexuality that had always lain dormant within me was finally able to blossom and take its place as my true identity.

And in those moments when my mind slips back into the old ways of feeling and thinking, He whispers words of love in my spirit, and I run back into His arms and embrace anew the miracle that is Christ in me (see Gal. 2:20; Col. 1:27).

Can a person who has struggled with homosexual orientation be delivered and set free from that bondage to lust and idolatry? Well, is the Pope Catholic?

Notes

1. For more information, see Jeffrey Satinover, *Homosexuality and the Politics of Truth* (Grand Rapids, MI: Baker Books, 1996).
2. D. H. Hamer, "A Linkage Between DNA Markers on the X Chromosome and Male Sexual Orientation," *Science,* 261, July 1993, p. 261.
3. For more information on his findings, see Robert Spitzer, interview by Laura Schlessinger, *The Dr. Laura Schlessinger Program,* January 21, 2000.
4. Jeffrey Satinover, *Homosexuality and the Politics of Truth* (Grand Rapids, MI: Baker Books, 1996), pp. 49, 51.
5. For more information, see Nancy Sutton, "Domestic Violence and Domestic Partners: Two Sides of the Same Coin," *Mission: America,* Fall 1998; Linda P. Harvey, "Lesbians As Violent Partners," *Mission: America,* Fall 1998; Claire Renzetti, *Violent Betrayal: Partner Abuse in Lesbian Relationships* (Thousand Oaks, CA: SAGE Publications, 1992); and Joanne M. Hall, "Lesbians Recovering from Alcohol Problems: An Ethnographic Study of Health Care Experiences," *Nursing Research* 43 (July-August 1994), pp. 238-244.
6. Anita Worth and Bob Davies, *Someone I Love Is Gay* (Downers Grove, IL: InterVarsity Press, 1996), pp. 82-83.
7. Joe Dallas, *When Homosexuality Hits Home* (Eugene, OR: Harvest House Publishers, 2004), p. 63.
8. Helen H. Lemmel, "Turn Your Eyes upon Jesus," used by permission in *The Celebration Hymnal* (n.p.: Word Music and Integrity Music, 1997), song no. 340.
9. John R. W. Stott, *Authentic Christianity* (Downers Grove, IL: InterVarsity Press), p. 169.

Chapter 20

CHILD SEXUAL ABUSE

Tom R. Hawkins

Diane was born into a Christian home, made a personal commitment to Christ at age six and graduated from high school and college at the top of her class. Considered brilliant and spiritually committed, she completed her master's degree in Christian ministries, went on to become a missionary and eventually married at age 30.

Within a year of marrying, however, her life began to unravel. Only after seven years of an intense search for answers in the medical and mental health community did she begin to understand the reason for her emotional turmoil and the extensive gaps in her childhood memories. Evidence of overwhelming trauma that her child psyche had been unable to cope with began to surface, including child sexual abuse.

Her story is neither unique nor unusual, as child sexual abuse affects the lives of millions of men and women around the world. While using a host of psychological defense mechanisms to cope with it, these children usually grow up to experience significant pain, dysfunction and misery in their adult lives. These profound and long-lasting effects impact their families, churches and communities as well.

BIBLICAL VIEW OF THE SEXUAL RELATIONSHIP

Child sexual abuse needs to be understood and addressed from the perspective of the biblical framework that God established for the human sexual relationship. His unequivocal standard is for sex to occur only between one adult man and one adult woman in a lifelong, monogamous, covenant union. Most Christians believe that God intends us to have this kind of sexual union for both pleasure and procreation (see Gen. 2:24-25). Any kind of sexual relationship outside of these strictly defined boundaries is, for our own well-being, strictly prohibited (see 1 Cor. 6:12-20).

God's powerful admonitions against sexual activity occurring outside of marriage by implication cover any sexual contact whatsoever with children (see Matt. 18:6). When adults exchange "the natural use for what is against nature . . . to do those things which are not fitting" (Rom. 1:26-28), negative consequences are inevitable.

Understanding God's joyous view of the sexual relationship within marriage is an important part of childhood development. However, children should be protected from exposure to sexual activity and stimulation. Children, being physically and emotionally immature, are greatly confused when thrust into the dynamics of a sexual relationship or any intrusive sexual exposure.

DEFINING CHILD SEXUAL ABUSE

Child sexual abuse involves any kind of sexual contact or exploitation of a minor for the sexual stimulation of the perpetrator. Fondling (touch of any area normally covered by a modest bathing suit); inappropriate kissing; and oral, genital or anal penetration all involve physical contact with the child. However, directing inappropriate comments laden with sexual innuendoes at a child or exposing a child to pornographic material or to any inappropriate exhibition of sexual organs or sexual activity between adults is also considered child sexual abuse. All such behaviors are generally considered criminal behavior.[1]

Sadly, the secular media and the Internet have contributed to creating a society in which sexual dynamics are exploited and made public in a very unhealthy way, manipulating adults into immoral behavior and exposing children to what they are psychologically and emotionally not ready to handle. Kinsey and his fabricated "studies" have also contributed greatly to the societal distortion of the biblical ideal.[2]

It is estimated that approximately 2 million children each year are abused.[3] Conservative estimates indicate that a large number of them are being sexually abused. Many such cases are unreported.[4] Numerous statistical studies indicate that 20 to 40 percent of females[5] and up to 25 percent of males will have been sexually abused by the age of 18. In the majority of cases the children are abused by someone they know and trust. Victims can be found among every social, racial, economic and religious group.

The Pervasive Effects of Child Sexual Abuse

Sadly, the physical, emotional, psychological and spiritual effects of child sexual abuse are devastating in their impact, even if the abuse does not include "penetration" of a body opening or occurs only once. I do not agree with the notion that these effects occur only as the result of a repressive, "puritanical" upbringing. I believe the multifaceted impact on a child is much more than a sociological phenomenon; it is the natural consequence of violating God's creative order. Each case is unique, however, as not all children evidence the same long-term consequences.[6]

Many specific symptoms have been documented, and lists can easily be found by searching the relevant literature. A child's self-concept and worldview are often significantly distorted when the sanctity of their bodies has been violated. When children are manipulated with lies or misrepresentations about moral standards, their sense of morality is understandably affected at a deep level as well.

When the abuse occurs at the hand of a significant caregiver, the child feels an overwhelming sense of betrayal. This sense of betrayal is compounded if the child tries to disclose the abuse and is disbelieved, blamed or ostracized. Intense distrust of adults may occur and manifest in the form of angry outbursts, or isolation and avoidance of close relationships. Another almost universal effect of child sexual abuse is the sense of powerlessness, or "disempowerment," the child feels.[7]

The invasion of a child's body and "personal space" against the child's will commonly affects his or her ability to establish and maintain proper boundaries throughout life. Exaggerated fears (phobias) are also common. In fact, nearly all of the negative emotions can be problematic in a sexual abuse victim's life if they are not properly addressed. Psychosomatic physical symptoms can also result and prevail throughout the individual's life, especially when the child copes by dissociating or repressing the event and its emotions.

David Finkelhor and Angela Browne have documented that sexual feelings and attitudes may be developmentally shaped in a dysfunctional manner for a victim of child sexual abuse.[8] Abused children become confused about their sexuality and later, as adults, are often unable to function healthily within a marriage relationship. Their dysfunctional symptoms can range from hatred of their body and avoidance of sex, on the one hand, to compulsive and inappropriate sexual behaviors/promiscuity on the other.

Bessel van der Kolk has written widely about the inability of many such victims to regulate their emotions properly, resulting in depression and low-self esteem coupled with outbursts of anger.[9] This anger may seem inappropriate or out of proportion to the present situation, but it is triggered when the individual encounters or experiences something that consciously or unconsciously reminds him or her of the abusive events in the past.

The difference in how males and females handle the inevitable anger they feel over being wronged and violated is noteworthy. There are always exceptions to every rule. However, males are generally more apt to "act out" with their anger, while females tend to turn their anger inward onto themselves. Consequently, sexually abused males often end up in the legal and judicial system, while females are more apt to seek help through social services institutions, the mental health field or prayer ministries to treat the resulting depression and poor self-image.

Females are also more apt to engage in eating disorders, either to drown out the pain with food or as a desperate attempt to gain control over their body through deprivation. Drugs, alcoholism or other addictive behaviors, including workaholism, may also be used to drown out the inner pain in both males and females. Suicidal ideation is an all too frequent result of sexual abuse as well. Females seem to make more suicide attempts, but males are more apt to succeed when they do try.

Another more subtle and hidden dynamic found when young children (before age 6 or 7) are sexually abused is dissociation. Dissociation is the opposite of association and refers to the compartmentalization of aspects of the function of the mind, including memory and feelings. In other words, the mind unconsciously separates what would normally be cohesively held together in a consistent perspective, sense of identity and worldview.

In its extreme form, such dissociation can lead to dissociative identity disorder (formerly called multiple personality disorder). It has been estimated that 97 percent of those with dissociative identity disorder (DID) have been severely abused, most of them sexually.[10] Many who have experience in this specialized field would estimate that approximately 1 to 5 percent of people in most local church bodies are struggling with these more complex dissociative issues.

Christians gifted with spiritual discernment who work in this field recognize that another consequence of sexual abuse is often demonization. Unfortunately, ungodly sex can be an avenue leading to this spiritual bondage. Understandably, then, the deterioration of Western culture in the past century has led to an explosion of demonization.

As is evident in the New Testament Gospels, a large part of Jesus' ministry involved delivering those who were demon possessed. The Greek word used in these accounts is actually better transliterated as "demonized,"[11] as in modern English, "demon possession" implies a kind of ownership—which certainly could not be true of a Christian. Rather, the biblical term implies varying degrees of control and influence. Just as doctors can document that Christians can have cancer, those in deliverance ministries can document that Christians can be demonized, or held in bondage under influence of demons.

Important Considerations for Treatment

Understanding the effects and prevalence of child sexual abuse is important, but even more crucial is the need for the Christian community to provide more effective ministry to the large segment of our population who have been so abused. The last 20 years, in particular, have seen a substantial increase in secular research in regard to effective treatment modalities—research that has documented and validated the work being done by a large number of Christian ministries that are now successfully addressing these issues as well.

The approach for addressing child sexual abuse must be adjusted to the age of the person at the time intervention is started. If the abuse is discovered while the child is still preadolescent, it needs to be addressed by someone with training in play therapy and other modalities that take developmental issues into account and provide the necessary skills to meet the challenge of working with the child while avoiding suggestion. If the abuse is from outside the family, parental support becomes a vital and important part of the healing process. When one or both parents are involved in the abuse, however, children desperately need other safe adults who believe them and can provide a safe environment in which they can talk about their feelings. Competent help in healing must be provided by someone who knows the mandatory reporting laws for that particular state, while keeping the best interests and protection of the child clearly in mind.

It is also important to understand that often the need for a sexually abused child to deny that anything happened can be very strong, especially when a parent or primary caregiver is the perpetrator. When dissociation is involved, one part of the person may be very angry and disclose the abuse, while another part may be very loyal to the perpetrator and deny, with all sincerity, that any abuse has taken place.

In too many cases, a child may dare to disclose the abuse, which leads to an inept investigation, followed by the child's being severely punished by the perpetrators (sometimes in a way that leaves no outward sign of abuse) to reinforce the lesson that the child must never talk about "family matters" to outsiders. This may be a major reason why many children never disclose their abuse in a way that brings lasting change to their abusive situation or why they recant an accusation they may have made. While false accusations are sometimes made, particularly in custody cases, it is important to remember that only 5 percent of sexual abuse perpetrators ever admit what they have done.

If the disclosure of abuse is made during adolescence, there is likewise a great need for someone to believe and support the teen. Although teens will have problems similar to those of younger children, the developing sexuality of adolescents usually adds to their shame and humiliation. Again, competent and well-trained help is needed to bring healing for the survivor, while being careful to follow all state-mandated reporting laws. Act wisely so that you do not put yourself (or your ministry) at legal risk.[12]

While not minimizing the complexity of the healing journey, the process of helping adults who reveal sexual abuse in their past is at least not complicated by state-mandated reporting laws. Although the adult may have greater emotional and spiritual maturity, their healing, nevertheless, is often made more difficult by a lifelong pattern of denying the reality of their abuse or minimizing it. For this reason, it is important that the survivor be in a safe environment and clearly understand that healing does not require accusation of alleged perpetrators (see Rom. 12:18-19).

For Christians, the main goal is resolution of the psychological and spiritual dynamics resulting from the abuse, and, ultimately, forgiveness of the perpetrator. Many Christians fail to understand that restoration of relationship with the perpetrator (which is often not safe) is a totally different matter and is not required for complete and thorough forgiveness to be given.

When the survivor is not in a safe environment, it is important to provide initial support without going too deeply into the trauma issues. Concentrate instead on making his or her present environment safe and helping the person stay functional. It is also not wise to delve into painful memories until you ascertain that the person has sufficient ego strength, spiritual maturity and community support to do so without being overwhelmed. Sometimes, developing a supportive relationship is most important initially in order to strengthen the person's capacity to complete the healing journey.

Keep in mind that demonization, when present in sexual abuse victims, is a result of the problem, not the problem itself.

Uncovering an abusive past is similar to peeling away the layers of an onion. Peeling away too many layers too quickly can cause emotional instability, decreasing functionality and, in extreme cases, push a person toward suicide. It is critical that those providing help have an understanding of the many dynamics involved in these cases. This is especially important if the person demonstrates signs of demonization, dissociation or DID.

Ministry to survivors of child sexual abuse is complex. Professional counsel is often needed since complications can be serious. A ministerial or prayer ministry approach can be effective with adequate training, however. Understanding mandated reporting laws is essential, as well as developing competent legal, medical and psychological support that can be accessed when needed.

For those coming from a deliverance perspective, it is vital to be alert to the possibility of dissociation, which requires a more careful treatment approach. If deliverance is necessary, it should be done appropriately in a calm and gentle way that does not further traumatize the child or adult. Your authority does not depend on the volume of your voice.

Shouting or raising the voice can be traumatic to wounded survivors.

It is also important to keep in mind that demonization, when present, is a result of the problem, rather than the problem itself. If you can discover and remove the grounds claimed by spirits of darkness, they can be easily removed. Soul ties and sexual experiences outside of marriage are a frequent source of demonic attachments in these individuals and need to be resolved. Other grounds include those passed down generationally—often involving covenants, oaths and vows—as well as permissions given by caregivers. Grounds can also be given by rituals, ceremonies or agreements made by the survivor. A more comprehensive list of grounds is available from materials on the Restoration in Christ Ministries website (www.rcm-usa.org).

The Healing Journey

No two people will experience healing in the same way. Age differences, severity of the abuse, age at onset, duration of abuse and coping skills used by the survivor will all affect the process of healing. There are, however, some common issues that need to be addressed for effective healing from child sexual abuse, whether dealing with a child, teen or adult. Langberg has observed that "the central experiences of childhood trauma are silence, isolation, and helplessness. Healing, then, must involve a restoration of voice, safe connection, and rightful power. Such healing cannot occur in isolation but rather must take place within the context of relationship."[13]

A major issue for all survivors is finding a way to identify and address the beliefs formed within the context of the abuse experience. Beliefs such as *It is my fault that it happened* or *the abuse proves I am bad* are common and may *feel* very true to the individual. These emotionally held beliefs are seldom changed using facts or logic. Rather, true healing usually comes when the person is emotionally in touch with the original event in which the false belief was established and asks God to speak truth to that belief. This is a powerful method of bringing healing to the pain of sexual abuse, or any other issue held in place by a lie message.[14]

If treatment is started soon after the abuse, it is important to remember that a child is not developmentally capable of resolving all aspects of the abuse, nor is a teen. Each adult in treatment will have to be dealt with as an individual, adjusting treatment depending upon his or her maturity level.

The good news is that even when child sexual abuse has left its trail of devastating effects, the person's life or usefulness to God does not end. Diane, with whom this chapter began, was a successful missionary and pastor's wife; she has been in ministry with her husband for over 25 years. She now lectures internationally, telling her story and helping thousands of other survivors gain hope, which is so essential for healing. She is a mature, joyous Christian with a servant heart whose life is reflective of the Savior whom she loves very deeply. I should know—she is my wife.[15]

Notes

1. For a further description of such abuse, see Diane Mandt Langberg, *Counseling Survivors of Sexual Abuse* (Wheaton, IL: Tyndale House Publishers, 1997), pp. 61-62.
2. Judith A. Reisman, *Kinsey: Crimes and Consequences: The Red Queen and the Grand Scheme* (Arlington, VA: The Institute for Media Education, 1998).
3. David Middlebrook, *The Guardian System: S.T.O.P. Abuse Risk in Your Ministry* (Lake Mary, FL: Creation House, 2000), p. 2.
4. Richard R. Hammar, Steven W. Klipowicz and James F. Cobble, Jr., *Reducing the Risk of Child Sexual Abuse in Your Church: A Complete and Practical Guidebook for Prevention and Risk Reduction* (Matthews, NC: Church Ministry Resources, 1993), p. 14.
5. Langberg, *Counseling Survivors of Sexual Abuse,* pp. 62-63.
6. Ibid., p. 66.
7. David Finkelhor, *A Sourcebook on Child Sexual Abuse* (Beverly Hills, CA: Sage Publications, 1986), p. 183.
8. Ibid., pp. 180-181.
9. Bessel A. van der Kolk, Alexander C. McFarlane and Lars Weisaeth, *Traumatic Stress: The Effects of Overwhelming Experience on Mind, Body and Society* (New York: The Guilford Press, 1996).
10. James G. Friesen, *Uncovering the Mystery of MPD* (San Bernardino, CA: Here's Life Publishers, 1991), p. 42.
11. James Strong, *The New Strong's Exhaustive Concordance of the Bible* (Nashville, TN: Thomas Nelson Publishers, 1984), Greek ref. no 1139.
12. For more information, see James Wilder, *Keeping Your Ministry Out of Court: Avoiding Unnecessary Litigation While Ministering to Emotionally Wounded People*, ed. M. Smith (Campbellsville, KY: Alathia Publishing, 2002).
13. Langberg, *Counseling Survivors of Sexual Abuse,* p. 61.

14. See Langberg, *Counseling Survivors of Sexual Abuse;* also see Paula Sandford, *Healing Victims of Sexual Abuse* (Tulsa, OK: Victory House Publishers, 1988); and Diane Hawkins, *Multiple Identities: Understanding and Supporting the Severely Abused* (Grottoes, VA: Restoration in Christ Ministries, 2002).
15. In addition to the resources noted above, I also recommend the following: Grant L. Martin, *Counseling for Family Violence and Abuse: Resources for Christian Counseling*, ed. Gary R. Collins (Waco, TX: Word Books, 1987); Frank W. Putnam, *Dissociation in Children and Adolescents: A Developmental Perspective* (New York: The Guilford Press, 1997); William Sudduth, *So Free!!!: A Teaching on Deliverance* (Pensacola, FL: Ram, 2002)—see www.ramministry.org.

HOW TO MINISTER FREEDOM TO THE OCCULT BOUND

Chapter 21

SHEDDING LIGHT IN THE DARKNESS OF THE OCCULT

Doris M. Wagner

Witchcraft, Satanism, Eastern religions and the occult in many forms are rapidly on the rise the world over. It seems as though Satan is working fast and furious in these days, probably because he knows his time is short (see Rev. 12:12).

In his pride, Satan rose up against God because he wanted worship for himself. And to this day, his agenda remains the same. There is a kingdom of God and there is a kingdom of Satan, a kingdom of light and a kingdom of darkness.

Satan and his dark angels continually labor to rob Jehovah God of worship and usurp it for themselves. They must do so by deceiving people and leading them into the kingdom of darkness. They try to get a person to ask them for favors and, in so doing, bondages are created. The ensnared person becomes dependent on these dark angels and returns to them over and over for power, guidance and the satisfaction of personal desires. Thus the dark forces are getting the attention—tantamount to worship and devotion—that they so strongly desire.

I have prayed for many people who have been caught in the trap of witchcraft and the occult, but have found their way out of the darkness into the glorious light of the truth and freedom from bondages. But it takes the light of the gospel shining into the darkness of the hidden occult to unmask the deception.

Encounters with Cockroaches

I well remember, as a young missionary in the jungles of eastern Bolivia, being introduced to huge cockroaches for the first time. I had been raised in a very temperate climate in the Mohawk Valley of New York State in a household run by a very clean German mom. I had never even seen a cockroach in my life because I never traveled far away from our dairy farm.

How well I recall my early encounters with cockroaches! Because there was no running water in our entire little Bolivian village, naturally there was no indoor plumbing, so we used outhouses as toilets. These were usually located quite a distance from living quarters for obvious reasons. Without the blessing of electricity either, at night we would need to carry a flashlight or a Coleman gasoline lantern to the outhouse to illuminate the path. There could be many nocturnal and potentially deadly creepy crawlies along the way.

The first few times I took the evening stroll, I used a flashlight and didn't see much on my journey. But when I took a Coleman lamp—what a different story! Things would scamper away and shun the light. But my biggest shock came when some of the strong light illuminated the entire interior of the outhouse, including what was down in the hole. Everything was teeming with cockroaches of various sizes—hundreds and hundreds of them. I then realized what they ate, and didn't cherish the thought very much.

But then I walked back the several hundred feet to our house. On the way, I passed our kitchen area, which was just a lean-to structure built to allow the heat of the kitchen to escape while we were cooking. Because of the lack of cupboard space, many items were hung on the walls on nails. You can imagine my shock and dismay when the bright light hit those walls and hundreds and hundreds of cockroaches scampered to take cover behind breadboards, wooden bowls, frying pans and other hanging utensils I had used that day. My thoughts flashed back to the outhouse. Horrors!

Those little guys each had six dirty little feet and one dirty little mouth, and they were lapping up bits of grease and food from my kitchen floor. I wondered where they all slept during the day, because unless one opened a drawer or a cupboard door, they were pretty much out of sight and hence out of mind.

The same thing happens when we shed light on the occult and demonic activity in a person's life. When the bright light from the kingdom of God shines on the deep darkness of the occult, the evil creatures and their activities are exposed and they can no longer remain hidden. Let's make no mistake about it—where occult activity is taking place, many demons are present. Those who engage in the occult summon, use and are then stuck with demons. It just comes with the territory!

But just as with cockroaches, simply exposing the demonic activity is not enough. For example, in a jungle lean-to kitchen, it took definite action to beat back the cockroaches and finally get rid of them. It took powerful bug spray, thoroughly cleaning the utensils and area of infestation, and vigilance in keeping it clean. It was necessary to keep bread and other food in tightly covered tins, jars, boxes or other appropriately sealed containers. Even dirt floors needed to be swept and kept free from food particles.

The desire for freedom from the occult on the part of the infested person together with thorough deliverance and inner healing are needed to rid that person of demons. In my experience, I have found that demons simply do not leave on their own when exposed; rather, they go into hiding for the time being, but come out in all their ugliness at a more opportune time. They need to be commanded to leave in the name of Jesus. Their source of subsistence—and by that I mean the reason why they are there—needs to be removed; and the environment in which they had taken up residence must be thoroughly cleansed.

What Is the Occult?

That brings us to the meaning of the word "occult." By "occult," I mean the practice of secret, magical arts through which the practitioner seeks to influence demonic powers to bring about their often-evil desires. Those who practice the occult—witches and warlocks, for example—attempt to manipulate demons and circumstances in order to bring about harm, such as sickness, calamity and even death, to specific persons. To achieve these ends, practitioners of the occult use any combination of tools such as potions, chanting, rituals, magic, sorcery, effigies, the "evil eye," consecrated candles, incense, herbs and geometrical shapes to cast spells and to curse. Their desire is often to gain power or control over others.

What is a curse or a spell? Here is a quote from a tiny book entitled *Witches* by Kevin Osborn, which defines spells from a witch's point of view:

> Spells, whether spoken or written, are not unlike prayers employed in most religious traditions. Both involve the invocation of spirits, deities, and other supernatural forces in order to achieve a desired end: love, power, a cure for illness, prosperity, fertility, or long life. Spells can divine the future, make a person invisible, permit astral projection (out-of-body experiences), or promote alchemy (e.g., turning lead into gold). They can also guard against various illnesses and disasters. Yet spells can equally be used to achieve more wicked ends. Witches became notorious for throwing powerful curses that brought ill fortune, loss of love, impotence, barrenness, sickness, or even death.[1]

That pretty much says it all!

It is not uncommon to see witchcraft turned into a very lucrative business. As people see that these practitioners have spiritual power, they are willing to pay good money for these services. For a certain price, a witch will agree to perform a ritual, curse, hex, vex, incantation or the like. As Osborn's definition states, the most common reasons for a consultation usually include matters involving desires for money, health, love or sex, and power or control over others.

The ever-increasing influence of Eastern religions in our country has produced a proliferation of demonic activity.

The name given to occult practitioners will vary from place to place and culture to culture, depending upon the type of occult activity involved. Some of the more common terms include, but are certainly not limited to these: witches (females); warlocks (males); sorcerers (those who befriend demons and get them to act); spiritists; magicians; necromancers (who claim to speak with the dead in séances); spiritual healers also known as *curanderos*, or witchdoctors; practitioners of Voodoo, Santería, Macumba, Umbanda; and workers of divination (these are many, just a few of which are crystal ball users, readers of tea leaves, palm readers, tarot card readers, psychics, fortune tellers and teachers of feng shui).

The Invasion of Eastern Religions

Invading the American culture at the present time is the ever-increasing influence of Eastern religions. Make no mistake about it, this has produced a proliferation of demonic activity. Sneaking into our homes, schools, businesses, hospitals and universities are teachings on yoga, ungodly meditation, Wicca, mind control, hypnosis and martial arts. Most Americans do not understand that involvement in such activities can open a door to demonic operation, and even oppression, in their lives and homes.

Because so many are being very deceived by them, let me speak briefly about a few practices of Eastern religions.

Martial Arts

Within the martial arts there is a variety of fighting sports that have their roots in ancient Eastern religion, including Buddhism and Taoism. The martial arts seek to harmonize life forces (yin and yang) and to harness Ch'i (universal energy). Masters in the martial arts accomplish tremendous physical feats. I am convinced that these feats are accomplished with demonic help. I have frequently had to cast out spirits of violence and false religion from those who have practiced martial arts.

Transcendental Meditation

Transcendental Meditation (TM) is a Western variation of ancient Hinduism. It is often presented with a veneer of pseudoscientific jargon. While meditating, the individual chants a "mantra" which has personally been assigned to that person at the initiation ceremony. This ceremony is a ritual offering worship to Hindu gods, and invoking their favor and presence. TM offers an advanced program, which allegedly teaches students how to fly, levitate and become invisible.

I once was praying deliverance over a young man who was struggling with lust. In college he had taken a course in TM "just for the fun of it" and had learned to meditate. I asked him what his mantra was, and he wrote it down on a piece of paper. I knew a lady from India and took the piece of paper to her. When she read the name, she gasped and said it was the name of one of the most filthy sexual goddesses in Hinduism. Was there any wonder this fellow had struggled with lust after invoking the name of a lustful, demonic spirit thousands of times over? I was able to easily cast it out when we knew why it was there—it had simply been invited! He had not been told the meaning of the mantra or that it was worship of that goddess.

Yoga

One of the most popular practices of Eastern religion is yoga. The word "yoga" comes from Sanskrit and literally means "yoking."[2] The aim of yoga is to empty one's mind of rational constraints and to yoke one's individual consciousness with what is called universal consciousness, or "God." In fact, it is intended to bring practitioners into the realization that "God" is within them, or that they are "God."

Yoga involves the use of special postures and positions, along with meditation, to produce an altered state of consciousness and, ultimately, to achieve union with "God." All forms of yoga, even those presented merely as breathing or stretching exercises, can easily open the door to the occult. The advanced levels of yoga are concerned with a mastery of cosmic forces and the practice of spiritistic and magical rituals. To empty one's mind is a loud invitation to a demon to slip in and set up housekeeping.

I have been told that there is a strong demonic spirit that can be invited into a person during yoga and meditation. It lodges in the spine, starting at the tailbone and moving all the way up and over the skull, terminating between the eyes, in the spot called the third eye. The spirit is named Kundalini and acts very much like a snake, causing its host to writhe and slither along the floor. That's a stiff price to pay for so-called exercise.

Avoiding the Traps

Just as Satan and his dark angels lust for power and worship, so also many people lust for power and sense a need to worship something that will help them get what they want. Mostly, they want things to go their way. When mature Christians want circumstances to change, they ask an all-powerful God, whom they worship, to change them in accordance with His will. All too often, when unbelievers want circumstances to change, they will seek counsel and help from the occult and will worship gods, goddesses, nature and idols. In many instances, they will be harmed and possibly enslaved. Unless they turn from these practices, come to Christ and get delivered, Satan has successfully exchanged some of his power for their worship.

The rate at which young people are entering the occult is alarming. They usually lack the knowledge of the Word of God, or they have no respect for it. Deuteronomy 18:9-14 contains God's very clear instructions to His people concerning the occult:

> When you come into the land which the LORD your God is giving you, you shall not learn to follow the abominations of those nations. There shall not be found among you anyone who makes his son or his daughter pass through the fire, or one who practices witchcraft, or a soothsayer, or one who interprets omens, or a sorcerer, or one who conjures spells, or a medium, or a spiritist, or one who calls up the dead. For all who do these things are an abomination to the LORD, and because of these abominations the LORD your God drives them out from before you. You shall be blameless before the LORD your God. For these nations which you will dispossess listened to soothsayers and diviners; but as for you, the LORD your God has not appointed such for you.

These instructions were given for the good of God's people, as guidelines to keep them from sin and the resulting personal problems. They are very clear. To obey is to keep clear of Satan's traps. Remember that his mission on Earth is to steal, kill and destroy (see John 10:10). There is absolutely no such thing as good witchcraft, or white magic. That is a lie from the pit of hell. Dabbling in the occult is very dangerous and often opens a door for demons—who come to stay.

But when God sets a person free from witchcraft and Satanism, he or she is free indeed (see John 8:36)! You are going to enjoy reading the stories of deliverance in the chapters to come, and you will be filled with faith anew as you once again see what a great and wonderful, mighty and powerful God we serve. He is more than able to deliver us!

Together let us raise our hearts and voices and say: "Jehovah, God Almighty, You are the Lord our God, and we will have no other gods before You. We praise, adore, love and worship You, now and for all of our days!" Amen.

Notes

1. Kevin Osborn, *Witches* (Kansas City, MO: Ariel Books, 1996), pp. 36-38.
2. *Merriam-Webster's Collegiate Dictionary,* 11th ed., s.v. "yoga."

Chapter 22

BREAKING WITCHCRAFT CURSES

Frank D. Hammond

There are only two spiritual power sources: God and Satan. Servants of the Most High God use their delegated spiritual authority to bless others and to defeat the devil. Emissaries of Satan employ Satan's power to curse, control and harm. This supernatural evil power over people and their affairs is known as witchcraft or sorcery.

God's Word absolutely condemns and forbids all witchcraft practices and involvement:

> Let no one be found among you who sacrifices his son or daughter in the fire, who practices divination or sorcery, interprets omens, engages in witchcraft, or casts spells, or who is a medium or spiritist or who consults the dead. Anyone who does these things is detestable to the LORD, and because of these detestable practices the LORD your God will drive out those nations before you (Deut. 18:10-12, *NIV*).

Under the Law of Moses, witches and wizards were condemned to death (see Lev. 20:27). The death penalty for witchcraft no longer applies, since Jesus paid the penalty. However, God's emphatic condemnation of all that is today referred to as the black arts holds true.

Control of others is witchcraft's appeal. The witch and wizard, and those who seek after them, attempt to control others in an endeavor to gain some advantage over them. The power is real, but it is the devil's power, and its end is ruin. The history of Israel records times when God's people ignored God and turned to the powers of darkness for help. They thought that the sorcerers would solve their crises. God rebuked and judged Israel for relying on witchcraft:

> When men tell you to consult mediums and spiritists, who whisper and mutter, should not a people inquire of their God? Why consult the dead on behalf of the living? To the law and to the testimony! If they do not speak according to this word, they have no light of dawn. Distressed and hungry, they will roam through the land; when they are famished, they will become enraged and, looking upward, will curse their king and their God (Isa. 8:19-21, *NIV*).

The influence of witchcraft has increased in our own nation and society in recent years. "The whole world lieth in wickedness" (1 John 5:19, *KJV*), for "the great dragon . . . that old serpent, called the Devil, and Satan . . . deceiveth the whole world" (Rev. 12:9, *KJV*). God said that the devil would deceive the whole world, and we are seeing exactly that happening today.

The Problem of Witchcraft in the Body of Christ

The devil's deceptions are also infiltrating the Body of Christ. Witchcraft is spreading into many local fellowships through New Age influences. Many Christians are turning to powers other than God as they search for healing, guidance and power.

We witnessed an example of this when were invited to minister in a church in a small Texas city. Before the service began, we noticed 8 or 10 people lined up in front of a man who seemed to be laying hands on them for healing. To our dismay, we learned that the man was dealing in

Myotherapy, a form of acupressure. He was pressing the palms of people's hands to heal them. This practice had been routinely taking place in the aisle of a charismatic fellowship. The leadership of the church had questioned the practice and was relieved when we brought it into the light of God's Word.

Our burden for the Church today is expressed by Paul's concern over the church at Corinth: "But I am afraid that just as Eve was deceived by the serpent's cunning, your minds may somehow be led astray from your sincere and pure devotion to Christ" (2 Cor. 11:3, *NIV*).

Witches employ incantations, potions, herbal concoctions and other magical arts to bring about curses. There are many plausible accounts of people who have suffered and even died due to witchcraft curses sent against them.

A couple who had been classmates of ours in seminary went to Africa as missionaries. Their first letter to us from Africa related their awe over the power of witchdoctors to afflict people with curses. They had seen people die from such curses. Their seminary training had not prepared them to confront these evil spiritual powers.

Most Christians today would consider it unbelievable that witchcraft would have such power. Yet thousands of years ago, Ezekiel prophesied to women who were doing some kind of witchcraft or voodoo:

> Woe to the women who sew magic charms on all their wrists and make veils of various lengths for their heads in order to ensnare people. Will you ensnare the lives of my people but preserve your own? You have profaned me among my people for a few handfuls of barley and scraps of bread. By lying to my people, who listen to lies, you have killed those who should not have died and have spared those who should not live (Ezek. 13:18-19, *NIV*).

Some Case Studies

Following are some case studies of deliverance needed as a result of occult activity.

Maria

Maria needed deliverance. A couple in our church brought her to us. She was a very nervous, fearful, and distraught individual who was tormented by severe headaches. Maria was from Venezuela, South America. She had met and married a man from the United States who, at the time, was employed by an American oil company doing work in Venezuela.

In a predeliverance counseling session, we learned that Maria had been a young believer in Christ whose family in Venezuela was deeply involved in witchcraft. She, her sister and her mother had held hands, standing in a circle, and made a pact that they would never be separated. When Maria accompanied her husband to the States, her mother and sister put curses on her for breaking her vow. Maria explained that her mother kept a live owl, bat and tarantula spider as instruments for putting curses on people.

When we commanded the demons to leave Maria, a spirit of death manifested by cutting off her breath, and her face contorted grotesquely as the demons were cast out. Deliverance from witchcraft spirits is often accompanied by strong manifestations. We were thankful that Maria started coming to our fellowship meetings to receive teachings that would help her to maintain her deliverance. She was a changed person. The powers of witchcraft had been defeated.

James

James, a young soldier, was another person delivered from witchcraft curses. We met him at a deliverance conference we were conducting in California. James was a native of Jamaica. His father, uncle and he were deeply involved in voodoo. Then, James became a Christian; and being uncomfortable with his family's heavy occult activities, he moved to the United States to get away from that influence. We found James to be very tormented and oppressed. An evil spirit came upon him every night and attacked him sexually. We explained that this spirit, called Succubus, is a female demon that comes at night to sleeping males and gives them the sensation of having sexual relations. (The male counterpart to Succubus is Incubus, an unclean spirit that comes at night to lie on sleeping women in order to have sexual intercourse with them.)

A feeling of uncleanness overwhelmed James. He had tried everything he knew to get release from this tormenting spirit, but to no avail. In his ignorance of the demonic supernatural realm, he had consulted a witch in New England where he was then stationed in the Army.

The witch instructed him to go home and get an egg. He was to bring the egg in his hand, traveling quite a distance on a bus. The egg must not be broken. The witch then performed a ritual over the egg. After the ritual was complete, she instructed James to place the egg on the floor and crush it with his foot. Supposedly, if a serpent came out of the egg, it would be a sign that he had been set free from Succubus.

James did as he was instructed; and when he crushed the egg, out came a serpent! However, he soon discovered that the spirit was stronger than ever. His going to the occult for help only compounded his problem. Satan does not cast out Satan (see Matt. 12:26).

We led James in a prayer of confession and renunciation of the sins of witchcraft. In the mighty name of Jesus, we cast out the spirit of Succubus and many other evil spirits. "If the Son makes you free, you shall be free indeed" (John 8:36).

We took time to teach James how to use his own spiritual authority as a believer in Jesus Christ. He then knew that should any of the spirits try to return, he could drive them away in the name of Jesus.

Rita and Alberto

We began to learn firsthand about witchcraft curses while pastoring in a city with a strong Mexican-American culture that had been steeped in witchcraft. Many of those in this community whom we were reaching for Christ had major problems due to witchcraft curses.

This fact was driven home to us one early morning when a ringing phone jarred us out of a deep sleep. A glance at the clock told us that it was 2:00 A.M. It was Rita, a young woman who had attended a few services at our church. She was very excited and her request was very urgent.

She wanted me to come to her house as quickly as possible.

When I arrived at Rita's home, I found her brother, Alberto, a husky farm laborer, lying on the couch. He was too weak to move. He seemed at the point of death. Rita had seen us cast demons out of people, and she had tried to cast demons out of her brother. She showed me marks on her legs where the demons had attacked her and bit her. She was hysterical.

I began to pray for Alberto. I commanded the spirits of witchcraft to release him. Within a few minutes, he sat up and asked for food since he had not eaten since getting home from the farm.

This incident reminded me of the story of the sons of Sceva who attempted to cast demons out of a demonized man "by the Jesus whom Paul preaches. Then the man in whom the evil spirit was leaped on them, overpowered them, and prevailed against them" (Acts 19:13,16). The sons of Sceva were not believers in Christ and, therefore, had no spiritual authority over demons.

This was Rita's problem. She was attempting to cast out demons in the name of the Jesus whom I had talked about. She did not yet have a personal relationship with Christ. Soon afterward, she gave her heart to the Lord and is now helping to minister deliverance to others.

Lupe

Lupe was a new convert in our congregation. She lived with her mother and elderly grandmother. Lupe confided in us that her grandmother was a witch. She used stuffed animals and other paraphernalia to work her witchcraft.

When the grandmother died, Lupe asked me and another person to pray over their house. She and her mother were experiencing some strange things. Three or four hours after sweeping and dusting the house, it would be dirty again. When one of them would sit in grandmother's chair, something would prick their legs. They had examined the chair and found there was no natural cause for the pricking. Furthermore, there had been several apparitions of the grandmother since her death.

Another pastor and I went through the house room by room. Every item that had belonged to the grandmother, which might have been used for witchcraft, was destroyed. We anointed the walls with oil and commanded every spirit of witchcraft to get out. No closet or cabinet was overlooked. The cleansing of the house was effective. None of the problems recurred.

Lessons from Balaam

There is a biblical account of attempted witchcraft from which we learn several valuable truths. It is the account in Numbers 22–24 of King Balak's hiring Balaam to curse the Israelites. Balaam was a prominent sorcerer in the region who, because of his ability to effect curses, was considered worthy of substantial payment for his services.

The Israelites had come up out of Egypt, had defeated the Amorite kings and were now camped on the borders of Moab. Balak, the Moabite king, was afraid. The only chance he could see of defeating the Israelites was for them to be cursed by Balaam. In those days witchcraft was regarded as an effective way of gaining an advantage over others.

Balaam had a solid reputation of being able to curse people. His ability to impose curses on others was no mere superstition. King Balak testified, "I know that he whom you bless is blessed, and he whom you curse is cursed" (Num. 22:6). Yes, witchcraft curses are real! But in spite of Balaam's lust for reward, he could only speak blessings upon God's people (see Num. 23:7-10).

Why was Balaam unable to curse Israel? Because God sovereignly intervened and prevented Israel from being cursed. Moses testified, "Nevertheless the LORD your God would not listen to Balaam, but the LORD your God turned the curse into a blessing for you, because the LORD your God loves you" (Deut. 23:5). God's love for Israel was so strong that He would not allow Balaam to curse Israel. Israel was blessed of God.

Balak became impatient and angry toward Balaam. Why had he not cursed Israel? Balaam announced, "How shall I curse whom God has not cursed? And how shall I denounce whom the LORD has not denounced?" (Num. 23:8).

What do we learn from Balaam's inability to curse Israel? First, we see the power of God's grace on Israel. God's undeserved blessings were with Israel to enter Canaan and take over the Promised Land, even though the people abused this privilege. Second, we see that God's power is a great protection over His people: "There is no sorcery against Jacob, nor any divination against Israel. It now must be said of Jacob and of Israel, 'Oh, what God has done!' " (Num. 23:23).

We must not become paranoid, fearing that someone is putting curses on us. Our protection from witchcraft is a combination of receiving the cleansing and protection of the blood of Christ over us and not allowing sin to become a cause for a curse to alight on us (see Prov. 26:2).

All the Protection We Need

Thank God, Christians today are learning their authority in Him. They are becoming wise in knowing how to protect themselves from witchcraft and how to cancel the powers of witchcraft. How can we as Christians protect ourselves from witchcraft curses?

Our protection is in putting on the whole armor of God. It is all the protection required. As Christian soldiers, we must keep on the girdle of *truth*, the breastplate of *righteousness*, the helmet of *salvation* and the shield of *faith*. Our feet must be shod with a readiness to proclaim the *gospel of peace* and wield the sword of the Spirit, which is the *Word of God* (see Eph. 6:13-17). The whole armor of God is our defense.

As brave soldiers of the Cross, we are not awed by the devil. We know our weapons and our authority. We must never tremble at the powers of witchcraft nor cringe at the threats they pose; rather, we must remain strong in the Lord and the power of His might. Jesus promised, "Behold, I give unto you power to tread on serpents and scorpions, and over all the power of the enemy: and nothing shall by any means hurt you" (Luke 10:19, *KJV*).

Steps to Breaking Curses

If you know that you have been exposed—or think that you might have been—to witchcraft and other occult curses, I urge the following prayers and confessions. I encourage you to act on each step by repeating the prayer/confessions aloud, and personalizing your prayers whenever appropriate.

Step One: Affirm Your Relationship with the Lord Jesus Christ

Overcome Satan with "the word of [your] testimony" (Rev. 12:11, *KJV*), which is "the testimony of Jesus Christ" (Rev. 12:17, *KJV*).

Prayer

Lord Jesus Christ, I believe with all my heart that You are the Son of God. You left Your throne of glory in heaven and became a man. You lived in this world and were tempted in all things just as we are, yet You were without sin [see Heb. 4:14-15]. *Then You went to the Cross and laid down Your life. Your precious blood was poured out for my redemption. You rose from the dead and ascended into heaven. You are coming again in all Your glory. Yes, Lord, I belong to You. I am Your child and heir to all Your promises. You are my Savior, my Lord and my Deliverer. Amen.*

Step Two: Repent of All Your Sins, Both Known and Unknown

Ask God's forgiveness through Jesus Christ.

Prayer

Heavenly Father, I come to You in an attitude of repentance. I ask You to forgive me of each sin that I have committed—the ones I am aware of and those which I have not recognized. I am sorry for them all.

Step Three: Renounce the Sins of Your Forefathers

Prayer

Heavenly Father, I confess the sins of my forefathers. I now renounce, break and loose myself and my family from all hereditary curses, and from all demonic bondage placed upon us as the result of sins, transgressions and iniquities through my parents and all of my ancestors.

Step Four: Accept God's Forgiveness, and Forgive Yourself

Prayer

Heavenly Father, You have promised in Your Word that if I will confess my sins, You are faithful and just to forgive me and will cleanse me from all unrighteousness [see 1 John 1:9]. *I believe that You have forgiven me for Christ's sake. Therefore, I accept Your forgiveness, and I forgive myself.*

Step Five: Forgive All Others Who Have Ever Trespassed Against You

Prayer

Lord, others have trespassed against me, but You have commanded me to forgive each person who has ever hurt me or wronged me in any way. I now make a quality decision to forgive [name them, both living and dead]. *Also, I bless each of these whom I have forgiven and pray that they will have Your peace, joy and love in their lives.*

Step Six: Renounce All Contact with Cults, the Occult and False Religions

Prayer

Father, I confess as sin and ask Your forgiveness for every involvement with cults, the occult and false religions. [Be as specific as possible.] *I confess having sought from Satan's kingdom the knowledge, guidance, power and healing that should come only from You. I hereby renounce Satan and all of his works. I loose myself from him, and I take back all the ground that I ever yielded to him. I choose the blessing and refuse the curse. I choose life and not death.*

Step Seven: Destroy All Books, Objects and Paraphernalia Associated with Any Cult, Occult or False Religious Source

Prayer

Heavenly Father, You are a jealous God, visiting the iniquities of the fathers upon the children unto the third and fourth generation of them who hate you [see Exod. 20:5]. *Therefore, I destroy all books and objects in my possession that are contrary to You and Your kingdom. If there is anything in my possession that is not pleasing to You and gives any advantage to the devil, reveal this to me, and I will destroy it.*

Step Eight: Cast Out Every Demon of Curse

Warfare Prayer

Satan, you have no right to my life and no power over me. I belong to God, and I will serve Him and Him only. By the authority of my Lord Jesus Christ, I break the power of every evil curse that has come upon me. I command every demon of curse to leave me now: ancestral curse spirits, personal-transgression curse spirits, witchcraft curse spirits and spoken-word curse spirits. [Be as specific as possible in identifying spirits of curses.]

Step Nine: Claim the Blessing

Now that the curses are broken, and the demons of curse have been cast out, it is time to confess your blessings in the Lord. Know this: The grace of God enables you to stand unashamed in the presence of God Himself. Since you have God's favor, you are assured of His blessings.

Prayer

Heavenly Father, thank You for delivering me from every curse through the redemptive work of Your Son and my Savior, Jesus Christ. You exalt me and set me on high. You cause me to be fruitful and to prosper in everything. By Your hand of blessing I am a success and not a failure. I am the head and not the tail—above and not beneath. You have established me in holiness. I am Yours, and I purpose to serve You and to glorify Your name.

God instructed Aaron and his sons to put His name on the children of Israel and bless them. Similarly, those in headship should bless those under their care. Let the pastor bless the people, the husband his wife, and the parents their children. I have found it especially effective and deeply appreciated to speak a pastoral or fatherly blessing upon the individual who has been delivered. It is a heart-moving experience for those who have never had a blessing spoken over them by someone in authority.

Let us use these same priestly words to speak blessings on others: "The LORD bless thee, and keep thee: The LORD make his face shine upon thee, and be gracious unto thee: The LORD lift up his countenance upon thee, and give thee peace" (Num. 6:24-26, *KJV*).

Amen!

Chapter 23

UNVEILING THE EVIL EYE

Chuck D. Pierce

I can still remember the eye doctor telling me, "You have a blind spot." A blind spot? What could that mean? He showed me the test results, which indicated that a huge portion of my vision was being blocked. He called this *a blind spot.* A blind spot is that small area that is insensitive to *light* in the retina of the eye. Another definition of a blind spot is a person's lack of sensitivity to a particular thing. Prejudice or ignorance about a subject can be a blind spot, of which this person is unaware. When the eye doctor told me that I had a blind spot, more than a physical malady was present—I knew that the Lord was going to uncover whatever was hidden in me.

I was diagnosed as either having a tumor on my optic nerve or a blood clot that was pressing on the nerve and blocking my vision. In either case, this seemed to be serious enough for the doctors to want me to go quickly to the hospital for further testing. Little did I know that, in addition to the doctor's tests, God had planned a week of deliverance. The week turned into a year. The year turned into a process of 10 years. The 10 years resulted in a testimony of freedom. And the Lord let in a lot of light.

THE EYE

The eye is a major gate, where information is perceived and channeled into the human soul and spirit. The Bible calls the eye "the lamp of the body." Matthew 6:22-23 reads,

> The lamp of the body is the eye. If therefore your eye is good, your whole body will be full of light. But if your eye is bad, your whole body will be full of darkness. If therefore the light that is in you is darkness, how great is that darkness!

In the Bible, one method of punishment in war was to blind or put out the eyes of the captive (see Judg. 16:21; 2 Kings 25:7; Jer. 52:11). If the eye is to be useful, it must see clearly. Biblically, the eye is of great importance for a person to prosper fully in God's plan. The eye also relates to the heart and mind, since the "eye of the heart" determines our spiritual perception. As we read in Matthew 6, if our spiritual eyes are open, we can receive enlightenment, and the Spirit of God can flow. If our eyes are darkened, our whole body becomes dark and eventually we lose our way.

THE EVIL EYE IN THE BIBLE

The purpose of this chapter is to reveal Satan's hidden snares, or to unveil the evil eye. The term "evil eye" is found in the Bible. The *New King James Version* of the Old Testament usually uses a literal translation of the Hebrew words for "evil" and "eye" ("your eye be evil," Deut. 15:9; "an evil eye," Prov. 28:22), whereas the *New International Version* uses a figurative translation ("ill will" and "stingy"). These Bible versions translate the New Testament Greek words in a similar manner. The *New King James Version* uses "is your eye evil" in Matthew 20:15 and "an evil eye" in Mark 7:22, whereas the *New International Version* uses "are you envious" and "envy" in these verses.

The Bible warns that God will judge people who have an evil eye:

> Woe to those who call evil good, and good evil; who put darkness for light, and light for darkness; who put bitter for sweet, and sweet for bitter! (Isa. 5:20).

From the Bible, we also learn that our heart can be subverted by the evil eye. In Mark 7:20-22, Jesus explains, "What comes out of a man, that defiles a man. For from within, out of the heart of men, proceed evil thoughts, adulteries, fornications, murders, thefts, covetousness, wickedness, deceit, licentiousness, an evil eye, blasphemy, pride, foolishness." "These things," Jesus says, "are within us and make us unclean" (v. 23). In these verses, we see that covetousness is linked to an evil eye, as are evil thoughts.

The Evil Eye Defined

As we have seen, having an evil eye can cloud our spiritual perception and cause us to look at things from a perverse, ungodly perspective. And that leads us to the definition for "evil eye" that I will use; the evil eye is a perverse perspective.

Merriam-Webster's Collegiate Dictionary defines the evil eye as "an eye or glance held capable of inflicting harm."[1] According to the *Columbia Encyclopedia,* the evil eye is

> principally [a] Sicilian and Mesoamerican superstition, although it is known in other cultures. According to the Native American version, a person who stares fixedly at a pregnant woman or a child or who is too admiring or physically affectionate with children may produce a malicious effect on their lives, whether or not by intent. In rural Sicily any person or animal was considered vulnerable to the evil eye, and many individuals wore protective amulets or charms to nullify its effects.[2]

Blinded by the Enemy

The word "occult" means to conceal or cause to disappear from view—to be secret, mysterious, supernatural. The Bible explains that we can be blinded by the deceptive ways of the enemy, but God gives us access to revelation that will uncover that which has been kept secret (see 2 Cor. 4:3-4,6).

The enemy likes to hide. He plans strategies to divert us from accomplishing God's will and entering into our heavenly Father's blessings. Many of us have a hard time *seeing* the enemy's snares, which are strategically planted along our path. Thus we *step into* his tangled web and spend much of our time struggling to free ourselves.

In the next portion of this chapter, I will expose several of the snares that the enemy lays: generational iniquity, covetousness, superstition, spiritism, magic and sorcery, and Freemasonry. And at the chapter's end, I will suggest how to remove these snares and unveil the evil eye.

Blinded by Generational Iniquity

Occult practices were not unusual in the generations of my family. There was an inherited weakness toward sins of the occult and witchcraft, which was passed down through our bloodline. A weakness like this is known as *iniquity*, and it forms a pattern in our lives that causes us to deviate from God's perfect path. Its root definition is linked to "unequal" or "twisted." In other words, we do something that is not equal to God's righteous standard and we are unwilling to be reconciled to God's ways. This causes our path to be twisted.

Rebecca Sytsema and I have previously written on this topic of generational iniquity in *Possessing Your Inheritance*: "Have you ever noticed how such things as alcoholism, divorce, laziness or greed tend to run in families? These aren't just learned behaviors. They are manifestations of iniquity [or iniquitous patterns] passed down through the generations."[3] Occult iniquitous patterns work the same way, only they are more difficult to detect because they are hidden.

Soon after my doctor told me about my eye problems, I discovered that the blind spot I was experiencing was linked to many inherited occult influences in my life. When I entered the hospital, it was as if the

Lord were pulling me aside so that He could go deep down and show me some things that had been hidden for a long time.

My family had all the potential in the world to prosper. My relatives were good, hard-working people. However, the enemy seemed to ravage and destroy all that God had planned. My dad was led astray and became involved in gambling and eventually in witchcraft. When I was a child, I watched certain family members operate in supernatural dimensions; therefore, the supernatural was easy for me to understand. My grandfather could speak words and bring about changes in the elements around him. I had cousins who would visit with an unknown source and then watch the table rise up off the floor. When I was 10 years old, I thought nothing about buying my first Ouija board. I had never been told that it was a harmless game nor had I been warned that it might be dangerous; I just knew I could ask it questions and it would speak back.

One side of my family was so steeped in superstition that all the rules became wearying to follow. Of course, I also had some family members who were totally devout, praying, godly saints. Talk about having your eyes unfocused and going in every direction. Mine sure were!

Familial and Familiar Spirits

My wife, Pam, used to tell me that at times there was something driving me to react. However, she could never put her finger on what it was. She would say, "It's linked to your family in some way. Every time we almost see what it is, like a bat it flies back into the cave. It never comes to the light enough so that we can detect it and pull it out of you—like the way certain members of your family operate!"

A family is defined as a group of people living in the same house, one or more people consisting of the same parents or a group of people that have a common blood tie. When a member of a family sins, the door is opened for demonic forces to work in subsequent generations of that family because of the iniquity produced. Spirits assigned to a family are called *familial spirits*, and they can remain at work in the family for generations. They know the iniquitous patterns in a family bloodline. They know when the patterns began. They know that, unless dealt with through the blood of Jesus, these patterns will be passed on to someone else in the next generation.

Familiar spirits work the same way, only they do not have to be part of the family bloodline. "Familiar" is applied to that which is known through constant association. These spirits are linked with some sort of intimacy, such as sexual soul ties. The old saying, Birds of a feather flock together, does have some validity. The iniquitous pattern in one person is drawn to the iniquitous pattern in another. I call this a cluster of iniquity. If one member of the cluster dies or lets go of this iniquitous pattern, the pattern is strengthened in the other members.

The Revelation of Hidden Things

Once I knew about my spiritual blind spot, I went to a cell group and asked for prayer. One of the leaders, a very spiritual woman who at one time had been involved in the occult, laid hands on me and declared that anything hidden within me would be exposed. Oh my, did this stir up a nest! It was as if my blood curdled or the bottom of the lake came to the top. Over time truths about my background began to expose themselves.

One day, not long after I received prayer, I was trying to finish some tasks around our house before I went to the hospital. My wife has always kept a most beautiful yard, but she noticed a small brown spot in the grass. She asked if I could determine the cause of that spot. The brown spot reminded me of my spiritual blind spot. The more I dug, the larger the hole got in our front yard. I became frustrated because I had dug a hole three feet wide though the spot looked to be only a couple of inches. I found a huge piece of concrete underneath our luscious green yard. It was not evident until the heat of August had reached a certain level.

When things heat up, reactions occur. So, when Pam walked out of the house and, of course, had a better way of digging so that the yard would not be ruined, I felt this strange feeling come over me. (Doris Wagner always says that this is one way to detect a demon—something "comes over you.") I felt as if I were outside of my body. My natural self wanted to take the sledgehammer that I was using and throw it as hard as I could at my wife. Thank God for wisdom and self-control—and a measure of fear. I know my wife; she, too, can react!

My natural self wanted to take the sledgehammer and throw it as hard as I could at my wife. Thank God for self-control!

I stopped where I stood and said, "Lord, I've had this familiar feeling before. Remind me of when and how this started." Immediately the Lord reminded me of times when I would have what my grandmother would call a spell. She would have me lay down in a bedroom and then she would chant certain words until the spell subsided. Instead of throwing the hammer, I went inside my house, laid down on my bed and remembered every word of the chant. Instead of chanting, I renounced those words and decreed that any power attached to them would no longer have the right to hold me captive. I prayed the blood of Jesus over my family and myself, and I asked God to fill me anew with His Holy Spirit. For me, this was the beginning of true freedom.

Covetousness

In Deuteronomy 8:18, we read how the Lord spoke to His covenant people and prepared them to go into the land that He had promised. He told them that He would give them the power to get wealth, but He also warned them about the pitfalls of worshiping mammon, which is wealth that has a debasing influence. God's assignment to Joshua and the tribes of Israel was to use their wealth for God's covenant Kingdom plan. To fulfill this assignment, a spiritual battle had to be fought, mammon had to be defeated and all riches had to be transferred to God's rule and stewardship plan. Proverbs 28:22 sheds some light by declaring that a man with an evil eye will greedily pursue earthly treasures. Matthew 6:24 further explains that no one can serve both God and mammon.

We face a similar battle with mammon today. Have you ever looked closely at a dollar bill from the United States? An eye is imbedded right there in the paper. While the origin and meaning of this eye is debated, it clearly resembles the traditional evil eye. Moreover, in a wealth-driven world, people easily use their natural eyes to look at money (mammon) with covetousness. Obviously we can't burn and destroy every dollar bill we have, so we must ask God how to deal with the presence of the eye.

Money is neither good nor bad in itself. The key issue for us is our relationship and dedication to the power behind money. We must guard ourselves against the *love of money* (see 1 Tim. 6:10). The Greek word for "the love of money," *philarguria,* refers to avarice, which is the insatiable greed for riches, or covetousness.[4] It also means to inordinately or wrongly desire the possessions of others.[5] If we are not careful, this covetousness is the fruit that money will produce in our hearts. Moreover, the *deceitfulness of riches* is an issue (see Mark 4:19). This is primarily a perceived power that comes with money. It produces an attitude of the heart that seeks to manipulate through false pretenses and appearances.

Envy is also linked with covetousness and the evil eye. When we look at something or someone else with an unholy desire, especially someone's riches, we fall under the power of its demonic grip. The power of envy is noted in Proverbs 27:4: "Who is able to stand before envy?" (*KJV*). To avoid this trap of the enemy, we must sanctify what God gives us and be satisfied with our portion (see Ps. 16:5; Phil. 4:11; 1 Tim. 6:8).

The term "mammon" predominantly signifies riches and wealth; but as Colin Brown, in *The New International Dictionary of New Testament Theology,* points out, "Material wealth can be personified as a demonic power, Mammon."[6] In addition, Bible scholar Ralph P. Martin has noted that the Jewish rabbis personified the Aramaic word for wealth as "a demon and rival of God."[7] Further evidence correlating wealth to false gods is the fact that ancient teachings connect the Aramaic word for wealth to a Babylonian god.[8] The point of this is that when our stewardship of wealth does not align with God's purpose and plan, we open ourselves to demonic activity.

Furthermore, as Ralph P. Martin points out in his commentary on Colossians and Philemon, covetousness encourages us to trust in our material possessions instead of in God.[9] When we turn our trust from God to money, we place ourselves in submission to a new master. Jack Hayford, in *Hayford's Bible Handbook*, refers to Luke 16:13 in the following manner: "Jesus said that no one can serve two masters—God and money—at the same time, and makes Mammon a potential 'master.' "[10] Mammon should be recognized as a god, then, when it leads us into worship of material possessions.

Money often has curses attached to it. If we don't break the curses before we get the money, we will get the curse that comes with it. The Bible lists some people who were cursed by wealth or were driven by impure motives to gain it; Judas, Esau, Gehazi, Ananias, Sapphira, Lot and Achan are some examples. Each of these men and women was trapped by impure desires. One way we can break this curse is by tithing and giving offerings (see Mal. 3). These acts change our attitude about money. As we move forward against the enemy, we must renounce every issue of covetousness that is tied to mammon, and we must break its curses.

Going back to the eye that is printed on the dollar bill, I do not believe that it has any power over God's children unless they are not stewarding their money right. Then this evil eye is just representative of the *watching* demonic host that longs to trap God's people. Money is good when it is a servant to us and to God. However, we can become slaves to its dominion. That is when it truly becomes an evil eye.

Superstition

Superstition is probably more closely linked with the evil eye than anything else. Superstition can actually mean "fearing demons." It is a belief, half-belief or practice for which there appears to be no rational substance, but which supposedly brings a person protection. Superstitions can fall into three categories: religious, cultural and personal. A religious superstition (against which Christians are not immune) may be something such as leaving an open Bible next to a bed to gain protection from demons. Cultural superstitions are folk traditions linked to irrational beliefs intended to ward off illness, bring about good results, foretell the future and prevent accidents. A personal superstition may include a perceived need to use a lucky pen or, when gambling, betting on a particular color of horse. Superstition develops a mind-binding fear within.

My family was steeped in superstition. Several of these superstitions really affected my life as I was growing up—they kept me in bondage to fear. In the following few paragraphs I present some examples and then show how the Lord broke me out of a mind-set regarding each set of superstitions.

Superstitions Involving Beds

- It is bad luck to put a hat on a bed.
- When making a bedspread, or a quilt, be sure to finish it or marriage will never come to you.
- When making the bed, don't interrupt your work, or you will spend a restless night in it.

Breaking the Superstition

Psalm 4:8 reads, "I will lay down and sleep in peace; for you alone, O Lord, make me dwell in safety." Claiming this Scripture was helpful in freeing me from the superstitions regarding the bed and rest.

Superstitions Involving Brooms

- Do not lean a broom against a bed. The evil spirits in the broom will cast a spell on the bed.
- If you sweep trash out of a doorway after dark, it will bring a stranger to visit.

- If someone is sweeping the floor and sweeps over your feet, you will have calamity in your life.
- If you take a broom from one house to another, you will allow the spirits of the previous house to come to the next house.
- To prevent an unwelcome guest from returning, you should immediately sweep out the room that he or she was in and bind that person from ever returning.

Breaking the Superstition

The Lord showed me that He stands at my door and knocks, and that I should always be willing to let Him in. He took me to Song of Solomon and Revelation. He showed me that a broom had no power in itself, and that if an evil spirit entered my house I had the authority to bind and cast it out.

Superstitions Involving Birds

- A bird in the house is a sign of death.
- If a robin flies into a room through a window, death will shortly follow.

Breaking the Superstition

The Lord showed me that, according to Matthew 6, He loves me more than any bird. He also took me to Psalm 84:3, which reads, "The swallow [has found] a nest for herself, where she may have her young—a place near your altar." God showed me how to build an altar to Him in my home through prayer and worship so I need not fear any intrusion. Now if a bird comes into my house, it can be at home with God and me, because my house is a sanctuary.

The next two were harder to break.

Superstitions Involving Cats

- If a black cat walks toward you, it brings good fortune; but if it walks away, it takes the good luck with it.
- Keep cats away from babies because they suck the breath out of the child.
- A cat on board a ship is considered to bring luck.
- If a black cat crosses in front of you, you must turn around for trouble would be on the path ahead.

Breaking the Superstition

Idiotic word curses such as these often turned my family from the path they were on. I was late one day going to work because there was a black cat in the path I normally took. At the time, I was living fully in the Lord; however, words that had been a part of my belief system would not die easily. These superstitions had built a stronghold. In the end, I just broke the devil's power, and the words. Then I heard a word from behind me telling me not to turn to the right or to the left, but to go forward. I was freed.

The next two superstitions led me into obsessive-compulsive tendencies and created a fear of death within me.

Superstition Involving Cracks

- Don't step on a crack on a sidewalk or a walkway.

Breaking the Superstition

I made it through the crack obsession when I was 12. I just simply stepped on one. At that time, things weren't going too well, so what was one more issue? I believe the breaking of this curse was the beginning of my realizing the ignorance of holding superstitions.

Superstition Involving Sparrows

- Sparrows carry the souls of the dead, and it's unlucky to kill one.

Breaking the Superstition

The sparrow curse was linked to the practice of spiritism in my family. To break this one, God gave me Proverbs 26:2: "Like a fluttering sparrow or a darting swallow, an undeserved curse does not come to rest." In other words, the sparrow did not carry the soul of a human, nor could its death bring a curse upon my life or family. Using God's Word itself is one of the strongest ways to break the power of a superstition.

Spiritism

The evil eye also works through spiritism. *The Catholic Encyclopedia* defines spiritism as "the belief that the living can communicate with the spirits of the departed, and to the various practices by which such communication is attempted."[11]

The Catholic Encyclopedia describes two types of phenomena that occur when spiritism is practiced: physical phenomena and psychical phenomena. The physical phenomena include

- production of raps and other sounds;
- movement of objects (tables, chairs) without contact or with contact insufficient to explain the movement;
- "apports," i.e., apparitions of [objects with no] visible agency to convey them;
- moulds, i.e., impressions made upon paraffin and similar substances;
- luminous appearances, i.e., vague glimmerings of light or faces more or less defined;
- levitation, i.e., raising of objects from the ground by supposed supernormal means;

- materialization or appearance of a spirit in visible human form;
- spirit-photography, in which the feature or forms of deceased persons appear on the plate along with the likeness of a living photographed subject.[12]

The encyclopedia describes psychical phenomena as those that "express ideas or contain messages." These include

- table-rapping in answer to questions;
- automatic writing; slate-writing;
- trance-speaking;
- clairvoyance;
- descriptions of the spirit-world; and
- communications from the dead.[13]

During spiritistic rituals and practices, such as séances, the dead do not actually communicate back; rather, evil spirits linked with familiar and familial spirits communicate to individuals to reinforce their fears and guide them on to twisted paths. In other words, the demon forces that were with the dead individuals during their lives know the answers to questions and pose as the dead people with whom the spiritists try to communicate.

This is a very dangerous and deceitful practice because it can seem real—after all, who but the real Aunt Nellie could have known that rocky road was her favorite flavor of ice cream? The problem is that those who are attempting to communicate with Aunt Nellie aren't reaching her at all, but they are contacting and inviting the presence and counsel of the demons who tormented Aunt Nellie during her life.

The only true outcome of these attempts to communicate with a dead person is opening wide a door to demonization by familial or familiar spirits. This practice can lead into delusion and even death. The torment caused by these spirits can bring great mental imbalance and vexation. Spiritism invites the evil eye and opens the soul to satanic influence and control.

Magic and Sorcery

When we look at occult relationships that utilize an evil eye, we must also review how magic and sorcery attempt to influence people and events. Biblically we find that these two activities are linked with many aspects of the supernatural, including witchcraft, enchantment using charms, enchantment using spells, charmers, Chaldeans, divination, secret arts, snake charming, Magi (or wise men), sorcery using drugs and potions, spiritual imposters, mind-binding spells, curious arts and religious bewitchment. Magic itself may be associated with some forms of divination. Divination is the attempt to use supernatural means to uncover events or discover information.

Magic is universal, and may be black or white. Black magic attempts to produce evil results through such methods as curses, spells, destruction of models of one's enemy and alliance with evil spirits. It often appears as witchcraft. White magic tries to undo curses and spells, and to use occult forces to advance the good of oneself and others. Of course, in reality there is no good magic. All magic is of Satan and leads to death and hell.

The magician tries to compel a god, demon or spirit to work for him. He follows a pattern of occult practices to bend psychic forces to his will. Magic and sorcery are not mere superstitions; rather, they have a reality behind them. And they must be resisted and overcome through the power of the Holy Spirit, in the name of Jesus Christ.

Freemasonry

The evil eye is very attached to ritualistic practices and secret societies. One powerful secret society that uses the evil eye to influence its members is Freemasonry. In the short space here, a long explanation is not possible. I will give a brief description below, but for more information you can read Selwyn Stevens's *Unmasking Freemasonry: Removing the Hoodwink* and Ron G. Campbell's *Free from Freemasonry.*

There is much secrecy involved in this society. This often opens a person to fear and bondage. Interestingly, Wicca and Mormonism have rites similar to those found in Freemasonry. The initiations that bring a person into Freemasonry are humiliating. If a person is married, he has to remove his wedding ring, because he has to be totally married to, or in covenant with, the words that he speaks. Often unwittingly, this initiation also commits a person to the false god behind Freemasonry. There is a wall of secrecy between a Freemason and his wife. This is how the occult works.

In Freemasonry, there are 33 degrees of attainable power and authority. In the Third Degree, a Mason swears that if he violates the Masonic brotherhood his body will be cut in two, his bowels will be removed and his body will be burned to ashes and scattered to the four winds. There are oaths taken in every degree. These oaths in Freemasonry are filled with curses that are attached to the generations. This is why it's so hard for anyone to get out of this false religion.

Those who are initiated live in constant turmoil, making blind contracts with the enemy by speaking things that can be very destructive in their life and the lives of their descendents. Yet if a member tries to leave, he faces censure. Freemasons will not associate with someone who has left the fold. They believe that the sacred oaths have been broken. The person is then criticized and cursed, and sometimes hounded, forever treated as untrustworthy.

Nevertheless, as Selwyn Stevens writes,

> God's Word requires a Christian to renounce a bad or sinful oath such as this. Leviticus 5:4-5 shows us that if a person is required to swear something which was hidden prior to the oath-taking, God says we should plead guilty to Him, confess it as sin and totally renounce and repudiate it, preferably publicly. When you have done this God says you are no longer bound by it. God wants us to know that repentance releases us from such a vow or oath. This is one of the major keys for removing the consequences of the curses invoked by Masonic oaths.[14]

How to Unveil the Evil Eye

I trust that through this chapter you have begun to understand that the enemy seeks to cloud our ability to discern. He hides himself. He plots and plans to divert us from accomplishing God's will and seeks to keep us from entering into God's blessings. Many of us have a hard time *seeing* the enemy's snare or diversion. As a result, we often *step into* the middle of this web and spend much of our time struggling to free ourselves. In response to the enemy's tactics, we must ask the Lord to help us look past the visible to see the invisible, and to discern any supernatural force that would seek to ensnare us or keep us from accomplishing the Lord's will.

Here are 15 ways we can remove the enemy's hidden snares in our life and unveil the evil eye:

1. The enemy has a voice to bring deception into our life. Ask God to reveal any deception or lie the enemy fosters.
2. Satan is the father of lies; however, he can only work with the resources that we give to him. We need to cut ties with anything in our soulish nature that holds us captive to the enemy.
3. We need to ask the Lord to fill us with His love so that we can break any sin strategy in our life and destroy the devil's work.
4. Jesus resisted the voice of the enemy. We can ask the Lord to fill us with the Holy Spirit in the midst of our wilderness so that we also can resist the devil.
5. We should not be ignorant. We must let God reveal to us the supernatural qualities that the enemy possesses—Lucifer's hidden characteristics.
6. We should be sure that we are operating our life in humility and submission so that we can put up an effective resistance.
7. Satan manipulates us and wants us to believe that God is not directing us or that God is holding out on us. We can ask God to break any manipulation that is aligned with our desires.
8. We need to be sure that our desires are correctly aligned with

God's. Temptation is linked to selfish desires that are not within God's boundaries.

9. It is wise for us to ask the Lord to deliver us from temptation.
10. We should change our mind or redevelop our thought process (repent). We can renounce acts linked with our wrong thinking. We also can forgive ourselves and other people who have seduced us and led us astray.
11. We can ask God to give us a mind-set for increase. We should ask Him to open our heart to any prophetic word that will bring us success and cause us to be able to rake in the spoils that the enemy is holding.
12. We must declare deliverance from the hand of the wicked one who seeks to rob us of our provision and health.
13. We should declare that any generational curse that robs God of anything rightfully belonging to Him will be released from our bloodline. This is one of the four major generational curses, sometimes identified as "God-robbing" (see Mal. 3:9). We need to tear down mind-sets of poverty that might tell us, "God is not able." This is a lie to withhold everything that should be freely given.
14. We can dismantle unbelief over provision. "Prove Me *now*," says the Lord! Look up and see the windows of blessing that He wants to open. Watch Him overcome the devourer (see Mal. 3:10-11).
15. Rejoice that we are free from the enemy's plans and purposes!

Let your eye be filled with light, and may the Holy Spirit direct every step of your path. "The path of the righteous is like the first gleam of the dawn, shining ever brighter till the full light of day" (Prov. 4:18, *NIV*).

Notes

1. *Merriam-Webster's Collegiate Dictionary,* 11th ed., s.v. "evil eye."
2. *The Columbia Encyclopedia,* 6th ed., s.v. "evil eye," quoted at *bartleby.com.* http://www.bartleby.com/65/ev/evileye.html (accessed February 16, 2005).

3. Chuck D. Pierce and Rebecca Wagner Sytsema, *Possessing Your Inheritance* (Ventura, CA: Renew Books, 1999), pp. 172-173.
4. James Strong, *The New Strong's Exhaustive Concordance of the Bible* (Nashville, TN: Thomas Nelson Publishers, 1984), Greek ref. no. 5365; *Merriam-Webster's Collegiate Dictionary,* 11th ed., s.v. "avarice."
5. *Merriam-Webster's Collegiate Dictionary,* 11th ed., s.v. "covet."
6. *New International Dictionary of New Testament Theology,* vol. 2, ed. Colin Brown (Grand Rapids, MI: Regency Reference Library, 1986), p. 829.
7. Ralph P. Martin, *Colossians and Philemon* (Grand Rapids, MI: Eerdmans, 1973), p. 104.
8. *Hayford's Bible Handbook,* ed. Jack W. Hayford (Nashville, TN: Thomas Nelson Publishers, 1995), p. 962.
9. Martin, *Colossians and Philemon,* p. 104.
10. *Hayford's Bible Handbook,* p. 962.
11. *The Catholic Encyclopedia, Volume XIV,* s.v. "spiritism" (by Edward A. Pace), public domain, quoted at *New Advent.* http://www.newadvent.org/cathen/14221a.htm (accessed March 2, 2005).
12. Ibid.
13. Ibid.
14. Selwyn Stevens, *Unmasking Freemasonry: Removing the Hoodwink* (Wellington, New Zealand: Jubilee Resources, 1999), p. 19.

Chapter 24

MY ESCAPE FROM SANTERÍA

Araceli Alvarez

I was born in Cuba and raised in a family that called itself Roman Catholic. But like many such families, we went to church only on special occasions. At the age of 12, I became a good practicing follower of Catholicism. I became very deeply involved in my church—teaching catechism, working with food banks, distributing toys, giving blankets to the elderly and food to the needy, and serving in the Catholic Youth Organization. My time was divided between teaching my students and working in my church.

In 1958, I married a Cuban Air Force pilot. In 1959, Fidel Castro overthrew the Cuban government. This was a crucial and frightening point in my life because my husband, who was as an active pilot, was imprisoned.

Castro's government was holding military trials for just about any reason, and a person could be sentenced to 30 years of hard labor or to death, to be executed by a firing squad the next morning. No investigation or witnesses were needed. Someone's saying that you were not a follower of the revolution was enough. Castro condemned the Cuban pilots before any trials were held. He just appeared in public and said they had to be judged and condemned as "an example to the rest of the world."

My mother always had believed in spiritism. She suggested that under the circumstances I should go to a *santero,* a priest in the Santería religion, and seek help of the "saints." I agreed out of desperation, fear, confusion and the knowledge that justice was not available due to the political situation at that time. I went for a *consulta*, a reading, which was done by a priest with small river shells. From that moment on, everything became a whirlwind. I was told that I needed to be initiated in order to save the life of my husband and myself. Without thinking, I paid the required fees and prepared myself for the initiation ceremony. And thus I entered into the world of Santería.

What Is Santería?

Santería is a religious tradition of African origin that developed in Cuba at the beginning of the 19th century, when hundreds of thousands of men and women of the Yoruba people, who come from what are now Nigeria and Benin, were brought as slaves to Cuba to work in the island's booming sugar industry. They were forced to convert to the Roman Catholic Church. In spite of the terrible conditions, they were able to keep their own religious rites, associating the stories of different Catholic saints to their own gods' stories. They used the statues that represented specific Catholic saints to worship their spirits, called *orishas*, which are represented with different kinds of stones and river shells.

The name "Santería" means "the way of the saints." The words *sao* and *santera* indicate an initiated devotee. Despite the frequent presence of Catholic symbols in Santería rites and the attendance of santeros at Catholic sacraments, Santería is essentially an African way of worship drawn into a symbiotic relationship with Catholicism; and the Latin American countries, which traditionally are Catholic, easily fall into the trap of this cult. The basis of Santería is the development of a deep personal relationship with the orishas, a relationship that will bring the santero worldly success and "heavenly" wisdom.

Devotion to the orishas takes four principal forms: divination, sacrifice, spirit mediumship and initiation. For the ordinary devotee,

Santería serves as a means for resolving the problems of everyday life, including problems of health, money and love. Divination claims to reveal the source of these problems, and it points the way to their resolution.

The different methods of divination that are used range from simple to complex. A simple method is the santeros' reading river shells. The most complex system of divination in Santería is *ifa*, which can be "read" only by male priests called *babalawos*. In response to an adherent's problem, a babalawo will throw an *ekwele*, a small chain that has eight pieces of shell, bone or other material affixed to it. Each piece is shaped so that, when thrown, it lands either concave or convex side up. This results in 256 possible combinations, each representing a basic situation in life. The combination that falls at any particular time is considered to be the purest expression of fate, and is thus the God-given destiny of the devotee. Most of the patterns refer to stories that tell of the problems faced by the orishas and heroes in the past, and to the solutions that were found. These solutions become the archetypes used by the devotee to resolve the problem.

As problems seem to be solved, the devotee becomes more deeply dependent on the orisha. As the dependence becomes greater and greater, the devotee's involvement soon includes offering sacrifices, being initiated and finally being dominated by the orisha. It was in this type of environment that I rose to the position of a high priestess.

My Journey Into (and Out of) Santería

One year later my husband and 27 other pilots were tried. He was sentenced to 12 years of hard labor. The excuse for the severity of the sentence was that he was probably going to be sentenced to death anyway. In 1961, I fled the country by boat, arriving at the Cayman Islands some 44 hours later. After 38 days on the island of Grand Cayman, I arrived in the United States and went to New York to live with my aunt.

I soon settled in and found work. I discovered someone who was practicing Santería and started visiting and worshiping with them. In 1967, I moved to California and was surprised to learn that Santería was being practiced very openly in the Los Angeles area due to the arrival of thousands of Cuban exiles.

After divorcing and losing most of my savings (you have to pay for everything that is done for you in Santería, from a simple reading to any other help), I fell away from worshiping in Santería and started visiting a Foursquare church with my daughter. However, my house remained full of idols and representations of different orishas.

A year later in 1986, a friend invited me to a Full Gospel Businessmen's Fellowship dinner. When I heard the testimony of a member, the Lord touched me, and I accepted Jesus as my Savior. My friend was attending Lake Avenue Church in Pasadena and the Sunday School class known as the 120 Fellowship. The teacher was C. Peter Wagner. Today I am still a member of this same church and the same class. I thank the Lord for taking me there. I believe that I am a Christian today because of the love, compassion and ministry that the members of the class showed to me.

One member, Roger Nelson, put me in contact with a pastor from Utah, who was one of the very few Christian pastors with a deliverance ministry at that time. This pastor graciously came to my apartment with Roger and prayed deliverance over my daughter and me.

My first two years as a Christian were very difficult, full of guilt and remorse for all that I had done. I still had difficulty accepting forgiveness from the Lord, and the concepts of being saved and forgiven by grace were still foreign to me.

The support, understanding and prayers of my sisters and brothers from the Sunday School class were so wonderful that only God could have moved them to so much sacrifice. At that time we in the 120 Fellowship were studying the book of Acts, and I understood what our teacher, Peter Wagner, was explaining. It was a wonderful awakening to walk through this book and to read daily from the Word of God, although I still did not fully understand what I was reading.

Two years later, during the class's annual retreat, the Holy Spirit touched me and brought me to a total confession in front of my class. Tom White, who was leading the retreat, prayed over me, and something broke. My cycle of learning and understanding the Word of God started. Since then, when I read through the Old Testament each year, the Lord brings back memories of Santería ceremonies, and I keep discovering more about how deceiving this cult really is.

The Counterfeit Santería Initiation Ceremony

The devil often counterfeits the things of God. Let's compare the Santería initiation ceremony with the Israelite priesthood consecration ceremony and discover some examples of Satan's counterfeiting God's ways.

Special Garments

God instructed Moses to make special garments for the priests:

> Make sacred garments for your brother Aaron, to give him dignity and honor. Tell all the skilled men to whom I have given wisdom in such matters that they are to make garments for Aaron, for his consecration, so he may serve me as priest These are the garments they are to make: a breastpiece, an ephod, a robe, a woven tunic, a turban and a sash. They are to make these sacred garments for your brother Aaron and his sons, so they may serve me as priests. Have them use gold, and blue, purple and scarlet yarn, and fine linen. Make the ephod of gold, and of blue, purple and scarlet yarn, and of finely twisted linen—the work of a skilled craftsman. It is to have two shoulder pieces attached to two of its corners, so it can be fastened. Its skillfully woven waistband is to be like it—of one piece with the ephod and made with gold, and with blue, purple and scarlet yarn, and with finely twisted linen (Exod. 28:2-8, *NIV*).

In Santería, special garments are also made. During the first year of initiation, the devotees have to dress in white; and since their heads are shaved during initiation, their heads must be covered for the first three months. Later, the devotees will wear specific clothes that the masters (which are demons) prescribe.

Offerings

God required Moses to give an offering in order to consecrate the priests.

> This is what you are to do to consecrate them, so they may serve me as priests: Take a young bull and two rams without defect. And from fine wheat flour, without yeast, make bread, and cakes mixed with oil, and wafers spread with oil. Put them in a basket and present them in it—along with the bull and the two rams (Exod. 29:1-3, *NIV*).

Similarly, in Santería, a bull is offered to the orishas in order to initiate the babalawo (the higher position); but for the other positions, offerings of lambs, goats, roosters, hens, doves and dogs are given.

Cleansing and Dedication

This is how God told Moses to begin the consecration ceremony of the priests:

> Then bring Aaron and his sons to the entrance to the Tent of Meeting and wash them with water. Take the garments and dress Aaron with the tunic, the robe of the ephod, the ephod itself and the breastpiece. Fasten the ephod on him by its skillfully woven waistband. Put the turban on his head and attach the sacred diadem to the turban. Take the anointing oil and anoint him by pouring it on his head (Exod. 29:4-7, *NIV*).

Similar to the ceremony that God described to Moses, the Santería ceremony involves the devotees' being brought to the entrance of the place where the ceremony will take place. The devotees are then washed and dressed in their special garments. The difference between the two ceremonies is that in Santería the devotees are blindfolded.

A ceremony of dedication follows the cleansing bath; and the devotees, with eyes closed, are dedicated to each orisha in general, and specifically to the one that will "govern" his or her life. All chants are in Yoruba, an African dialect. The devotees never know what they are agreeing blindly and faithfully to do.

When the secret ceremony ends, the devotees open their eyes and, lying face down to the floor, bow first to the altar where all the stones and shells that represent the orishas are, and then to each of the santeros that participated in the ceremony. Then the sacrifices start.

Animal Sacrifice

Let's examine Satan's counterfeit of the sacrifice that God ordained. God's instructions to Moses were,

> Take one of the rams, and Aaron and his sons shall lay their hands on its head. Slaughter it and take the blood and sprinkle it against the altar on all sides. Cut the ram into pieces and wash the inner parts and the legs, putting them with the head and the other pieces. Slaughter it, take some of its blood and put it on the lobes of the right ears of Aaron and his sons, on the thumbs of their right hands, and on the big toes of their right feet. Then sprinkle blood against the altar on all sides. And take some of the blood on the altar and some of the anointing oil and sprinkle it on Aaron and his garments and on his sons and their garments. Then he and his sons and their garments will be consecrated (Exod. 29:15-17,20-21, *NIV*).

Through animal sacrifice, the priests were consecrated in service to the Lord. Santería devotees are initiated in a similar manner. First, the animals are brought into the ceremony room and presented to the devotees, who lay their hands on the heads of the animals as the priest prays in Yoruba. Once again, the devotees do not know what is being said nor the commitments they are making, but they agree with all that is spoken. Next, the devotees place their foreheads to the foreheads of the animals and touch their shoulders to the heads of the animals. Then the animals are slaughtered in the presence of all the orishas, or idols, that the person is going to receive. The blood is sprinkled on the altar (or throne, as it is called) and poured into bowls that contain the shells and stones representing the orishas. Each orisha has its own bowl, and specific animals are sacrificed to it. The santero who represents each devotee wets his index finger in the bowl and touches the devotee's forehead, hands and feet, and behind the ears. While the santero does this, all the santeros pray a prayer in Yoruba.

God's instructions to Moses continue like this:

> Take from this ram the fat, the fat tail, the fat around the inner parts, the covering of the liver, both kidneys with the fat on them, and the right thigh. (This is the ram for the ordination.) From the basket of bread made without yeast, which is before the LORD, take a loaf, and a cake made with oil, and a wafer. Put all these in the hands of Aaron and his sons and wave them before the LORD as a wave offering. Then take them from their hands and burn them on the altar along with the burnt offering for a pleasing aroma to the LORD, an offering made to the LORD by fire (Exod. 29:22-25, *NIV*).

Very similar to the dedication of the Israelite priests, in Santería, after the sacrificed animals are cleaned, the fat of the tail, the fat around the inner parts, the liver, the heart, the kidneys, and the left and right thighs are given to the devotee and presented at the altar, along with a basket of bread.

A Portion for the Priest

In the Israelite ordination ceremony, a portion of the sacrifice was given to the people who led the ceremony. Here are God's words to Moses:

> After you take the breast of the ram for Aaron's ordination, wave it before the LORD as a wave offering, and it will be your share. Consecrate those parts of the ordination ram that belong to Aaron and his sons: the breast that was waved and the thigh that was presented. This is always to be the regular share from the Israelites for Aaron and his sons. It is the contribution the Israelites are to make to the LORD from their fellowship offerings (Exod. 29:26-28, *NIV*).

In Santería, the sacrificed animals are cooked, and the initiate has to eat the food in the company of the other priests who participated in the ceremony. More food is then prepared for the big celebration that takes place three days later. At that time, all the santeros, families and friends are invited to feast. The portion given to the santero is not only part of the sacrificed animals but also a sum of money that has been agreed upon before hand. Today this amount is usually between $5,000 and $15,000.

As we have seen, the biblical ceremonies and those in Santería are very similar. God directed the former by His holy Word, which Satan copycatted in the Santería ceremony. I believe that when this initiation ceremony is performed, Satan is very happy, because he desperately desires to be worshiped in place of God.

I have made these comparisons so that you can see the deception that is practiced in Santería. There is a great difference between having your fortune read, with the accompanying simple payment, and asking for help for a personal situation and becoming an initiate to help resolve the problem. It is a very serious thing to ask information or help of priests of Santería, because the whole system is built on satanic lies designed to imitate God's system and to lead the requester deep into bondage.

I was a priestess for many years (even though I never sponsored anyone for initiation). Because of my experience, I can testify that the moment people sit across the table from a santero to have the shells read, they begin to invite in and ask for a master other than Jesus. Though they can't understand the prayers that are being prayed by the santero in the Yoruba dialect, they accept and promise to follow, obey and comply with anything the santero says, which leads to their total domination by the orisha demon that works though the santero. They are caught in a trap from which there seems to be no escape—and no other choice.

The moment you sit across the table from a santero to have the shells read, you begin to invite in and ask for a master other than Jesus.

Ministering Deliverance

When ministering deliverance to people who have been involved in Santería, I always ask how deep their involvement was. If they have gone just once for a reading, I make sure that they confess, renounce their promises and ask forgiveness for accepting a master besides Jesus.

If they have been deeply involved, I break any spirit of control, submission, dependence, lust, homosexuality (this cult is full of homosexuals), slavery, poverty, financial loss, broken families, divorce, loneliness and abandonment. Then I have them destroy all objects that they have kept from the ceremonies.

You may be wondering, *Why take such extreme measures?* In order to free themselves from the bondage that they enter into when they devote themselves to the orisha demons. When they answer yes to domination by the orisha, they accept all of these evil spirits. All the prayers may be in a dialect that they do not understand. Nevertheless, they are promising all of their lives, families, finances and faithfulness to the demonic orisha. We shouldn't be surprised, because this is the kind of worship and obeisance that Satan demands from his followers.

At the beginning of involvement, the devotees may begin to prosper. But as they get deeper into the ceremonies, they "grow" within the scale of authority. As they are initiated into higher positions, the ceremonies—and the "help"—become more and more expensive.

Eventually they start spending all their finances on sessions with the santero. When they have lost almost everything, they find themselves with more needs to resolve but no more money to pay for ceremonies or readings. And then they find out that no money means no "help."

The trap becomes deep and dark. This was my case—and the case of so many of the followers that I knew at the time. They lost their businesses or their good jobs, and those dealing with drugs were apprehended and taken to jail. The favor of the orishas lasts only as long as the money flows.

Escaping Santería

In order for people to escape from the bondage of Santería—whether they only went for a reading or whether they advanced to higher levels of initiation—they should follow three simple steps:

1. They need to confess their involvement in ungodly ceremonies, renounce their promises to orishas and ask forgiveness for accepting a master other than Jesus.
2. They need to get rid of any objects connected with their participation. If they have been given a piece of jewelry (an object that has been consecrated in a ceremony with a blood sacrifice), they should either destroy the object or take it to a jeweler to have it melted down and designed as something else. It is necessary to destroy such sacrificial dedications with fire.

   If they have received *collares*, necklaces, they can just cut them up and throw them in the garbage. Shells can be smashed with a hammer until they are broken and then thrown away. Porcelain objects also must be smashed. Metal objects should be placed in a safe container and burned using rags and charcoal fluid, or paint thinner if necessary. When the material has cooled, the remains should be thrown into the garbage. *Under no circumstances should the people seeking deliverance return anything to the santero who gave it to them.*

3. They need to seek deliverance with a ministry that knows about witchcraft. They will need to learn how to stand against the attacks of the enemy, because he will attack them—trust me. Their health and finances will be the primary targets, but if they trust the Lord, they will be victorious.

The morning after I accepted Jesus as my Lord and Savior, I disposed of all that I had received during 20 years of priesthood. Within a week, the santeros sent someone to tell me that the orishas, or idols, spoke in the previous night's ceremony, saying that I would be dead in three months. But I believed that Jesus was stronger. I accepted Jesus in March of 1983, and I'm still alive! The power of the Holy Spirit is certainly far greater than that of our enemy.

I praise the Lord and thank Him for His forgiveness, deliverance and healing (healing not only of my body but of the wounds of my soul from childhood to adulthood as well). I have no words to describe the freedom, and especially the peace, that Jesus has brought into my life. I daily enjoy His peace and presence. I am so grateful that He delivered me from the satanic religion of Santería.

Because of His great mercy, He has chosen me to help others also find His freedom and peace. I now have the great privilege to lead a ministry of personal deliverance called Fountain of Freedom Ministries. Praise God for His everlasting faithfulness!

Chapter 25

THERE'S NOTHING NEW ABOUT NEW AGE

Chris Hayward

I was 14 years old and spiritually hungry. Our family had left Canada for California only three years earlier. Our stay in Canada had been an unplanned, four-year stopover after leaving our homeland of England. My parents had joined a Community Church in Lakewood. For me it was a spiritual wasteland. While it possessed all the markings of a "house of the Lord," it had none of its characteristics (although I must admit, I was not able to identify truth from error at this point in my life).

All I knew was that there was more to life than the "natural" universe. I was on a search, but I could not tell you exactly what I was searching *for*. I wanted something or someone to explain why I was here—and if there was a purpose to my existence. In church I sang hymns and listened to sermons that seemed to have no relevance. The Word of God was unknown to me and disregarded by the pastor and his followers. So I began my quest to obtain some meaning to life. I began to read everything available about spirituality.

Looking back, I can tell you that in the absence of truth, the spirit of error will find a way to captivate the "open-minded." My mind was open, and the enemy of my soul purposed to fill it with whatever would lure me away from God.

Standing in the wings of every yearning soul is the kingdom of darkness. Like a vulture circling its prey, it is ready and willing to devour *those to whom the Church should be reaching out.* In the absence of truth, lies will flourish. I bought into these lies with great abandon. What I embraced was everything that is espoused by the New Age movement. Of course, in 1960, the term "New Age" had not yet been popularized.

What Is Meant by "New Age"?

"New Age" is actually a catchall phrase. This term was first made popular by Alice Bailey, who, in the 1930s, founded an offshoot of the Theosophical Society (which had begun in New York in 1875 under the leadership of the Russian-born occultist H. P. Blavatsky). In 1960 the term "New Age" again became popular with the rise of Baba Ram Dass (alias Richard Alpert) and others as it became identified with the coming "Age of Aquarius." It was said that humanity would finally "come of age." Such ideas as "new world order," "peace and harmony," "higher or cosmic consciousness" and "universal love" became popular.

At that time in America many people rejected materialism and science. Institutions that seemed to have no relevance to the meaning of life or exhibited nothing of power or fulfillment were cast aside. Unfortunately, Christianity seemed to fall into that category—"having a form of godliness, but denying the power thereof" (2 Tim. 3:5, *KJV*).

In the midst of such a void many people became attracted to spiritualism and the Theosophical Society. Soon there were many offshoots. Drawn into the vortex were Christian mystics, Jewish Cabalists and previously obscure Christian heretics. Gurus appeared from the East. Zen Buddhism and Sufism became popular, which prepared the ground for the Dalai Lama. Parapsychology flourished, along with channeling, mediums, paganism and Wicca (witchcraft).

The Core of New Age

Although years have passed since its birth in American, the core beliefs of the New Age have not changed. These core beliefs include reincarnation, spiritual evolution, self-realization, self-improvement or spiritual healing (this form of spiritual healing cannot be confused with the Christian approach of dependence on the Holy Spirit). Many New Age beliefs made their way into major corporations through self-help gurus and motivational speakers who sought to assist key personnel to become motivated and fulfilled. Other widely embraced avenues of New Age thought are matriarchal forms of religious thinking such as the Mother-Goddess concept and a female priesthood. Even much of the interest in extraterrestrial beings has its roots in New Age beliefs. So-called encounters of the third kind always seem to accompany New Age philosophies and doctrine.

Encounters of the third kind always seem to accompany New Age philosophies and doctrine.

Sir George Trevelyan is a well-known English leader of the New Age movement. He is the founder of the Wrekin Trust, a New Age center. He sums up his New Age worldview in *A Vision of the Aquarian Age:* "Behind all outwardly manifested form is a timeless realm of absolute consciousness. It is the great Oneness underlying all the diversity, all the myriad forms of nature. It may be called God, or may be deemed beyond all naming. . . . The world of nature, in short, is but a reflection of the eternal world of Creative imagining. The inner core of man, that which in each of us might be called spirit, is a droplet of the divine source. As such, it is imperishable and eternal, for life cannot be extinguished. The outer sheath in which it manifests can, of course, wear out and be discarded; but to speak of 'death' in relation to the true being and spirit of man is irrelevant."[1] Strongly suggested in this quote is the most popular belief within the New Age movement: reincarnation.

Sir George goes on to this: "The soul belongs properly to higher and purer spheres. It incarnates for the purpose of acquiring experience in the density of earth matter—a necessary educational phase in its development. Such incarnation, of course, entails drastic limitation of a free spiritual being. Birth into a body is, in fact, more like entry into a species of tomb."[2]

He explains his reasoning as follows: "More precisely, we must recognize man as a threefold being of body, soul and spirit. . . . The immortal 'I' is neither the soul nor the transient personality. In order to descend into the density of the phenomenal world, it must clothe itself, so to speak, in a protective sheath. The 'soul' is therefore the sheath or 'astral body,' which the eternal 'I' draws about it in order to experience the psychological level of reality. (It also draws around itself an 'atheric' body of vital forces to hold together the physical body.)"[3]

As you probably observed in these quotes, some New Age terminology sounds similar to Christian terminology. For example, the terms "body," "soul" and "spirit" are used by Christians and New Agers alike. The difference, however, is the definition ascribed to each. So, while most Christians will consider the language used in these quotes to be hogwash, people outside the Body of Christ who are seeking something profoundly meaningful, unable to discern deception, may find this rhetoric appealing.

A Personal Quest for Identity and Ability

Let me give you an example. In 1964, I joined the Army. My basic training took place at Ft. Polk, Louisiana. After that, I received specialized training at Ft. Benjamin Franklin in Indianapolis, Indiana. I was trained as a personnel specialist. Within a few weeks, my orders sent me to White Sands Missile Range, New Mexico. My basic duties were simple enough, and I was enjoying other activities as well. I had begun flight training prior to joining the Army and found a way to continue it at White Sands. I had also landed a job at the base pool as a lifeguard during the summer months.

Life was pretty good—until I received new orders. It seemed that I was about to be transferred to an outpost in the middle of the desert, away from all my enjoyable activities. I couldn't allow this to happen. Knowing that the base chaplain needed an assistant, I set out to fool him with spiritual lingo and thereby convince him I would make an excellent assistant—thus getting my orders changed, which would allow me to stay at White Sands.

The chaplain was convinced of my spirituality—so much for discernment—and he then convinced the general to have my orders changed. When questioned about my faith in Christ, I simply converted the terminology to my own understanding. I knew the intent of the questioner, but I simply justified my response on the basis of my "superior understanding." Such pride is commonplace among New Age devotees.

The reason for this is quite simple—and understanding why enables us to share our faith effectively: *Those caught up in New Age teaching have an insatiable appetite to know their value as individuals and to find fulfillment.* They do so by discovering their personal identity and their purpose for being born. Those who are articulate, exhibit personal confidence and claim to possess particular powers have an immediate following. I found that whenever I was around others in this field, I felt an underlying pressure to impress them with what I knew or could do.

Of course, the hunger for identity is remedied in the foundation of the gospel: "For God so loved the world that He gave His only begotten Son, that whoever believes in Him should not perish but have everlasting life" (John 3:16). The fact that Christ died for us gives us amazing joy as we realize the enormous value He places upon us. How can we not feel great about Someone who cares enough to be tortured and murdered for our sakes?

Our identity and fulfillment are further emphasized throughout the first chapter of Ephesians: "Blessed be the God and Father of our Lord Jesus Christ, who has blessed us with every spiritual blessing in the heavenly places in Christ (Eph. 1:3)." Not only has our heavenly Father established our identity in Him, but now He has also piled up every blessing imaginable and freely given them to us. Now that is *identity* fulfilled and *purpose* realized!

New Age Understanding of Christ

As a New Age disciple, I was proud and arrogant and absolutely convinced that what I believed was right. I would have died for it. I had a counterfeit term for just about every biblical term or phrase. Jesus Christ was savior, inasmuch as He came to enlighten those who were less spiritually aware. He was a master of the highest plane, having gone through the required reincarnations. Though not God, He was godlike, but not totally unique. There were other "masters." If a Christian spoke about Christ, I would automatically think about "Christ-consciousness," the higher plain of understanding, which enveloped and influenced the "enlightened."

It is hard to convince New Agers who are as convinced as I was; they will just patronize you if you attempt to witness to them. They'll nod kindly as you speak, having assessed that you are simply an immature child in your spiritual growth and thinking that you still have many more reincarnations to go through before you will be able to understand the deeper truths.

The god worshiped by those involved in the New Age movement is themselves. Christ is seen as being within each and every person, though not perhaps recognized. To many New Age authors, "the Christ" who spoke through Jesus of Nazareth was the highest of true teachers. In a work called *Esoteric Christianity*, Annie Besant writes, "The historical Christ, then, is a glorious Being belonging to the great spiritual hierarchy that guides the spiritual evolution of humanity, who used for some three years the human body of the disciple Jesus, . . . who drew men to Him by the singular love and tenderness, and the rich wisdom that breathed from His Person; and who was finally put to death for blasphemy, for teaching the inherent Divinity of Himself and of all men."[4]

And so New Age disciples have not read nor understood the Gospel of John, which makes clear the truth of the Incarnation: "In the beginning was the Word, and the Word was with God, and the Word was God. He was in the beginning with God. All things were made through Him, and without Him nothing was made that was made. In Him was life, and the life was the light of men" (John 1:1-4).

How Should Christians Respond?

New Age teachers think nothing of reinventing the Scriptures. Very few of them have even read the Word of God. Most have read a little and taken the meanings out of context, or they have taken what they believe Scripture says and twisted it out of proportion. Those who read the writings of such teachers know even less. It is a fundamental fact that although those who are involved in the New Age purport to be open-minded, they are most definitely close-minded when it comes to historic Christianity.

As Christians we can respond in one of two ways. We can denounce such activity as being abhorrent to God and proclaim that New Age followers are destined for the eternal flames, or we can acknowledge the failure of the Church to recognize a legitimate hunger in the lives of searching souls.

Those who fall prey to New Age thinking in all its forms truly hunger to know the meaning of life, to have true power and to experience love in its deepest form. No one has the answer to these needs except God's people. Jesus Christ, raised from the dead by the power of the Holy Spirit, who is now given to us that we may know the width, the length, the height and the depth of God's love, is the answer. He alone can satisfy the longing of the New Ager.

Rather than looking askance at the followers of New Age, we can use their longing as a platform for evangelism. We should love them and not denounce them for searching for truth. Our challenge is to place the true light on Jesus, the lover of their souls.

The gospel demonstrated with power will place New Age beliefs where they belong—in the shadows of darkness. Why would anyone want to hug and kiss a shadow, if the real can be embraced?

My Emergence

I would like to end this chapter by sharing with you how I came to leave the New Age movement and to embrace Jesus Christ. Perhaps it will provide some understanding as to how we might help those caught up in New Age philosophy.

The last 18 months of my Army duty were spent in Vietnam (1967-68). Near the end of my duty there, I found myself in the home of a missionary. Paul Travis and his wife had been in Vietnam for over 42 years. They had been through the Japanese occupation, the French occupation and now the American occupation of this small but strategic country.

This godly couple had been instrumental in establishing a number of churches throughout the land. The husband was highly respected, and I was grossly ignorant. Although I was a chaplain's assistant, I was still as lost as a rock. Since the age of 14, my life's ambition had been wrapped up in the occult and I wanted to become a medium. Being fairly well versed in the "truths" of the New Age, I gave a lesson to Mr. Travis, thinking he could learn from my vast experience and knowledge.

For almost 30 minutes, he somehow endured my endless nonsense. I sat on his counter while he cut vegetables in his little home in Qui Nyon. I was giving him a lesson on reincarnation, the necessity of karma and spiritism, and teaching him all about the great teachers and thinkers of our time. Finally he'd had enough. He put known his knife, looked at me and said, "What a shame!" Shocked, I replied, "What do you mean, 'What a shame!'?" He simply responded, "You don't believe in a personal God, do you?" With one simple remark I was undone. No Scripture, no sermon—just one simple question.

For two weeks his words rocked me. All my life I had been yearning to know God. I knew there had to be something or Someone out there. From that moment of reckoning, I felt like a bucket full of holes, and whatever I tried to fill myself with quickly flowed out. The security of feeling like I had everything figured out evaporated. My head and my heart were corrupt, and I was empty inside.

Now sitting on a sandbag wall around the perimeter of the 504th Military Police Battalion where I was assigned, I was at the end of myself.

Despite my extensive pursuit of spirituality, I had never spoken with God before. And so it was that a sandbag became my altar.

My prayers up to that time had been all about myself, and I had done the talking. Now God had something to say to me. In the presence of His infinite holiness, a mirror was put up to my life. All the ugliness and falseness was there. My belief system was empty—it just wouldn't hold up under the strain of this life.

God gave me a choice that night: to embrace His Son, Jesus Christ, or to choose to forever walk the path I had been traveling. I recall running into the chapel tent, falling on my knees and crying out, "Jesus, Jesus." At the time, that was the depth of my theological understanding. But it was sufficient, "for whoever calls on the name of the LORD shall be saved" (Rom. 10:13).

I needed Jesus, and He came in. Then my Christian walk began. It took some time for many of the erroneous New Age teachings to fall away. But in time, and through the Word, they were quickly replaced.

There is hope for those entrapped by New Age thinking. With a loving approach, explaining that they can really know the love of God in a personal way, and through much prayer, they can be won for Christ.

Notes

1. Sir George Trevelyan, *A Vision of the Aquarian Age* (London: Coventure, 1977), pp. 5-6.
2. Ibid., p. 6.
3. Ibid.
4. Annie Besant, *Esoteric Christianity* (London: Theosophical Publishing Society, 1905), pp. 140-141.

Chapter 26

RESCUED FROM SATANISM

Jeff Harshbarger

With David the psalmist, I can proclaim, "I shall not die, but live, and declare the works of the LORD" (Ps. 118:17). The words that follow comprise my testimony of how the Lord saved me from death after my descent into Satanism.

I grew up in a military family. We moved a lot, and I mean a lot. Between the ages of 6 and 12, I moved—together with my family—five times. This type of lifestyle made it very difficult for me to have friends and establish any kind of positive roots.

My father came back from the Vietnam War a very different person from the man he was when he had left. He was thousands of miles away when I was a baby, so I never had a chance to bond with him. He returned very angry and began to drink heavily. This resulted in violence becoming a normal part of our family life. My parents fought, and I myself was physically and verbally abused. And as we moved from small town to small town, I felt the shame of being the town drunk's kid.

My First Encounter with Jesus Christ

By the time I was in third grade, the violence and abuse had taken their toll. I was not doing well in school. To sit in a classroom full of "normal" kids and to perform were just too much to expect of me, and I would just want to cry. I began to see a school therapist. It was then that I noticed that I was becoming as angry as my father.

During this time I also began to notice something about my life. It was something that was unexplainable. There were times when I would get up to go to the bathroom or to get a drink of water and I would feel a presence in my house. I didn't know what I was experiencing, but it was like something—or someone—was aware of me and was following me around. I wasn't fearful of the experience, though I simply did not know what to think about it.

Curiosity began to cause me to get up more frequently, just to see if the presence would be there. And it was. As this continued, I became more and more curious.

Near the end of the school year, I was invited to attend Vacation Bible School. I wasn't too excited about the idea, but my mother had found out about it, and she made sure that I attended the first day. Once I was there, I liked it. We had crafts, we ate cookies, and we had a story about Jesus. It didn't take long before I wanted to know this Man named Jesus. I accepted Him as my Savior and would pray to Him. I was given a Bible, but I did not know how to read it. It was very confusing to me. So I fostered my relationship with Him primarily through prayer. I went to church on my own for a short time, because my family wasn't attending. But when I did go to church, I just didn't connect with the church and no one was following up on me. So I quit going to church, but I would pray to Jesus before I went to sleep.

My Search in the Dark

I was in my bedroom one night by myself playing with a Ouija board and had the shock of my life! Thinking that this was just simply a game, I took the pointer and I began to ask the board questions. To my amazement the oracle moved by itself! I was scared to death, but I was thrilled at the reality of this happening. I knew at this point that there was a "power" behind what I had just experienced. And it immediately reminded me of my previous experience of a presence that was in my house. What was I on to? I had a million questions, and I wanted to know more.

With the desire to know more about the power behind the Ouija board and about the presence that I had experienced in my house, I opened the door for the dark supernatural to become a common occurrence.

I soon had an incredible experience when I astral projected into a house. Then I began to be able to see things in dreams—before they happened! For example, I had a dream that I saw through the wrapping on a Christmas gift. I knew what was in the present before I opened it! This just kept feeding my desire for more until I got to a point of experiencing the presence of demons and exhibiting my own supernatural abilities. I was very excited about all of this and began to pull away from my family and live in my own little world.

My Descent into Satanism

By high school, I was done with Jesus Christ. I had attempted to go to church, but it just wasn't working out for me. I had many supernatural experiences and I wanted to pursue finding out more about them. I was very aware of the media's coverage of Jeanne Dixon and Uri Gellar, and I thought, *I possess the same abilities as they do. Maybe I am a clairvoyant or have psychic abilities.*

It was during this time that my parents finally divorced. I thought that the divorce would bring peace to our home situation. At least there would not be constant fighting anymore. But the divorce only caused further isolation among the family members. In an attempt to find some stability in my life, I determined that I was going to pursue the abilities that I possessed. I was actually hoping that I could fine-tune my clairvoyant or psychic abilities and make a living at foretelling the future.

My mother received Jesus Christ as her Lord and Savior soon after her divorce, and it was then that our household environment changed. She began to attend church and pestered me ferociously to attend as well. I really wasn't interested, though. But my mom wouldn't give up that easily. She constantly played Christian music or television. She would have prayer in the kitchen with her friend before I would get out of bed for school. This was too much for me. I pulled away. I even watched a Christian show in order to tell the Lord that I wanted no part of Him.

I soon took a job at the local department store and met the man who would "evangelize" me and eventually lead me to Satanism. He was the associate manager of the store, and I found him to be very charismatic. He had an ability about him that I admired. I found myself wanting whatever he had to offer.

The offer to become a Satanist came one evening as I was working. We had experienced a snowfall that had rendered the roads impassable; as a result, there was no way for me to get home. And so the associate manager asked if I would like to stay in his apartment. I immediately took him up on his offer. When I went to his place, I recognized that he had the same presence in his apartment that I had experienced as a child. I was intrigued! I began to discuss with him the things of the supernatural; and he took over the conversation, which led to his inviting me to become a Satanist. I accepted. That evening I was filled with an unholy spirit through a satanic initiation ritual.

My Life as a Satanist

I immediately recognized a change after the night of my initiation. Within a very short time, I went from being a fearful, wallflower type personality to possessing a bold, commanding presence. I dressed for success and I knew that the earth was mine because I served the god of this world. We had a covenant—I would exchange my soul in return for his power and abilities.

It was my responsibility to offer myself to my new god as a living sacrifice and to be filled with his presence. I was to die to my nature in that

I was to die to what is human. I was to give over to Satan my need for love, and in exchange he would give me power. My heart was to die. This was the ultimate sacrifice demanded by Satan.

The demons that I had invited to possess me soon began to torment me. We were no longer walking in covenant, and they were looking to destroy me.

I began my walk in Satanism as a religious, rather than a philosophical, Satanist. This type of Satanism is referred to as modern Satanism and does not adhere to the belief in a real Satan. It holds to a satanic philosophy: self-deification through indulgence. The "scripture" for this ideology is the satanic Bible written by Anton Szandor LaVey. He began the move of modern Satanism in San Francisco in 1966. Because there are rituals and a belief system that this type of Satanism promotes, it is termed religious Satanism.

However, I was soon confounded in my walk as a Satanist. I began to change my perspective and practice from that of a philosophical Satanist to that of a traditional Satanist. Philosophical Satanism accepts the reality of Satan and demons. It is, in essence, devil worship. The basis of this type of Satanism is the exchange of one's soul through possession in exchange for demonic power.

I did not succeed in my Satanism. After several years as a Satanist, my heart was still alive, and my growth was hampered. I was told by my satanic mentor that I could not grow as a Satanist because I was "angelically oppressed." I had been, up to this point, serving the most powerful being I knew of. And yet, I was being told that there was a power that was stronger than what I was possessed by. I had to find out what this Higher Power was. And when I recognized that the Higher Power was Jesus Christ, I wanted no part of Him. I had been conditioned to hate the name of Jesus Christ.

Yet even as I rejected Jesus, I realized that everything that I had put my hope and heart into had failed me. I was being tormented by the absence of meaning and purpose. I had received no answers to the questions that I had in my life.

The demons that I had invited to possess me soon began to torment me. We were no longer walking in covenant, and they were looking to destroy me. It was at this point that I attempted suicide twice. I wanted to die. Death would come easily, or so I thought. I purchased my gun, took the usual means of sedating my fears—marijuana and whiskey—and headed for a place where I could finalize my ruin. I checked into a hotel room and smoked and drank myself to a place where I would have the nerve to pull the trigger. I wondered whether I would make the evening news. But as I sat there, I began to wrestle with the thought of this being the end.

When I put the barrel to my head, fear came to me. I wasn't afraid to die. I was afraid of where I would go after I died. So I didn't, or rather couldn't, pull the trigger. Again, I felt the failure of my life, even in my death.

With the realization of my desire to die being still unfulfilled, I attempted to destroy myself again the next afternoon. I took a rope and attempted to hang myself. I tied the rope over the garage rafter. I made sure that the knot was tight as I tied the other end around my neck. I felt as though I were ready. My issue with my eternal destiny was meaningless at this point.

I kicked the chair out from under my feet, expecting to experience the jerk of the rope on my neck. I found myself on the floor of my garage instead. I sat there wondering why I was not dead. How could I fail, again?

I was miserable. I had failed at suicide twice. Not only had I desired to die, I had also failed twice in fulfilling that desire. Was there a way out? What could or should I do at this point? I found myself struggling with a million new questions. *Where would I go to find the answers*? I needed a beer.

That evening, after failing at suicide for the second time, I thought I would try to drink myself into a stupor. However, I couldn't. Every time that I put the beer can to my lips, the smell of the alcohol nauseated me. This was highly unusual, since I had been a drinker for years.

I attempted to light a cigarette, but it would burn my lips and the smell was as bad as the beer. I attempted to smoke some marijuana in order to get a high that might curb my pain. But, just like the beer, the smell of the joint was nauseating. Nothing could sedate my condition. My old friends, alcohol and drugs, were suddenly inconsumable. I couldn't even smoke a cigarette. I was confused.

I went outside to clear my head. However, the questions were too strong. I couldn't die and I was not in my planned drunken stupor. I didn't want to feel what I was feeling at that point. I was unable to take my life, and I did not know what to do.

Then I thought that perhaps sleep would relieve my pain and confusion. I fell onto my bed, desiring only to close my eyes and sleep. As I lay there, I began to cry. All the years of my seeking answers had produced nothing. I had such a strong desire to die, and yet I had failed at this—not once but twice. Failure. All I felt was failure.

As I began to cry, I felt a tremendous relief in my tears. However, as I wept, I experienced something that I had not before. I heard a voice from the foot of my bed, demanding, "Get out!"

I immediately quit crying, expecting to see a demon appear in order to destroy me. I had attempted to kill myself and thought that I had angered the demonic host by my attempt to take my life.

Again the voice insisted "Get out!" However, this time I heard the voice from right beside my face. I did not hesitate to respond to what I was told. I got out of the room and went outside of my house. I actually stepped through my bedroom window so as not to delay a single moment. When I stepped outside, I experienced the presence of God. There was the presence of a Being more powerful than any I had ever met in all my years as a Satanist. But I somehow knew that this Being cared for me.

I fell on my face and began to weep. As I raised my head from my driveway, I asked Jesus Christ to make my life okay. I knew who it was that I was meeting. I knew at that moment that I was in the presence of Jesus Christ, and I just wanted Him to make my life okay.

I wasn't conscious of accepting Him as my Lord and Savior at that moment. I just needed Jesus to help me through that time in my life. When I asked for His help, He was there to give it. The same Jesus Christ whom I had walked away from numerous times before spoke to me in my despair.

A Very Present Help in Time of Need

Jesus Christ led me out of Satanism and led me to a small church so that I could find the help that I was so greatly in need of. I sat in the back row of a small church in Muncie, Indiana, in 1981, and listened to the first sermon of my life. It was after that service that a man by the name of Harry Richardson approached me. He asked me to dinner at his and his wife's home. I gladly accepted the invitation.

I sat down with Harry and Jo Richardson for dinner and for a night that would change my life. To this point, I still had the demons inside me, and they were still tormenting me. As I sat there, I was not sure how the evening was going to turn out. It went well. We talked in order to get to know one another, even though it was somewhat awkward. But soon, I was sharing with them that I had been involved in Satanism. Jo told me that I was in need of prayer. She began to pray, and I was delivered from the demons that had been tormenting me.

I immediately experienced a change when I knew they were gone. I ran to the nearest mirror and looked at the reflection of my real self for the first time in years. Since I had been initiated, I could only see the demons in me. It was good to see only me, and I smiled for the first time in years!

It was through Harry and Jo Richardson that I received the help to be delivered from the demons and the effects of my involvement in Satanism. They offered me the love that my heart was seeking, and I was counseled and discipled in the Word of God. I thank God that He led me to individuals who knew how to be used by Him in the area of deliverance.

There is a way out of Satanism. I was so glad when I found that way. The Bible is true when it says Jesus is the way, the truth and the life (see John 14:6). I will forever be grateful for His mercy toward me and for His incredible love for me.

Chapter 27

OUT OF THE DARK PRISON OF VOODOO

Ana Méndez Ferrell

What happened one night when I was 13 years old is an experience I will never forget—nor stop pondering the significance of, even years later. I was in my bedroom preparing for a final exam. As I sat studying, something began to distract me. I felt a powerful, supernatural force drawing me toward my window. Despite the cloudy darkness of the night sky, I saw a spectacular, bright light shining through. It resembled a gigantic star. As I intently pondered what it could be, the light suddenly broke away, pierced through my window and filled my room with a dazzling splendor. I fell to the floor unable to move. All I could do was weep as an indescribable love and infinite goodness surrounded me. This presence caused me to feel filthy and insignificant, yet blessed beyond anything I could have imagined.

Suddenly, I was not able to see any of my surroundings as they were. My eyes only saw the Lord Jesus in all of His majesty! Christ Himself had come to visit with me! I awkwardly wrote down what He spoke to me. I do not know how many hours went by as little by little the vision began to vanish. I found myself on the floor, soaked in tears and holding a piece of paper that said, "I am your Lord, Jesus Christ, and I have come to tell you that, in time, I will make Myself known to you. You will be My servant, and I will come to you through a man with blue eyes."

From that moment on, I fell deeply in love with Jesus, and I began a desperate search to find God and to serve Him. Having been raised as a Catholic, I started my quest in the Roman Catholic Church, but I only found emptiness. For me, the rituals sorely lacked the presence of the supernatural, majestic God for whom I was looking.

The Path to the Occult

In Mexico, where I grew up, I never heard of any kind of church other than Roman Catholic. This gave the devil an opportunity to drive me into a horrendous snare and into the paths of the occult. My thirst for a kingdom of invisible power coming from God, my brokenhearted youth and my ignorance of the ways of the Lord were the perfect ingredients for Satan to trap my soul.

My Search for Power

Disappointed by the powerlessness I found in Catholicism, I made my way into Eastern religions. I wanted to find Jesus no matter what it took, and these philosophies speak about an avatar named Jesus, an anointed spirit that visited the earth in the form of Buddha, Krishna and others. So I gave it a try, in the only way I know how to do things—totally sold out. But after two years of yoga and meditation, I realized that the marvelous Jesus who once visited me was not in the Eastern philosophies either. Nevertheless, those practices were the first step the devil used to create a fascination in me for the unknown, for the mysteries of the universe and for the search for the occult—the ways of the so-called Great Universal Mind.

Shortly after I left Eastern religious practices, I was introduced to a man who is best described as a powerful warlock, a shaman and a master of the occult. He was known as an enlightened one, one of the few chosen who could enter into the realm of the spirit and have contact with the gods.

Talking to this man was very appealing. He spoke of God, the universe, magical powers and magical worlds in a way that left me speechless. As his words came out of his mouth, a seducing spirit captured my soul. I was caught in something so powerful that it created the desire in me to be part of it. Then this man opened a Bible and read to me John 3. He said, "You must be born again in order to enter the kingdom of God," which he then explained is the kingdom of magic, where all things are possible. Satan's arrow pierced my soul at that moment, and I fell into the web that drove me into the depths of the kingdom of darkness.

The Prison of Voodoo

A couple of weeks later, I was initiated into voodoo magic, through the traditional "initiatrix death." The initiation ceremony, based mostly on the animal sacrifices recorded in the book of Leviticus, called for the one being initiated to be bathed in blood, which represented atoning blood.

After a series of rituals, I found myself outside of my body, floating in the middle of the room.[1] I watched as a series of demonic beings entered my body. When my spirit returned to my body, I felt as if a fully charged, high-voltage battery had jolted me. After the ceremony drew to a close, I was no longer myself. My soul was in covenant with the devil and under the power of a force that would guide my steps in the world of the occult. I had been terribly deceived.

That is when my work with the warlock began. We did witchcraft, read cards and initiated others whenever possible. The warlock insisted that we were practicing white magic and that our alliance was only with spirits of light, who came from beautiful saints and virgins and whose mission was to help us in our daily walk on Earth. Little by little I realized that this was not true, but the phrase that echoed within me was "Once you enter into this path, there is no way out."

The spirit voices within me were becoming clearer as time went on. These spirits were powerful and had the ability to heal the sick and perform deliverance (which was deceitful, because we would pull out one spirit only to replace it with another). The people who were delivered left rejoicing, believing that they were free, but the spirits that were "cast out" of them eventually returned and took revenge against them.

As I ascended to higher levels of the occult, the devil began to manifest himself just as he was, rather than as the beautiful being he had pretended to be.

I walked farther and farther into the deepest prisons of voodoo magic. I developed a thirst for blood and enjoyed animal sacrifices. The power that was exuded as the animals died was like a drug to me. As I grew in knowledge and ascended to higher levels of the occult, the devil began manifesting himself just as he was, rather than as the beautiful being he had pretended to be in the beginning. I was in tyranny, forced to obey at any price. My home was completely bewitched. I spent endless nights terrorized by spirits that were assigned to torture me to exhaustion.

On the other hand, I was favored with fame, money and influential friends. By the time I achieved the level of priestess in voodoo magic, I had the authority to ask for whatever I needed for my works of magic. It was then that I began to notice that there were some things the devil simply could not do. All the power he boasted about had limits. There were places he could not go and people he couldn't touch, no matter how many sacrifices or ceremonies we performed. I became very angry with him when I understood that he was not able to make good on all his claims of power.

Impending Death

When the devil realized that I knew the truth about his weaknesses and the limitations of his power, he decided to kill me. This he made clear to me one day when one of his emissaries announced to me, "I come to claim what belongs to me. I am coming for you; your time has come."

That year was filled with horrific, deadly attacks against me. The first came during a prayer journey in El Salvador, where part of my family lives. I fell seriously ill with pneumonia and needed to be hospitalized. While I was there, the city was attacked and a bomb exploded right next to the hospital where I was staying. Soon after, while I was visiting Los Angeles, two men assaulted me at gunpoint. Their intentions were to rape and kill me, but I now know that God's hand was on me. They beat me up and left me in the street, but strangely nothing further happened. A few months later, the assailants were caught and imprisoned for having killed seven other people in that same neighborhood.

Shortly after the attack, a gas tank in my apartment caught fire. I put it out with a blanket and my body, while I heard the devil scream, "You are going to die." Then, Mexico City's terrible earthquake hit, killing over 30,000 people. My apartment was located in the disaster zone, where hundreds of buildings were demolished. While I was trying to rescue people trapped alive in the rubble, the building exploded, and my body was expelled. Even so, the fire did not touch me. I once again experienced God's hand over my life.

The devil's voice became increasingly stronger and more frequent, "I have come for you; you belong to me, and you are going to die." My nerves, along with the demons tormenting me, were destroying me. My health began to fail, and I suffered strong nervous breakdowns. I decided to fly to Puerto Rico for a rest; in Puerto Rico a torrential storm destroyed a nearby mountain. Once again, I was surrounded by corpses and by those crushed by rubble.

I suffered a partial facial palsy because of my deteriorating psychological condition. I experienced extreme pain for an entire year and finally understood how the soul becomes anesthetized when suffering takes you to your breaking point. The devil took me into the deepest chambers of hell, where I saw lost souls beaten and burned to their executioners' joy. I knew the true meaning of darkness, where there is no longer a single ray of hope, nor escape from oppression, loneliness or sadness.

I went back to Mexico in an attempt to stop the torment, but I ended up far from the peace I sought. The demons that had been tormenting me turned their power against me to kill me once and for all. There was a fierce battle within me that lasted until I, unable to bear it any longer, attempted to take my life by slitting my veins.

I lost a lot of blood by the time my twin sister found me and took me to the hospital. While I was in the emergency room, battling between life and death, the unexpected happened. A glorious presence started descending over me. It was the same light I had seen so many years earlier, when Jesus first visited me in my room. I then heard an audible voice say to me, "Your heavenly Father is not going to abandon you." Sleep finally overcame me as the strong sedatives that were administered to me took effect.

The Start of Feedom

I woke up 48 hours later in the psychiatric wing of the hospital—a remote building with security bars and mentally ill patients. I was one of these patients and still in extremely poor condition. After several medical evaluations, the doctor determined that my prognosis was very serious and that I would certainly remain in the hospital for a long time. But God's plans were different. Several days later, my beloved aunt Gloria Capriles came to see me. She was a beautiful, sweet lady full of love and compassion. She told me there was a man who had changed her life and she wanted to bring him to see me. I agreed, more out of curiosity than faith.

The next day she walked in with a Christian pastor. His eyes were a striking blue. I listened attentively as he presented the message of salvation. I knew what he was saying was true. Nonetheless, my reaction was to weep bitterly in intense sadness. "This is a terrible thing you are preaching," I told him. "I know everything you are saying is true, but I am unable to run to Jesus. I have made unbreakable covenants, and if I try to break them, the devil's wrath will come on me."

In that moment of deep despair, the minister interrupted me by saying, "That's not true! The Word of God says, 'If we confess our sins, He is faithful and just to forgive us our sins and to cleanse us from all unrighteousness' [1 John 1:9]. The blood of Jesus breaks every covenant! Jesus, our Lord, died for you to deliver you from the devil's chains!"

His words shook me, and the Holy Spirit began a deep work in my soul. "What must I do to receive Jesus in my heart," I asked through my tears, with a deep longing for my beloved Jesus to put an end to the nightmare.

"Repent and ask Him to live in your heart. Tell Him you want to make Him your Lord and Savior."

When I did, the Holy Spirit came on me with such conviction of sin that I broke down in a mixture of pain and shame. My conscience was being purged as I poured my soul out to God and begged for mercy. It was during that deep and sincere prayer that God removed the deception and I was able to clearly see how the devil had ensnared me. After that time of confession, the minister prayed for my deliverance from the demons that had held me in their grasp. At that moment, I felt as if lightning had fallen from heaven and broke the chains that held me captive. As the demons fled, joy and peace filled my heart, and I was convinced that Jesus had totally set me free.

My Declaration of War

During the days I spent in the hospital, God's presence was extremely powerful in my life. The first thing the Holy Spirit told me was to not even think of turning back in the slightest, because the enemy was furious with me because of the decision I had made to follow Christ. Far from being frightened by this, I was filled with a divine zeal. I decided to declare war against the enemy until the end. I wanted to snatch back every soul I could. I vowed to deliver the captives and serve the Lord with all my heart; I have been doing so ever since.

What Is the Draw into the Occult?

In my deliverance ministry, I have found that no matter what type of occult activity an individual has been involved in, the battle against demonic influences is tremendous, and the demonization can be quite severe. Because I was so bound, and by God's grace have been set free, I want to share the wisdom I have gleaned in understanding the path to total victory.

First, it may be helpful to understand what causes people to become susceptible to becoming ensnared by the occult. This helps us understand how best to minister to the whole person as these people emerge from Satan's grasp.

1. *Everyone involved in the occult suffers from deep rejection.* Rejection is the number one cause of occult involvement. A broken home, the lack of true fatherhood, all types of abuse during childhood, the early death of one or both parents, or any traumatic experience can be the cause of a deep feeling of rejection. Rejection leaves individuals longing for acceptance and significance. Satan will deceive them into believing that following his paths will provide them with both.
2. *Those involved in the occult are generally hooked into Satan's lies through a lack of identity.* Everyone needs to have an identity. Identity is the understanding of who we are, what our destiny is and what our function in this life is. Of course, God created us to have our identity in Him. But because of sin, abuse or lack of understanding, we often do not look to God for our identity. Instead, we tend to strive to be accepted by others, to be respected, to "be somebody." The cry of many souls is, "Somebody please tell me I'm worthy."

   This ties back to rejection. When people are rejected, the need for—but lack of—true identity grows stronger. They may begin looking for identity in money and possessions or in fame and power.

   The devil is looking for people who have been rejected and to whom he can promise a source of identity. He sends one of his messengers, who whispers promises such as "You are a chosen one" or "You have such unique powers; you are not like all the common people" or "You are the perfect candidate to receive all the power of the universe—you will know the future; you will have power to heal; you will master the destinies of others." What attractive promises these are to people who have been rejected and who have no identity!

3. *Inner anger is a driving force.* Here is an important truth to understand: The devil needs anger and hatred and envy to energize his demonic power. That is why James states this in his epistle: "But if you harbor bitter envy and selfish ambition in your hearts, do not boast about it or deny the truth. Such 'wisdom' does not come down from heaven but is earthly, unspiritual, of the devil. For where you have envy and selfish ambition, there you find disorder and every evil practice" (3:14-16, *NIV*).

   As long as these sins remain in the heart, the devil has a major grip that allows him to torment and beat people down into deep places of anguish, depression and despair. Those who have been tormented by demons tend to throw themselves into the pit of desolation. There is so much anger and vengeance within them that they tend to punish themselves in order to relieve the inner valves of pain. Demons love this self-destructive cycle and gladly oblige these tormented souls, drawing them even further into Satan's grip.

4. *Satan uses imagination that is mixed with reality.* Those involved in the occult give the enemy a lot of ground in their minds. It is there that he builds his master structures, where he can use these people for his evil plans. I call it the twilight zone. This is an area in the mind somewhere between the conscience and the subconscious, between the real and the unreal world, between reality and imagination.

   People who are involved in the occult have amazing experiences in their own spirits as well as in the realm of imagination. These experiences are so real that the person can no longer tell the difference between what really happened and what was just a deep trip into the imagination.

This is so important to deal with when helping people emerge from the occult, otherwise the devil will devastate them with fearful and horrifying imaginations and dreams. For true deliverance to occur, they need to renounce the power that they gave the devil to operate in and from their minds.

How to Free Captive Souls

Whether you are one who is emerging from the occult or one who has been called to set these captives free, here are some important steps along the path to freedom:

1. *Truthfully encounter the sacrifice of Christ.* A true encounter with the sacrifice of Christ is the most powerful and, in fact, the only source of deliverance and salvation. This encounter is a confrontation between the sinful nature, the dark and filthy state of the soul, and the terribly painful sacrifice of Christ on our behalf. We cannot be called Christians, followers of Jesus, if we do not understand that each and every one of our sins bruised, chastised and nailed Him to the cross. We crucified Christ. We can avoid this encounter, but salvation and deliverance start with it.

   Salvation occurs when we respond, with our entire bodies, souls and spirits, to what Jesus did for us. When we can see our filthiness before His purity, our shame before His perfect love, then and only then can our lives be changed. The Cross has to have a weight in our hearts that will enable us to live for it and through it. This is what delivered me—and anyone who encounters it.
2. *Truly repent from occult involvement.* True repentance is not an option. It is the primary foundation of deliverance. In addition to repenting for our individual actions, we must repent

for having been servants of Satan and for having made Satan our father, instead of making God our Father. All sins, not just practicing the occult, make us servants of Satan. And living sinful lives makes Satan our father. We all have to really gain an understanding of this if we want to succeed in our freedom. And we need to hate that condition with every cell of our bodies.

3. *Want deliverance with the whole heart.* Unfortunately, because of ignorance, many people masochistically enjoy the torment of demons. By always being the victims, they are able to control other people by drawing attention to themselves and evoking their sympathy. People who do this have never made God the true center and the number one focus in their lives. They are totally centered on themselves. Whatever happens to them takes on paramount importance.

   They ignore the fact that by doing that, they will never be delivered and they will always serve Satan in his purposes of making everybody around them miserable. They have to desire deliverance with their whole heart, loving God and loving the people around them.

   The devil will always try to attack the children of God. He comes to steal, to kill and to destroy every child of God, not only those who once served him through the occult (see John 10:10). But God has put in each and every one of us divine anger. This is the very wrath of God to despise and destroy every work of the enemy. We need to learn to cast him out with divine anger once and for all.

4. *Confess and break all covenants made with the devil.* Confessing sins to one another is essential for deliverance. James 5:16 reads, "Confess your faults to one another, and pray one for another, that ye may be healed" (*KJV*).

   General confessions to God in privacy don't work for deliverance from the occult. It is crucial that those involved in the occult confess their sins to another in as much detail as possible. They need to ask the Holy Spirit to help them remember every time they asked a favor from a deity in the occult and every time they paid someone to do a "work." This may take some time, but it will help leave no stone unturned.

Then, once these have been confessed, they need to do these things: break the covenants; cancel the works; renounce and cast out every deity; break soul and spirit ties with every ceremony and every person who performed the ceremony; and burn every object, garment, piece of jewelry or idol that was used to participate in these ceremonies.

5. *Renounce the deities of voodoo.* If there has been specific involvement in voodoo, they need to renounce Legbas or Elegua, Yemaya or Erzulli, Obatala, Shango, Dambalah, Ochung, Ogun, Orula, Olofi, Olla, all "Loas" (voodoo spirits), and all the spirits of the dead that work along with them.

My life is a testimony. I stand as someone who has been completely freed from the occult. The Son of Man came to destroy all the works of the enemy, and He is still able to do so, if you allow Him to do it in your life.

The anointing of the Lord God is on Jesus to set the captives free. My prayer is that these words, joined with His mighty presence, will help you to come out from the horrible bondages of evil that you may be under. It *is* possible. I am God's witness of His amazing grace and power, and I will live to the very last day of my life committed to destroy the works of the devil.

To God be the glory for the magnificent salvation He performed in my life! He can do the same for you!

Note

1. These initiation rituals are described more fully in my book *High Level Warfare.*

Appendix

HOW TO CONDUCT A DELIVERANCE SESSION

Doris M. Wagner

Let me share from my experience some pointers on preparing to minister deliverance to someone. I will comment on a number of items.

Getting Ready

You are the deliverance leader of the session. Please keep in mind that of primary importance is your own spiritual preparation and condition. Above all else, do not attempt deliverance on someone else if there are demonic footholds in your own life. Demons seem to know when the person who is counseling and praying has "critters" hanging on to him or her. That could prove embarrassing to everyone because the demons you are working to expel might just tell you so.

Therefore, you must be free from demonic presence in your own life. You must be living a pure life with no known sin lurking anywhere. That gives you a "right" to minister to the life of another person and assures you of the authority to do it in the name of Jesus.

You need to be "prayed up." Ask the Lord for His special help and guidance as you look over the questionnaire [see chapters 9 through 14 and appendix 3 in *How to Cast Out Demons*] and pray for wisdom, discernment and compassion to minister effectively.

I usually fast on the day of a deliverance. As I look into the practice of other deliverance ministers, I find that some do and some don't. Those who do deliverance on a daily basis need to eat sometime. I am able to do it only occasionally at this point in my life, so fasting is a luxury I can well afford.

Originally published as "A Deliverance Session," *How to Cast Out Demons* (Ventura, CA: Renew Books, 2000).

A feature that comes along with experience is confidence. You must be a person of faith and confidence. Your faith grows in this area until you are sure that God will come to your aid each time you pray and that He will increase your authority. The job gets easier as time goes by and as your experience mounts.

Remember our two chief weapons: the *authority* our Lord has given and the use of the *name of Jesus* as we address each demon by name, commanding it to leave.

The Support of Intercessors

I like to have some of my intercessors know when I will be doing deliverance so they can uphold the session in prayer. If the person for whom I am praying is comfortable in asking for prayer from his or her Christian friends, that can help also. I do not divulge the name of the person I am praying for or the nature of the problems. I am very careful to maintain privacy and dignity as much as is possible. I usually just say something like, "I am praying for a woman on Tuesday at 9 A.M. and it could be a difficult case. Please pray for wisdom, discernment and the help of the Holy Spirit in great measure."

Working with a Team

If you are working with a small team of people, be sure that only one person is in charge of the session at a time. It is never to become a free-for-all with several people praying or speaking at a time. When I am working with a team, I ask that any suggestions that my team has be written on a piece of paper and handed to me. If I request someone to say something, that is a different story. Demons thrive on confusion because they can get a bit of an advantage in chaos. My advice is to keep things calm and in order.

Training Others

It is wonderful if team members can be "apprenticed" in actual deliverance sessions, but this should be done with just one or two at a time. As they are sitting in on a session, their job is to intercede. If they have questions, they are to be written down and never asked out loud during the session. Debriefing is to be done in private after the session is over.

It is also a good learning technique to have the person being apprenticed go over the questionnaire with you ahead of time. You can point out what is "as plain as the nose on your face." I usually write down the name of the demon I will be going after in the margin. I highlight in pink (you can use any color!) significant items that require either further explanation or attention in prayer.

The person being apprenticed needs to promise to maintain strict confidentiality. This must never be betrayed, even for "prayer purposes" (too many prayer meetings become gossip sessions). If you have private information and you feel it needs prayer, you are probably the person God wants to do the praying. Of course, if the person requesting deliverance asks you to have some intercessors pray, that is a different story, but we still insist on confidentiality. Generally, a person will ask for prayer if there has been involvement in witchcraft or satanism. Fear is always present in abundant supply. Seasoned intercessors usually know how to keep their lips buttoned. Those who cannot don't qualify as deliverance intercessors.

We need to assure the person requesting deliverance that to be with us is to be in a safe place where confidentiality is respected and guarded. The devil would like nothing more than to bring insecurity to the individual by having misgivings about our keeping confidence. He also enjoys embarrassing his victims. We just won't give him that satisfaction!

An interesting thing happens after I pray for an individual. Since I am naturally a rather tender person who can't stand conflict, God supernaturally removes almost all of what I pray from my mind so that I just don't remember it. If I ever had to carry the load of garbage I pray about, it would make me an emotional basket case! God is very kind, and I can meet the person I prayed for later on and look him or her straight in the eye without any "baggage" attached. I also make it a point to never converse about a past deliverance session. This may be a reason why it "evaporates" from my memory—I just don't reinforce it by talking about it.

The Person Requesting Prayer

There are several requirements I insist upon before agreeing to pray for a person.

This does not mean I refuse to pray for that person. It usually means the person is not yet ready. When the person agrees to the following requirements, I will set up an appointment.

The person must desire to be free.
It can't be the idea of the spouse, grandfather or a friend. It must be his or her sincere desire.

The person must be willing to forgive those who have been the root causes of their problems.
This can be hard to do; but until the person is willing to forgive, prayer must be postponed, since unforgiveness can be an invitation for the problem to return.

The person must be serious about promising to stop sin, break bad habits, perhaps let go of certain friendships, or do whatever will assist in the healing process.
I am unable to hold people's hands after I pray for them. I advise them to follow the post-prayer instructions [see appendix 4 in *How to Cast Out Demons*] and expect them to do so in order to maintain satisfactory results and lasting freedom.

The person must promise to keep close to God.
A steady diet of regular church attendance, daily Bible reading and prayer will be expected. Small-group attendance is desirable, when available, to assist in accountability.

The Physical Place of Prayer

I always insist on being in a safe place for prayer. If I need to pray alone for a man, I do it in my office. There are windows with no shades, and I pray during business hours only. I was fortunate enough to design my own office, and from my desk I can see through windows to the right and left of me. I can see everyone in a straight line through these windows. This protects us all, and we cannot be accused of "being behind a closed door." Even our conference rooms have large floor-to-ceiling windows so that any passerby can see when the room is occupied.

I always place my chair directly opposite the person for whom I am praying. In this way I can look straight into his or her eyes. I am certain my guest is not looking into the sunshine or the bright light of a window. I always provide a glass of water, a box of tissues and a wastebasket within handy reach of us both. If there are any other persons present, they sit off to one side of me, easily within arm's reach in case they need to discreetly hand me a note.

I push the "do not disturb" button on my phone and hang a "do not disturb" sign on my door. I convey to my guest that I am giving my undivided attention to the matters at hand.

Gathering Further Information

I would have received the confidential questionnaire some days before the scheduled session and will have prayed over it, marked places for prayer, and analyzed it pretty well. However, there are always items that will need further clarification and explanation.

I usually pray for a person for about two hours. The first item of business at hand is to pray and ask God's blessings upon the time we spend together. I pray that God will lead and guide us and bring to our minds anything that might need prayer that was not mentioned on the questionnaire.

Next I make a declaration to all evil spirits, commanding them not to manifest. The prayer will go something like this: "And now, in the mighty name of Jesus, I bind, muzzle and gag every evil spirit present in the heart and life of [name]. I say you are forbidden to manifest or cause discomfort, and you will leave when I command you to do so! Holy Spirit, please come and accompany us as we pray together and guide all our thoughts, conversation and prayer, in Jesus' name."

The object of the next half hour is to place the person at ease. I usually have not seen the individual before, so I am a complete stranger. I try to act as much like a caring grandmother as I can, always trying to get to the bottom of things. Usually the main objective here is to locate the entry point(s), ascertain if someone needs to be forgiven and forge a "plan of attack" in my mind.

Where Do We Start?

What we pray for first varies from case to case. As a rule, I start with the oldest problems from childhood, if there are any. Generally these have to do with inherited problems of rejection; problems that still hurt concerning family members, schoolmates, injustices and so forth. Then we cover the rest of the categories one at a time.

Occasionally you will run into persons whose special delight in life is going from counselor to counselor, talking about themselves and their problems. If their conversations are lengthy and they give you more detail than you need, politely tell them that you have enough information in the questionnaire and are looking for specific details concerning specific items. Sometimes, I'm convinced, the evil one wants to derail our thoughts or weary our minds so we don't stay sharp. It is important to keep control of the conversation and stay in charge of things.

I personally do not charge for my time. I feel that since I receive a salary, the ministry pays for my time. My board of directors has approved my praying deliverance over people as part of my job description. I also feel that the Scripture's injunction "Freely you have received, freely give" (Matt. 10:8) includes deliverance and praying for the sick, so I personally feel it is unacceptable to charge anyone. I have accepted spontaneous donations to the ministry, but I have not invited them, nor do I keep anything myself. Sometimes people like to give out of gratitude, and it would be wrong not to accept a gift for the ministry. It is sort of a "thanks offering" on their part.

Since I am giving them my time, I expect them to respect it and allow me to "call the shots." If anything gets too lengthy, I simply say something like, "My time is really limited, and in order to cover all the bases we will need to hurry along, so please let me ask a few more questions." Always be very kind in the way you say this, because some poor souls are already very rejected and a harsh reprimand is the last thing they need.

Healing the Memories

The last half hour is spent praying for healing of the memories and blessing the person. Everything I have marked in pink or every demon noted in a margin is prayed over, this time with the very opposite of the problem or stronghold. For example, if there was rage, I pray for quiet control in the person's mind and tongue. If there was hatred, I pray for love and so on.

Lastly, I pray a benediction over the person. I ask God to bless and keep them, bless their going out and their coming in, bless every aspect of their day-to-day life, and that the person would please the Lord in all they do, say and think.

I often get a rather strange comment as people are leaving. They frequently say something like, "I feel so light!" I have never actually gotten out a scale and weighed a demon, but apparently after a demon leaves an individual, there is a weight removed from the soul that makes the person feel lighter all over. And they like the new feeling.

I ask the person to write to me in about a month to let me know how things are progressing. I keep portions of these letters because they are so sweet—many of them give profuse thanks to the Lord for drastic changes in their lives that they never dreamed possible. Freedom sure beats bondage! The epilogue [of *How to Cast Out Demons*] contains some of these anonymous testimonies.

In all honesty, this is something I would rather not do. While I dislike the process and listening to all the yucky things the devil does to people, I also must confess that I like to see what God can do to reverse all of that and bring freedom. Besides, the last time I looked in the Bible, I was still told to "cast out demons" (Matt 10:8; Mark 16:17). The best thing to say is, "Yes, Lord, I'll keep on doing it as long as I am able."

SCRIPTURE INDEX

SUBJECT INDEX

Made in the USA
Middletown, DE
11 November 2020

23717007R00189